DESIGNING
AND BUILDING
YOUR OWN FRAMESET

An Illustrated Guide For
The Amateur Bicycle Builder

Richard P. Talbot, P.E.

The Manet Guild

DESIGNING AND BUILDING YOUR OWN FRAMESET

An Illustrated Guide For
The Amateur Bicycle Builder

Library of Congress Catalog Card Number 79-63015
©1979 Richard P. Talbot
All Rights Reserved
Printed in The United States of America
First Edition
ISBN: 0-9602418-1-7
Second Printing, May 1980

ACKNOWLEDGEMENTS

I am particularly grateful to Mr. George P. Wilson, Bicycle Framebuilder, for his assistance in expanding the Appendix listing of professional framebuilders and his valued review and commentary on the draft manuscript. A sincere thanks also to Mr. James Redcay, Framebuilder, and to Mr. Robert Shipley of Lil Henry's Bicycle Emporium for their reading of the manuscript, to Mr. Henry James Folson of Henry James Bicycles, Inc., and Mr. Robert A. Prednis, Vice President, Sales, Gray-Syracuse, Inc., for the background data on investment casting; to many of the professional framebuilders listed in the Appendix, too numerous to mention here, for their encouragement; to the manufacturers and suppliers who graciously offered illustrations and data and who are individually credited in the text; to Miss Evelyn Lowell for her yeoman service in transforming the initial handwritten manuscript into typed copy; and last, but certainly not least, to my fellow cyclists — tourists, commuters, racers — who provided much of the inspiration which made this book a reality.

R.P.T.

CONTENTS

Foreword i

Introduction iii

A Note On Illustrations v

PART I
Developing a Design and
Preparing for Construction

Chapter I   Frameset Design Principles 3

Chapter II   The Design Drawing 19

Chapter III   A Primer on Brazing —
Key to Successful Construction 23

Chapter IV   Tooling Up 35

PART II
Frameset Construction

Chapter V   Jigs and Miscellaneous Aids 41

Chapter VI   Selecting Frameset Materials 47

Chapter VII   Preparing The Tubes And
Building The Fork 59

Chapter VIII   Building The Main Triangle And
Seat Stay Attachment 71

Chapter IX   Building The Rear Triangle — Braze-Ons —
Special Designs. 85

PART III
Finishing Touches

Chapter X   Finishing The Frameset —
Operations Requiring Special Tooling 103

Chapter XI   Surface Preparation, Painting
and Detailing 115

Chapter XII   Decision Time 125

Appendix 127

Index 153
Graph Paper 157

Foreword

"Nothing in the world can
take the place of persistence.
Talent will not;
nothing is more common
than the unsuccessful man
with talent. Genius will not;
unrewarded genius
is almost a proverb.
Education alone will not;
the world is full of educated derelicts.
Persistence and determination
alone are omnipotent."

Calvin Coolidge
1872 - 1933

INTRODUCTION

Designing and Building Your Own Frameset is expressly written to provide practical guidance for prospective first-time bicycle builders. While all bike enthusiasts should find it a helpful general reference, the book is primarily intended for use by those who are about to undertake (or *think* they are about to undertake) the formidable task of designing and building their own custom framesets. I stress the word *think* because the book is also meant to serve as a decision tool — to help readers make an intelligent choice on whether they really should do the construction work themselves or have a professional framebuilder undertake that task. Framebuilding will certainly not be every reader's forte and those who, on the basis of this book, decide to contract that work out, will have benefited just as much as the stalwart souls who choose to do the fabrication themselves.

While not a comprehensive treatise on every facet of bicycle engineering — selected readings listed in the Appendix will provide information on that diverse topic — the book does furnish a detailed and, I think, unique expose of the narrower but all important subject of frameset design and construction. Why unique? Because the text is written completely by a bona fide amateur builder, one who only a short time ago was in the same straits as the reader. In fact, the initial concept for writing an illustrated design/build manual developed while I was struggling through the final stages of fabricating my first home-built bicycle — a project still vividly remembered for its bittersweet mixture of challenge, satisfaction, elation, and yes, no small amount of frustration.

It is my belief that the first-hand experiences of one who is only a step removed from his former status as neophyte builder, will illuminate many facets of this subject and answer fundamental questions that a more advanced dissertation might take for granted. For example, brazing is a topic with which many readers may not be familiar — neither its theory nor its application. In this book, brazing receives special emphasis because its mastery is of critical importance in achieving a structurally sound and visually pleasing frameset.

Another major feature of the book is its abundant illustrations. One hundred seventy three captioned photographs provide close-up views that depict every step of frameset development — from initial design drawing to the last coat of wax. Additionally, numerous supplementary sketches, tables, graphs and manufacturer's illustrations augment the text to further enhance the reader's grasp of design principles and construction techniques.

Finally, regardless of how confident you now feel about your ability to build a frameset on your own, I urge you to read this text in its entirety *before* starting construction. Those who opt for the professional builder solution will still find it an indispensable reference for developing their own design drawings and frameset specifications. These documents will help buyers of custom-built machines obtain framesets that are truly fitted to their specific requirements. To further assist those readers in selecting a professional framebuilder, the Appendix features an up-to-date and verified directory of fifty-nine cycle craftsmen located throughout the United States.

Whatever your ultimate use of *Designing And Building Your Own Frameset* — decision tool, design treatise or complete design/build reference manual — I earnestly hope it serves you well, and, in a broader sense, that it will further your knowledge of that marvelous and most energy-efficient machine yet devised for human locomotion — the bicycle.

A NOTE ON ILLUSTRATIONS

With the exception of illustrations otherwise credited, all photographs, drawings and sketches appearing in this book are by the author. Of the 173 photographs published, 166 document construction of the first frameset built by the author. All were taken under available-light conditions using ASA 400 black and white film. Photographic equipment consisted of a tripod-mounted 35 mm SLR camera equipped with a 55 mm, $f/1.8$ lens and an integral self-timer.

Each photograph is identified with a unique code number consisting of the prefix letter P followed by a decimal fraction. Digits to the left of the decimal point denote the chapter in which the photo first appears, and the numbers to its right, its order of appearance in that chapter.

Photographs are usually referenced solely by parenthetic insertion of the code number at those text locations where a picture will serve to clarify the procedure being discussed. A typical insertion would appear as — (P8.20) — which means, refer to photograph P8.20. In this example the photo may be found in Chapter VIII and is 20th in the series of photographs appearing in that chapter.

PART I
DEVELOPING A DESIGN
AND PREPARING FOR CONSTRUCTION

Chapter I

FRAMESET DESIGN PRINCIPLES

Preliminary Notes on Terminology

In common parlance the word *frame* is nearly always used to describe what is actually a *frameset*. This text uses both words — but only in their strictest technical connotation. To avoid confusion, *frameset* always means the combined assembly of fork and frame; while the word *frame* refers solely to the assemblage of tubes comprising the main and rear triangles.

Furthermore, to simplify the writing and avoid unwieldy sentence structure, the masculine noun is used throughout the book. In all such cases it is understood that the feminine gender applies equally.

The Goal and Key Design Objectives

The ultimate goal of frameset design is an *energy-efficient* machine. To achieve it two fundamental design objectives must be met. They are as follows:

• OBJECTIVE 1: Establish a geometry that will fit the cyclist's anatomy in such a way as to facilitate the use of his muscles in the most efficient manner possible for the purpose of propulsion.

• OBJECTIVE 2: Develop a design that will best fulfill the specific use to which the bicycle will be put while wasting a minimum of the cyclist's energy.

The first objective addresses the problem of anatomical fit, a function unique to the body geometry of each individual. Humans come in a vast array of sizes and shapes; obviously, no single geometric arrangement of tubes will satisfy such wide physiological diversity. For proper fit the frameset must be custom tailored to the anatomy of the cyclist. Gross adjustments to handlebars and seat can never compensate adequately for a poor fit and are no substitute for a correctly sized frameset.

The second design objective pertains to the purpose for which the bicycle will be used. Touring and racing are the two broadest categories here, but there are many variations in usage under these rather general groupings. For example, cycle-touring may entail long-distance treks lasting weeks or months. In this case the cyclist uses the bicycle as a veritable packhorse to carry heavy camping gear and supplies. At the other end of the touring spectrum is the long-distance day-tripper. As he is concerned solely with covering great distances, and does not need heavy touring equipment, his frameset needs approach those of the time trial racer. Both uses fall under the general heading of touring, but for optimum performance and enjoyment the design of each frameset must necessarily be different.

A similar situation arises in racing where there exists an even wider range of usage — rough and tumble cyclo-cross, hill climbs, road races, criteriums, time trials, and track events. Each application has its own special design requirements. Finally, just to make matters a bit more complicated, there is sports riding — a racing/touring mélange.

Each use, whether it be in racing, touring, or sports riding, imposes a unique set of circumstances on the cyclist and his machine. Each calls for a unique design response. This does not mean that a frameset designed for one purpose cannot be employed successfully for another. In situations where differences in applications are rather small, a single frameset may be suitable for several purposes. However, it is imperative that the novice builder define the *principal* use of the bicycle and make that the sole basis for his design. A shotgun approach, trying to design a frameset for a multitude of radically different purposes, is destined to satisfy none.

When both design objectives have been met, we have achieved our goal — an *energy-efficient* design. This will produce a machine capable of converting most of the cyclist's energy-output into useful work at the rear wheel (propulsion) while minimizing losses caused by distortion of the frameset when the bicycle is used for its intended purpose. Energy-efficiency is an elusive goal, but through thoughtful application of the following design criteria, it is an attainable one.

Rational Criteria for Frameset Design

Where does one turn to obtain guidelines for meeting the two fundamental design objectives and thus achieve an *energy-efficient* design? One pragmatic and wholly acceptable approach is to simply copy the design of a particular frameset that has given you good performance in the past. Sometimes this will yield a better solution than any formula or table, but chances are most of you reading this have not found that perfect bicycle and are hoping to obtain an answer from these pages. Cyclists do seem to have a penchant for "buying and trying." They seldom seem satisfied. If you have been active in the sport for some time, just reflect on the number of bikes and framesets you may have purchased over the years.

What I am driving at here is that no set of formulas, graphs, or tables is going to lead to a "perfect" design without some judgment on your part. Bicycle design and frameset building are a curious mixture of science, art, and intuition. Until recently, the field has also been rather rigidly constrained by tradition. It does take some compromising and a little luck to blend the mix successfully and make the various elements work together to achieve an *energy-efficient* design. There is no single cookbook approach that will work for everyone. With that qualification in mind, let's move on to some fairly objective criteria that have stood the test of time and which may be used as a basis for design.

Frameset Geometry
Anatomical and Performance Considerations

Simplified methods for "sizing" framesets abound. One scheme uses leg in-seam length minus an arbitrary dimension to arrive at a *correct* size. Another advises you to straddle the top tube and if there is some clearance between it and your crotch, then that is your proper size. These methods are simple, but are they sound and do they really address the problem of fit? What about the long-legged rider with the short torso? Will he require the same size frameset as an individual with similar leg length but an average upper body? What about body anomalies?

Surely, any rational design method must take into account more than just the differences in leg length. Many such methods do exist and have been used successfully by professional and amateur builders alike. All have their pros and cons, and the subject remains a source of strong opinions and endless controversy.

The C.O.N.1. Method

One approach that has worked well for me, and which I recommend, is the method advocated by the Italian Central Sports School and published in their book *Cycling* C.O.N.1. Central Sports School — FIAC, Rome 1972. Any serious amateur would do well to spend some time reading this interesting manual to gain a wider perspective on the science of cycling. Intended primarily for racing, the C.O.N.1. design criteria are also generally applicable to the design of touring framesets. The method is not foolproof — you still have to make some decisions on your own — but it is rational and can be applied easily once some fairly straightforward anatomical dimensions have been taken.

Before getting into specifics and starting design work, you must familiarize yourself with the technical terminology and design factors that will be used throughout the remainder of this book. Refer to the drawing in Figure I-1 as you study the following definitions and principles. It will help make the text presentation more understandable. Also, keep in mind that in most instances the factors being discussed are interrelated, and a change in one usually affects others.

Definitions and Design Factors

Wheelbase

This is the distance between the front and rear wheel axles. Modern racing designs favor short wheelbases. What was once considered normal only for track racing has found its way into the design of road framesets. Contemporary road racing wheelbases in the 38½ to 39½ inch range are commonplace. Modern touring wheelbases are generally longer, 40 to 41 inches or more, although some recent sports-riding designs are being built on a one meter standard.

For a given cyclist the minimum wheelbase dimension is limited primarily by anatomical considerations. However, wheelbase may be lengthened (within practical limits) by making the head tube angle shallower, increasing the fork rake (which, as we shall see, is related to the head tube angle), lengthening the chain stays, or some combination of the aforementioned.

Wheelbase influences several important bike handling characteristics. A short wheelbase yields a stiff but energy-efficient ride (on smooth surfaces) because little work goes into frameset flexure; more power is available for useful output at the rear wheel. Also, other things being equal, a shorter wheelbase within a given *size* frameset minimizes weight through the use of shorter fork blades and stays. Unfortunately, these benefits are not gained without some cost. Short wheelbase machines can be devilish to control on rough surfaces, may be uncomfortable on long rides, and with their usually steep head and seat tube angles, sometimes raise havoc with headsets, wheels, and other components in general.

By contrast, longer wheelbase framesets exhibit greater resiliency. They offer a more sensible alternative for touring (where all-out sprinting is less likely to occur). Road shocks are greatly reduced by greater frameset flexure, resulting in better control and a less fatiguing ride for cyclist and machine alike.

Weight Distribution

This is the actual percentage of the total weight of the bicycle plus rider and equipment that is shared by each wheel. For a "good handling" bike, ideal distribution is generally considered to be 45% of the total weight on the front wheel and 55% on the rear. Weight distribution is principally influenced by the location of the cyclist's center of gravity (CG) relative to the wheels when he is in his normal riding position. In touring designs, loading caused by packed panniers and bags is also a factor. Deviations from ideal weight distribution can be caused by designs that place the rider too far forward or too far to the rear. It is a complex but nonetheless important factor in frameset design which will require some judgment on your part.

If you are light-shouldered with heavy hips, then some design steps should be taken to prevent excessive loading of the rear wheel. Three possible remedies are to steepen the seat tube angle, lengthen the chain stays, or do both. On the other hand, if your anatomy is that of a heavy-shouldered, light-hipped person, possible solutions would include lessening the seat tube angle, shortening the chain stays, or both. These moves have the opposite loading effect to those described previously. Another consideration is whether the bicycle will normally be used with touring or camping gear. If it is, an analysis of loaded pannier and handlebar bag weights must also be made to determine their impact on weight distribution.

Combined CG

This is the center of gravity of the combined mass of the bicycle, its rider, and any attached gear normally carried (such as panniers, handlebar bags, carriers, etc.).

Crank Axis

This is the longitudinal center line of the crank axle. It coincides with the longitudinal center line of the bottom bracket shell and is sometimes referred to as the *axis of central movement*.

Top Tube Height

Top tube height is the perpendicular distance from the ground to the top of the top tube. Regardless of the specific geometry of the rest of the frameset, this distance should always be such that at least one-half inch clearance exists between the top of the top tube and the cyclist's crotch while he is straddling the bicycle with both feet flat on the ground. The clearance should exist when he is wearing the shoes he normally uses while riding.

Bottom Bracket Height

This is the perpendicular distance from the ground to the center line of the bottom bracket shell and is one of the key dimensions for establishing top tube height — the other two are seat tube length and seat tube angle. Factors to consider in selecting an appropriate bottom bracket height are crank length and use of the bike. If cranks longer than the standard 170/171 mm length are to be used, then consider using a high bottom bracket to permit ample road clearance under the pedals when cornering.

If you are designing a cyclo-cross, criterium, or track frameset, then regardless of crank length, a high bottom bracket should be used. Uneven terrain, sharp cornering during racing, and the constraints of a banked track all have the effect of minimizing pedal-to-road clearance. Bottom bracket heights range from 9½ inches for smaller touring framesets up to 12 inches or more for cyclo-cross, criterium, and track designs.

Raising the bottom bracket makes for a slightly less stable ride by elevating the combined CG. Lowering it slightly improves stability and has a subtle effect on the "feel" of the bicycle under sprinting conditions. When you start to lay out a design using the C.O.N.1. method, selecting a bottom bracket height will be the first decision you will have to make.

Drop

This is the vertical distance between the crank axis and the horizontal wheel axis center line. It is a frame-related measurement (always remains constant) while bottom bracket height will vary in accordance with the actual wheel diameter used. Comparison of drop dimensions provides a ready means of evaluating relative performance characteristics of different framesets.

Laid Back

This term refers to head and seat tube angles that are shallower than normal.

Upright

Upright refers to head and seat tube angles that are relatively steep.

Seat Tube Length

This is the distance from the crank axis to the *top* of the seat lug. It is measured along the seat tube center line and is the dimension most commonly used to designate frame *size*. Seat tube length is directly related to the cyclist's leg length.

Top Tube Length

Top tube length is the distance between the head tube center line and the seat tube center line. It is measured along the top tube center line and is related to the length of the cyclist's arms and upper torso. Sometimes the *size* of a particular frameset is stated by specifying the lengths of both its seat tube and top tube (a more accurate method than that of specifying the seat tube length alone).

Seat Tube Angle

The seat tube angle is that angle formed between the seat tube and the ground. It usually falls between 68 degrees and 75 degrees, although some of the more avant-garde American builders have produced time trial and other special purpose racing designs with seat (and head) tube angles as steep as 78 degrees. A study of Figure I-1 reveals that increasing the angle displaces the top tube upward and forward and moves the top of the seat tube more directly over the crank axis. Decreasing the angle has the opposite effect. Changes in seat tube angle alter weight distribution by shifting the CG of the cyclist and that of a handlebar bag (if used) relative to the wheels. Also, an upright angle results in a stiffer ride while a laid back tube provides more frame flexure which tends to reduce road shocks transmitted to the cyclist's pelvis.

Head Tube Angle

This is the angle formed between the head tube and the ground. It falls within the same range as the seat tube angle but need not be identical. The head tube angle deserves special consideration because it and the fork rake are interrelated. (Rake is simply the perpendicular distance from the head tube center line to the front wheel axle.) Jointly, the two factors — head tube angle and fork rake — exert a profound influence on how a bicycle handles, both in a straight-line direction and, most importantly, through turns.

To grasp the significance of the relationship of the head tube angle to the fork rake and its influence on performance, it is first necessary to understand that for every given head tube angle and wheel radius there exists but *one* rake dimension that will provide *neutral steering*. Neutral steering simply means the fork will neither rise nor fall as it is turned. Just exactly how the fork rake dimension is determined will be covered a little later. What is important now is to keep the following relationship between head tube angle and fork rake in mind. As the head tube angle is *increased,* the required rake dimension to maintain neutral steering becomes *shorter.* As the angle becomes *shallower,* the required rake becomes *longer.* To simplify, steep angles mean short rakes; shallow angles mean long ones.

Steep angles and their accompanying short rakes have the desirable effect of providing front-end stiffness and quick steering. A steeply angled head tube pulls the front wheel more underneath the cyclist. Whether he is powering along in the saddle — or out of it, well over the bars in a wild sprint — the tucked-under wheel imparts stiff and sprightly handling. Also, as the cyclist thrashes on the pedals, a tucked-under wheel reduces the tendency of the bike to whip from side to side; it thus improves stability in a sprint. The steep angle of the fork blades coupled with the small rake dimension yields a short fork that undergoes only minor deflection under full power applications. These performance attributes are desired by most racers and many sports riders because they improve the energy-efficiency of the machine.

However, if the angle is too steep and the rake is very short, the front end will be excessively stiff and the steering ultra-sensitive. The condition can lead to a shoulder-pounding ride, diminishment of stability and control, and excessive wear in the headset and other components. When brought to extremes, steeply inclined head tubes and ultra-short rakes create designs that are so sensitive to road irregularities they are suitable only for the most experienced of cyclists.

Shallow head tube angles minimize steering sensitivity and provide more front-end flex by throwing the wheel farther ahead of the rider. There are limits in this direction also. Designs that use a shallow head tube angle and a neutral fork rake are quite resilient (sometimes referred to as giving a *bedspring ride*), but their high-speed cornering characteristics tend to be sluggish. Excessive turning force is needed to navigate corners even at modest speeds. The trend is away from the neutral or near-neutral steering geometry of the past. Unless you plan to use the bike mostly for low speed travel (as in beach cruisers), or for front-end loads which may be

extremely heavy (such as delivery bicycles), or if you desire unusual shock absorbing qualities, a steeper head tube angle and a shorter raked fork may be more satisfactory. Specific methods for determining the precise rake dimension will be discussed when that topic is covered in detail at the end of this chapter.

Before we leave the subject of head tube angle there are three additional factors with which you need to be concerned. First, from our previous discussion of the tucked-under wheel you have probably already surmised that the head tube angle affects weight distribution because it (and the accompanying fork rake) control the distance between the front wheel axle and the combined CG. Secondly, a steep angle may pull the front wheel so close to the crank axis that toe clip interference results. Lastly, an upright tube also brings the front wheel in close proximity to the down tube, sometimes interfering with the mounting of a fender. The last two conditions may not be important to racers, but tourists usually find either situation difficult to tolerate.

Chain Stay Length

Chain stay length is the distance from the crank axis to the intersection of the seat stay and chain stay center lines. Long stays permit greater flexure while short ones result in a stiffer but more energy-efficient ride. Chain stay length also affects weight distribution because it governs the distance between the rear wheel axle and the combined CG.

Additionally, with very short stays and conventional road drop-outs two special problems may arise. The rear wheel can be pulled so close to the seat tube that the wheel cannot be dismounted without deflating its tire. It may also become impossible to mount a rear fender due to lack of adequate space between the seat tube and tire. If you use a fender, the chain stays must be long enough to provide sufficient mounting clearance.

Fork Length

Fork length may be defined in two ways. The conventional method is simply to state it as the straight-line distance between the front wheel axle and the front brake hole. A second way is to measure the distance between these points along the blade center line, taking blade curvature into account. Of the two methods, the second is a more accurate indicator of performance characteristics, because a given fork rake and crown may use any number of blade curvatures.

For example, the blade may be made with a large radius bend that starts immediately below the fork crown, or it may be straight for most of its length and then curve abruptly at the tip. Each shape has a different center line length and each will give a different *feel* to the bike. Fork length is dependent on the type of fork crown used, the amount of wheel clearance under the crown (also affected by the type of brake used), and most importantly, head tube angle and fork rake.

Fork Rake

As mentioned earlier, fork rake is the distance between the head tube center line and the front wheel axle. It is measured perpendicular to the head tube center line. In our discussion on head tube angle we saw that rake is directly related to the head tube angle and wheel radius. To achieve neutral steering (remember, no rise or fall in the fork as it is turned) there can be but one rake dimension for a given head tube angle and wheel radius. Now, there is really nothing superior about neutral steering but it is a useful concept for examining the rather vexing question of fork rake and how it is determined.

There are three ways to establish a rake dimension — copy an existing design whose handling characteristics satisfy you, calculate it by using an appropriate formula, or select the rake from a special graph constructed for that purpose. The first method is valid provided you have had experience riding many different bikes with various head tube angle and fork rake combinations. But, if you lack that experience or just prefer the analytical approach, then Figure I-2 may be used. It contains the necessary formulas and graph.

An understanding of some basic steering terminology and handling characteristics is necessary before applying the rake selection data. The term *neutral* steering was defined earlier. Now examine the graph in Figure I-2 and observe the solid sloping line drawn on it. That line, identified as the Neutral Steering Line, is a graphical representation of the neutral steering formula, which is also displayed just to the right of the graph. The

Neutral Steering Line is a continuous plot of all *neutral* rakes for head tube angles ranging from 75 degrees to 68 degrees. The graph's ordinate (vertical axis) shows head tube angle in degrees; the abscissa (horizontal axis) displays corresponding fork rake in inches. An example rake selection problem is illustrated in the figure and demonstrates how the graph is used. The Neutral Steering Line was plotted based on an assumed wheel diameter of 27 inches ($13\frac{1}{2}$ inch wheel radius). It is thus applicable *only* to that size wheel. If rakes are desired for wheels other than 27 inch diameter, then the formula must be used. A table of tangents is included in the Appendix for your convenience.

As you study the graph note that the top of the Neutral Steering Line is marked with two directional arrows. The one pointing to the left indicates the direction of increasing *oversteer* (making rakes shorter than neutral); the one pointing right shows the direction of increasing *understeer* (making rakes longer than neutral). The terms are practically self-explanatory. To *oversteer* a turn means to cut it tighter than its true radius. To *understeer* a turn means to swing wider than its true radius.

The following examples will illustrate the practical aspects of forks built with *neutral* rakes and those designed for *oversteer* and *understeer*. When a bicycle enters a turn at high speed the gyroscopic effect of the spinning wheels and the linear momentum of the moving bike, its rider, and any attached gear combine to resist the turning forces. These forces tend to keep the bicycle headed in a straight-line direction. If the bike's fork is built with a *neutral* rake the machine will tend to swing somewhat wide through the turn, *understeering* it.

The tendency to swing wide, or understeer turns, becomes more pronounced as bike speed is increased. The characteristic can fortunately be offset by making a fork with a rake shorter than that indicated for *neutral* steering (building in *oversteer*). In so doing, builders create a turning geometry that permits counteracting forces to come into play. These forces offset the wide-swinging tendency and keep the wheel headed in the direction of the turn. The result is a more responsive bike that is much easier to maneuver through curves than its neutral steering counterpart.

When a bike with *built-in oversteer* is brought into a turn the amount of force that must be applied to the handlebars to keep the machine turning is significantly reduced and energy-efficiency is improved.

It is for this reason that racing designs in general and criterium framesets in particular are built with relatively short rakes (purposely designed with a substantial amount of *built-in oversteer*). Snappy handling around sharp turns at high speed necessitates it. A fork built for *neutral* steering would unnecessarily burden a racer, forcing him to waste energy muscling around every turn. An *understeering* racing bike also presents a serious hazard to the pack due to its lack of maneuverability.

Just how much *oversteer* should be built into your fork depends on the specific handling characteristics desired and what the bicycle will be used for. By the way, I have purposely not spent any time discussing forks designed with *built-in understeer* (those which fall to the right of the Neutral Steering Line) because their turning performance is so wretched. Only those builders who plan to duplicate an antique design, need super shock absorbing qualities in the front end, or want a bike that will hold a straight line while traversing uneven terrain will even consider a fork with *built-in understeer*. I also doubt that most cyclists will be satisfied with the rather unresponsive turning characteristics of *neutral* steering, unless perhaps, they are novice riders or are designing a delivery type frameset.

To furnish guidance in selecting an appropriate amount of *oversteer*, a second formula known as the Quick Steering Formula, and its accompanying Quick Steering Line (shown as a dashed line on the graph) are illustrated in Figure I-2. If you are designing a racing frameset, you might calculate the rake using the Quick Steering Formula or determine it using the graph (good only for 27 inch diameter wheels). For touring, a rake that falls midway between the values calculated by the formulas, or the graph's lines, might be appropriate. You can also plot your own pair of steering lines using the formulas, your exact wheel radius, the tangent table contained in Appendix Table V, and the attached graph paper.

Sports riders might choose a rake based on quick steering, or one that falls between quick

steering and that used for general touring. Unless you are designing for some really unusual condition, keep your rake selections within the boundaries of quick steering and neutral steering. Fork rakes lying beyond those limits will be inappropriate for most riders. And finally, what constitutes an appropriate rake for *you* depends upon your riding proficiency — *a judgement only you can make.*

Taking Your Anatomical Dimensions

With essential design factors and definitions covered, the important task of translating *your* anatomical dimensions into frame tube lengths may be undertaken. Key information for selecting appropriate tube lengths is presented in Table I-A. Column 1 in the table is used to determine seat tube length and Column 2 to find top tube length. To use the table, it is first necessary to obtain three anatomical dimensions. These are identified in Figure I-3 as A, B, and C. Enlist the help of an assistant to assure the measurements are accurately determined. It is possible to measure yourself, but there is a greater chance for error than with assistance since the process is most unwieldy. Reference to *Gray's Anatomy* will help identify the vital points on your body if there is any question about specific locations.

"A" Dimension — Pubis Bone to Floor

Standing erect, barefoot, and with feet flat on the floor, obtain the exact distance from the pubis bone (located at the base of the pelvis) to the floor. This dimension determines the required seat tube length which may now be taken from Column 1 of Table I-A.

"C" Dimension — Sternum to Pubis Bone

Next measure the distance between the pubis bone and the top of your sternum. The top of the sternum is at the base of your neck, that boney "V" you can feel just below the Adam's apple. This length must be added to the "B" dimension discussed below before entering the table.

"B" Dimension — Shoulder to Wrist Fold

The "B" dimension measures your reach and, when combined with the "C" dimension, is the basis for selecting an appropriate top tube length. It is a difficult measurement to obtain without assistance. The "B" measurement is taken from the tip of the acromion bone (at the back of your shoulder) to the fold of your wrist (turning your hand back on itself will reveal the fold). Your arm must be straight and held out at about 30 degrees from your side while the dimension is taken. Measure both arms and if there is a length difference between the two (a common occurrence) use the average. Now add the "B" and "C" dimensions together. Use the sum (B + C) to enter Column 2 of Table I-A and select the appropriate top tube length.

Geometry Adjustments for Weight Distribution of the Cyclist

The last anatomical factor to evaluate is the distribution of weight on your own "frame." Take an honest look in the mirror and try to come up with at least a general statement of your body anomalies. The judgment here is an important one for selecting an appropriate seat tube angle. C.O.N.1 recommends 73.3-degrees for riders of "normal" build to achieve proper weight distribution on the bike. If your anatomy departs from "normal" the seat tube angle must be adjusted accordingly. Cyclists with heavy hips, big buttocks, and narrow shoulders should steepen the angle to bring their CG a little further forward than that of the rider of normal build. Those who are wide-shouldered with narrow hips and smaller buttocks should lay the seat tube back on a shallower angle to move their CG closer to the rear wheel. Study Figure I-1 and imagine rotating the seat tube about its crank axis end. The rider is pushed farther from the rear wheel by increasing the

angle and pulled closer to it by decreasing the angle.

Also be mindful that changing the seat tube angle changes the relationship between the cyclist's legs and the crank axis. As the angle is steepened the horizontal distance between the crank axis and seat tube top is decreased; as it is made shallower, the distance increases. In touring designs handlebar pack weights should also be evaluated at this time to determine their influence on wheel loading. With a fixed top tube length, changes in seat tube angle will necessarily alter the handlebar's distance from the rear wheel and, of course, that of a handlebar bag, if one is carried.

Impact of Construction Materials

In addition to the geometric design factors just covered, the materials used in constructing the frameset also affect its handling characteristics. Metallurgy of the tubes, their wall thickness, cross-sectional shape, size and the manner in which they are assembled all influence bicycle performance. Other components, such as the fork crown, bottom bracket shell, lugs, and drop-outs have a similar impact. These design factors will be covered in Chapter VI where the selection of frameset materials is discussed in detail.

Sufficient information has now been developed to determine the seat and top tube lengths and, at least, a *trial* seat tube angle. These three dimensions establish the *fit* of the frameset to a particular cyclist's anatomy. With that data available, plus an understanding of the other geometric variables influencing bicycle performance, a design drawing may now be started.

NOTES

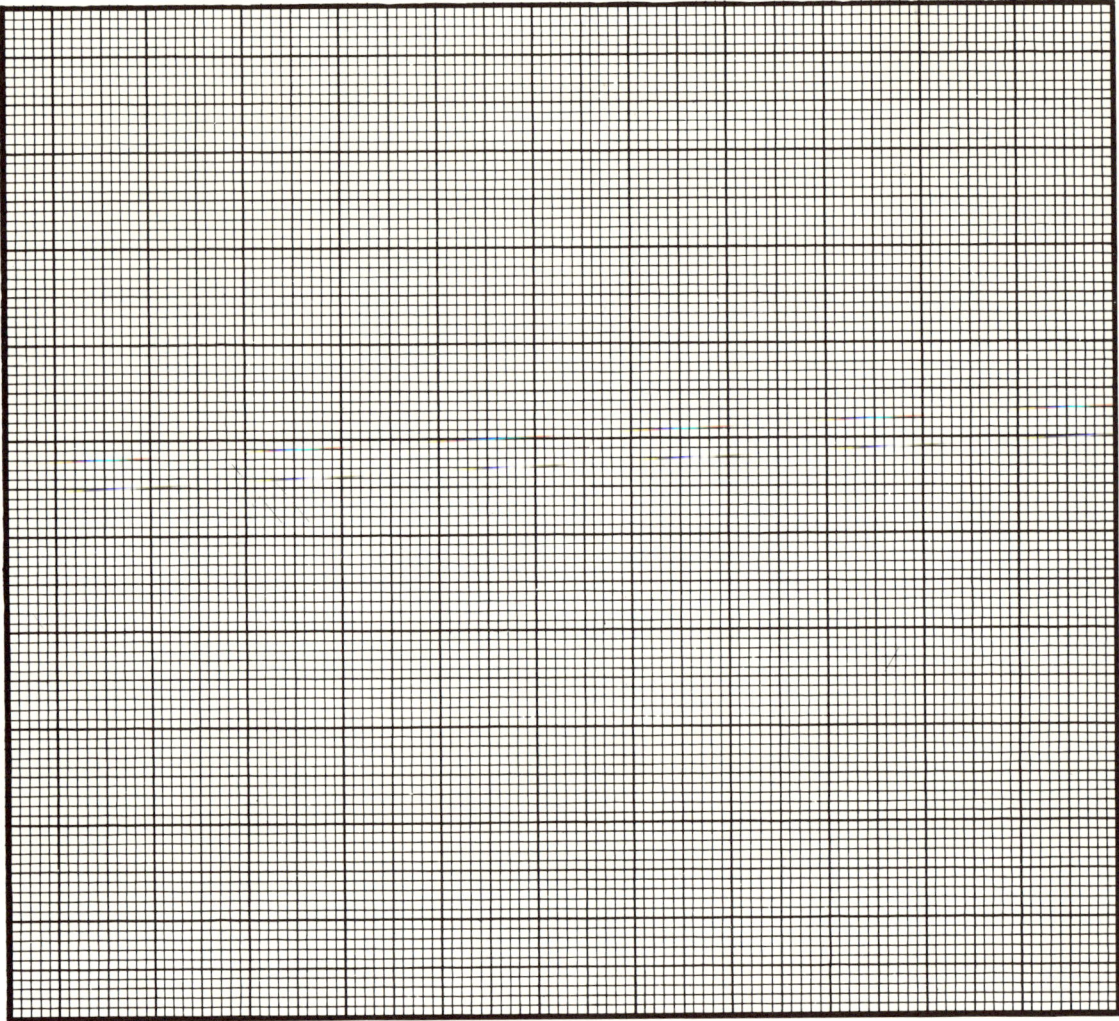

FRAMESET GEOMETRY AND
PRINCIPAL DESIGN ELEMENTS

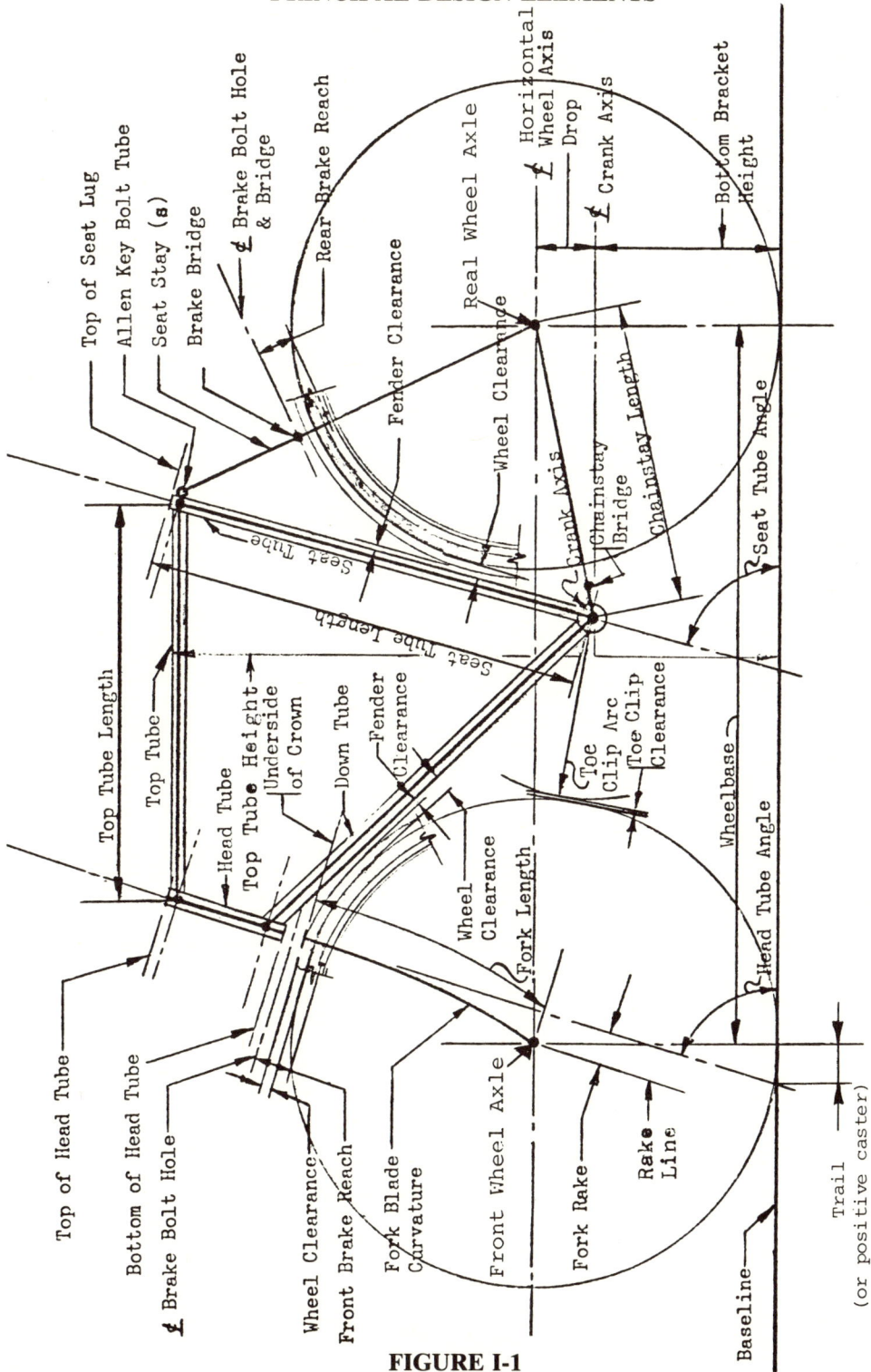

FIGURE I-1

NOTES

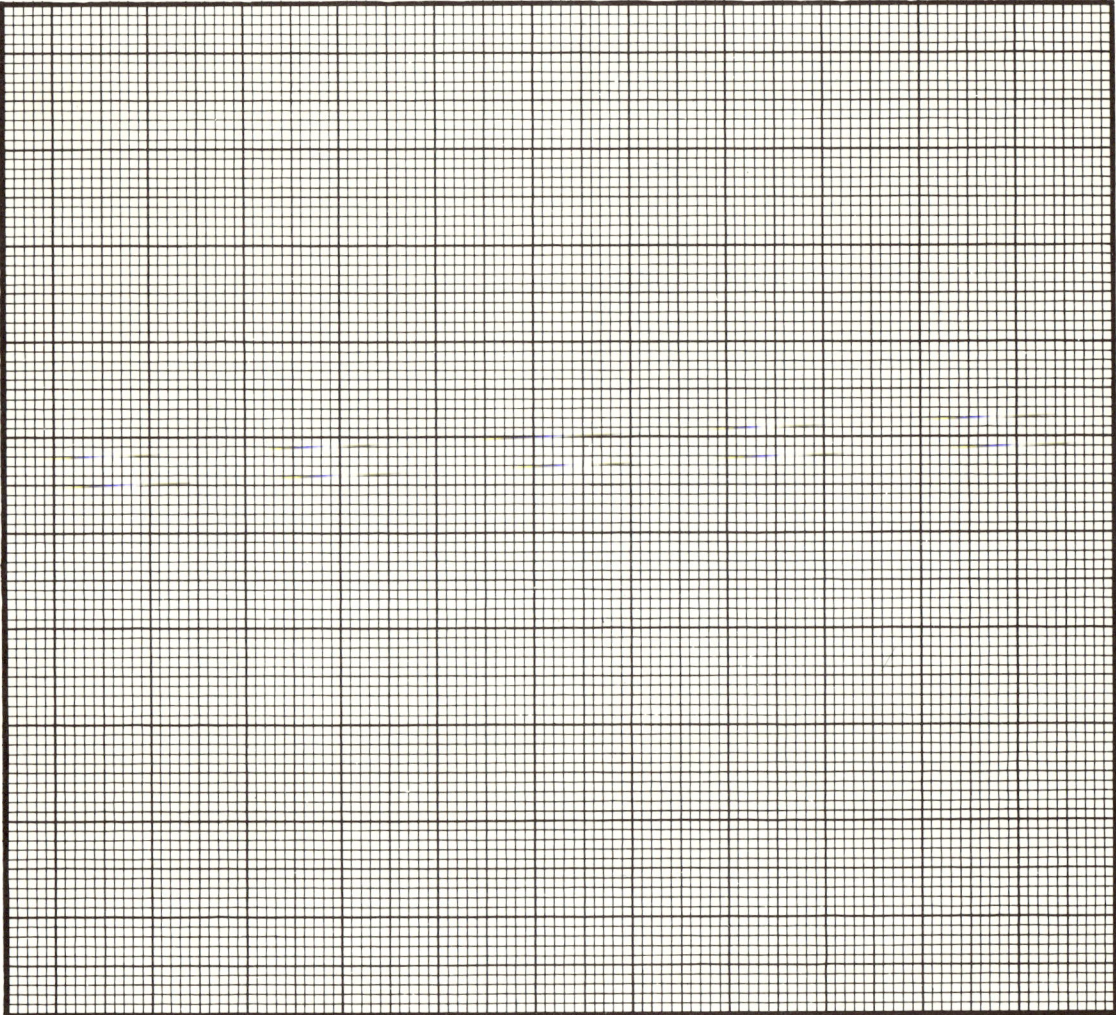

FORK RAKE GRAPH

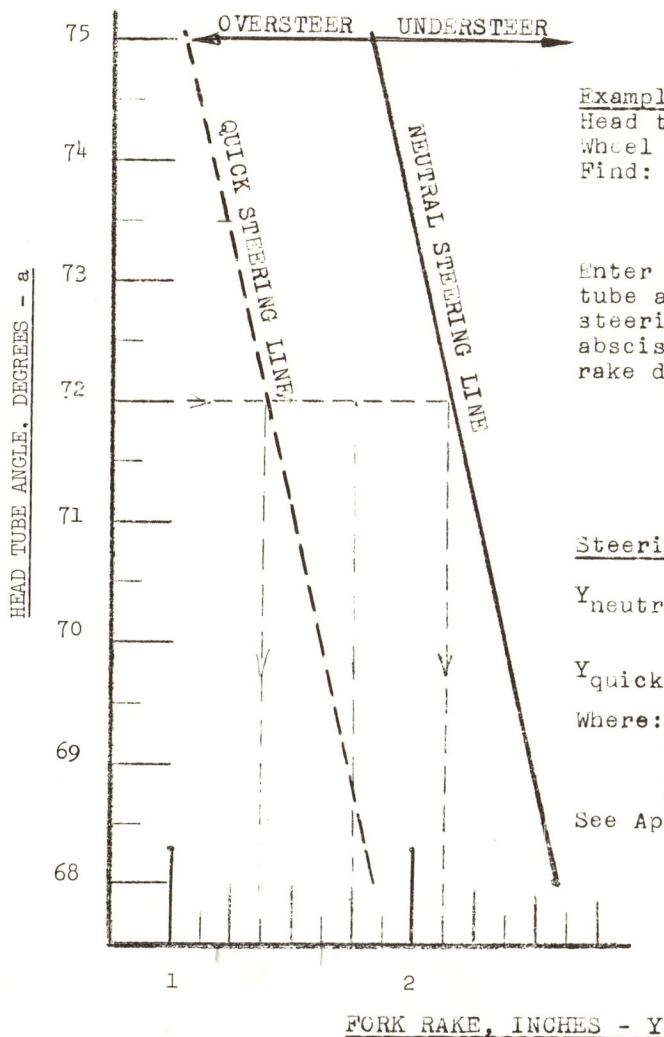

Example: General touring.
Head tube angle: 72deg.
Wheel dia.: 27 inches
Find: Rake dimensions for
      Neutral Steering
      Quick Steering &
      Touring use.
Enter graph at 72 deg. head
tube angle and move right to
steering lines. Drop to
abscissa and read the following
rake dimensions:
      Neutral: 2 1/8 inches
      Quick: 1 3/8 inches
      For touring select mid-
      point: 1 3/4 inches

Steering Line Formulas

$$Y_{neutral} = R \tan \left(\frac{90deg - a}{2} \right)$$

$$Y_{quick} = R \tan \left(\frac{90deg - a}{2} \right) - .75$$

Where:
      Y= fork rake, inches
      R= wheel radius, inches
      a= head tube angle, degrees
See Appendix Table V for tangents

Note: For general touring designs select rake approximately
      midway between the Neutral and Quick Steering Lines.
      Criterium and road racing designs require more over-
      steer and rakes should be based on Quick steering.
      Sports riders should stay within the range of Quick
      Steering and General Touring. Avoid rakes that fall
      in the understeer region or are shorter than Quick
      steering. GRAPH IS FOR 27 INCH DIAMETER WHEELS ONLY!

FIGURE I-2

15

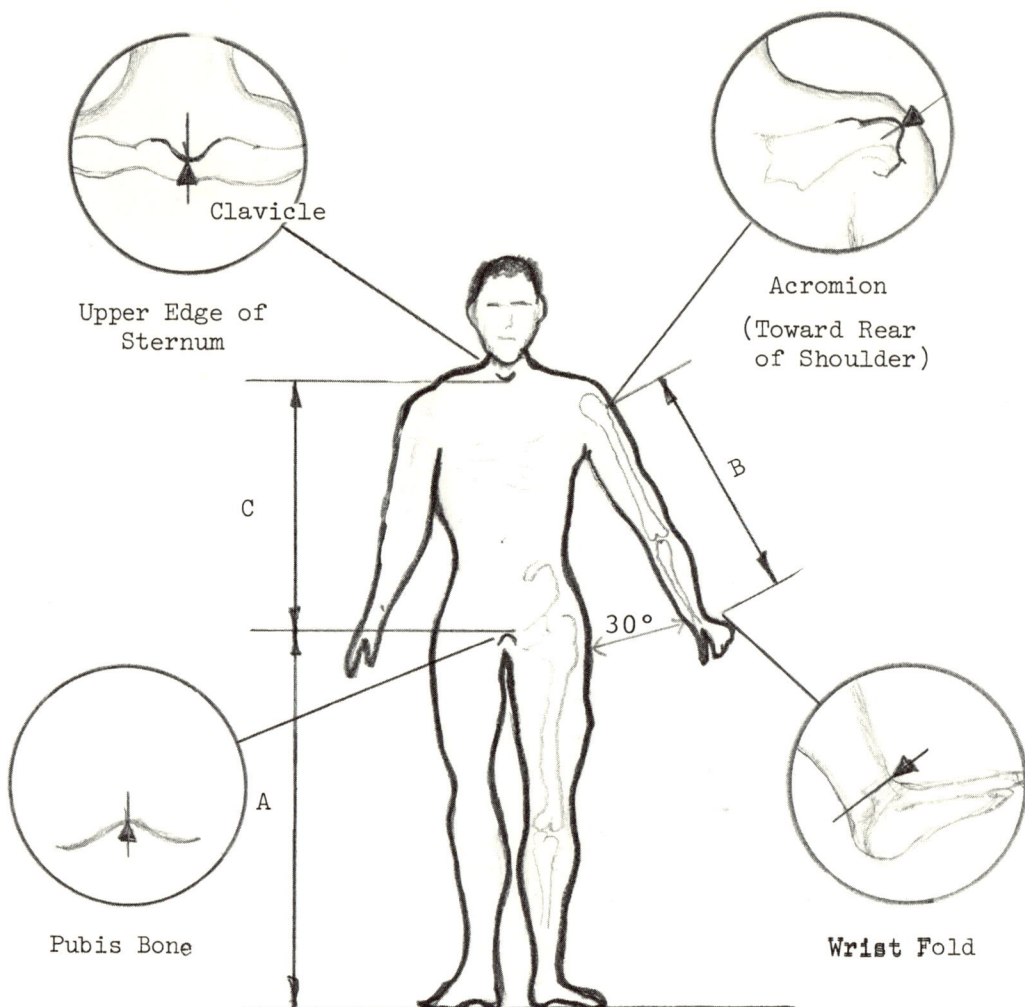

**ANATOMICAL DIMENSIONS REQUIRED
FOR USE OF TABLE I-A**

Important
Note: Weight Distribution Factor: In addition to the A,B, and C
dimensions you must make an estimate of deviations from
"normal" build. Individuals with heavy hips and narrow
shoulders will require steeper seat tube angles than those
with more massive shoulders and lighter hips and buttocks.

FIGURE I-3

TABLE OF ANATOMICAL DIMENSIONS AND
TUBE LENGTHS — CENTIMETERS

Column 1		Column 2	
Lower Limb (A)	Seat Tube Length	Upper Torso (B+C)	Top Tube Length
80	51	100	53
81	51.7	101	53.4
82	52.4	102	53.8
83	53.1	103	54.1
84	53.7	104	54.4
85	54.3	105	54.7
86	54.9	106	55
87	55.5	107	55.3
88	56.1	108	55.6
89	56.7	109	55.9
90	57.5	110	56.2
91	57.9	111	56.5
92	58.5	112	56.8
93	59	113	57.1
94	59.5	114	57.4
95	60	115	57.7
96	60.5	116	58
97	60.9	117	58.3
98	61.3	118	58.6
99	61.7	119	58.8
100	62.1	120	59
		121	59.2
		122	59.4
		123	59.6
		124	59.8
		125	60

Notes

1. To use table for English measurements, multiply inches by 2.54 to obtain centimeters; then enter table in centimeters. Obtain tube length in centimeters, and convert back to inches by dividing tube length by 2.54.

   Example - Find seat tube length for "A" dimension of 37 inches. (A = 37 x 2.54 = 93.98 cm) Enter table at 94 cm. Read seat tube as 59.5 cm. Now convert the seat tube length to inches.
   $$\frac{59.5}{2.54} \text{ cm} = 23.43 \text{ inches}$$

2. Refer to Figure I-3 for location of A, B, and C dimensions.

TABLE I-A

The frameset geometry developed from information in Chapter 1 can now be used to make a design drawing of the frameset. For ... ... half scale side view ... the center lines onl... The ... familiar... technique may ...wish... pproach an... make a ... raphic multi... iew...ooking b... ot absolutel... ...an. Fi... nches or ce...imeters — is up to... vhat you ar... most comfortable... ength data in Table ... A are in ... working in inch units, convert to centimeters y multiplying your dimensions by 2.54 efore entering the table. Figure I-1 illustrates ll principal lines, angles, and dimensions iscussed in the following step-by-step layout rocedure.

Make the drawing on a 20 x 30 inch sheet of opaque drawing paper or transparent vellum. Vellum is more practical because reproductions can be made easily from it. You will need the following drawing supplies: a drafting board or other suitable drawing surface, T-square or straight edge, protractor or adjustable triangle graduated in half-degree increments, compass, ruler, irregular curve, pencils, and erasers.

Since the drawing will be made half-size, all full-size frameset dimensions must be halved before laying them out on the sheet. Similarly, when scaling up measurements from the drawing, lengths are doubled. Begin by securely attaching the sheet to the drawing surface with masking tape. Arrange the 30 inch edge so it is horizontal.

Using a T-square or straight edge, draw a heavy horizontal line across the width of the sheet 3 inches above its bottom edge. This is the baseline (ground) on which the wheels will rest. Next, draw a thin line across the width of the sheet to represent the horizontal wheel axis center line. Assuming the frameset is designed for 27 inch wheels, the line will be $6\frac{3}{4}$ inches (to scale) above the baseline. It is important to realize that differences do exist between the 27 inch norm and the many rim and tire combinations available. If you are to be accurate, measure the actual diameter of the rim and tire combination you plan to use on the frameset. Now determine the actual wheel axle height by halving that dimension. Some purists may also want to subtract an additional $\frac{1}{16}$ or $\frac{1}{8}$ inch from the wheel's radius to allow for the slight flattening of the tire. Now draw the center line.

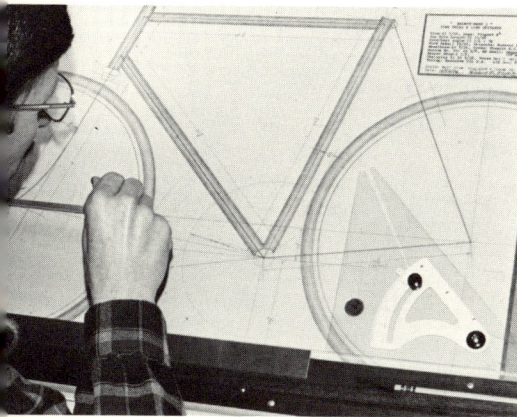

2.1 Laying out a design.

Eric? If not, donate to the Beulah Library for their book sale. The Grits

The next step is to establish the bottom bracket height. Select an appropriate height based on the crank length and bicycle use considerations presented in Chapter I. Then, at that distance above the baseline, draw a horizontal line across the width of the sheet. Next, draw a short vertical line in the middle of the sheet so it intersects the horizontal line just drawn. The intersection marks the exact location of the crank axis (axis of central movement), the key point around which the frameset will be designed.

Using a protractor or adjustable triangle, draw the seat tube center line starting at the crank axis and sloping upward to the right at your selected seat tube angle. Remember, 73.3 degrees is what C.O.N.1 recommends for a rider of "normal" anatomical proportions. The exact amount of angular deviation from the norm, if any, is simply a matter of your best judgment — based on your unique body geometry. Normal range is from 75 to 68 degrees. Review the discussion on seat tube angle in Chapter I before you select an angle. It may be necessary to experiment, using several *trial* angles before arriving at a final decision.

Next, using the seat tube data obtained from Table I-A, lay out the seat tube length. Place the end of a ruler on the crank axis and mark that distance off along the seat tube center line. The mark indicates the top of the seat lug. Now, measure down the seat tube center line ⅛ inch from the top-of-lug mark just made, and make a second mark. The second mark is the point at which the center line of the top tube intersects the center line of the seat tube. The ⅛ inch setback (an approximation; your specific design may differ) takes into account the fact that the seat tube length is actually measured to the *top* of the seat tube rather than to the center line of the top tube. To be more precise, obtain the dimensions from the actual seat lug you plan to use.

Now, using the mark just made as a starting point, draw the top tube center line to its correct length as obtained from Table I-A. Set the protractor, or adjustable triangle, to the selected head tube angle (based on the discussion in Chapter I), and draw the head tube center line starting at the end of the top tube center line just drawn. The head tube center line should slope downward to the left, all the way to the baseline. The head tube center line is multi-functional: it represents the center line of the steering tube, the fork crown and the central axis of the upper part of the fork blades. At any point along the head tube center line and *perpendicular* to it, construct a line 3 inches in length. The fork rake will be laid out along this line.

Determine the required rake using either the graph or formulas in Figure I-2 and the exact wheel radius determined when you set the wheel axle height. Lay the rake dimension out along the 3 inch line just constructed; then, draw a second sloping line parallel to the head tube center line so it passes through the rake mark. This line is the rake line. Where it crosses the horizontal wheel axis center line is the location of the front wheel axle. Now draw the outline of the front tire; place the point of your compass on the front wheel axle, open its pencilled tip to the wheel's radius, and draw a circle. Also draw the wheel rim now.

Continue laying out the rest of the fork assembly by deciding on the amount of clearance desired between the front tire and the underside of the fork crown. The dimension will vary according to whether or not you plan to use fenders, the brake reach, and stiffness considerations. Once established, the clearance dimension must be laid out on the head tube center line, *not the rake line*. Start at the point where the tire circle crosses the head tube center line, and mark the clearance distance with a heavy pencil stroke. This sets the location of the underside of the crown. As a last step, double check the front brake dimensions to be sure the brake pads will reach the rim with the selected wheel clearance.

Now determine the distance from the underside of the crown to the bottom of the head tube. To do this accurately, you need the exact dimensions of the fork crown and the lower headset assembly. One way of obtaining them is to visit a local bike shop and measure a bike equipped with the same type of crown and headset you plan to use. If you have the crown and headset on hand, then measure them directly. If neither of these options is available, then use ⁹⁄₁₆ inch for the headset height, and ⅜ inch for the distance from the crown's underside to its headset race seat.

When you have established the overall distance, lay it out on the head tube center line, making a second mark to locate the bottom of the head tube. Measure up from the second mark 1⅜ inches, and place a third mark on the head tube center line. This locates the *approximate* intersection of the head and down tube center lines (may vary depending upon specific lug design and intersection angle). Now, draw the down tube center line by connecting the crank axis to the intersection point just described.

Next, lay out the desired fork blade curvature. This is most easily accomplished using an irregular curve and hand-fitting a curved line between the front wheel axle and the point at which the blade attaches to the crown. To achieve accuracy, draw the blade-end of the particular crown you plan to use. Once the crown-to-blade connection point is established, sketch in several different-shaped curves to get an idea of which one will best serve your particular purpose. Recall from the discussion on fork stiffness in Chapter I that the specific blade curvature, either a long radius bend starting near the crown or a shorter sweep located close to the front wheel axle, influences the shock absorbing qualities of the fork. It is unlikely you will be able to purchase blades that match the desired curve exactly. You may have to make some compromise between what is theoretically possible and blade shapes commercially available. Two alternatives are to buy straight blades and bend them yourself, or find a supplier who will custom bend them for you.

Before we leave the front end, if you plan to mount a fender, be sure the selected head tube angle permits sufficient space for it to clear the down tube. Also, check the length of cranks you will be using to see if the front wheel, or fender, will interfere with the toes of your cycling shoes when the fork is turned (toe clip interference). To check this, open your compass so that it will describe an arc equal in radius to the crank length plus the distance between the pedal's axle and the toe of your cycling shoe. Place the compass center on the crank axis, and sweep an arc in the general direction of the front wheel. If the arc overlaps the tire or fender circle, then you may have toe clip interference. On some racing designs this is unavoidable but usually

presents no problem to the racer who takes it into account in his riding style. On the other hand, if yours is a touring design, toe clip interference can be a hazard.

Within the limits imposed by a fixed top tube length, seat tube angle, bottom bracket height, and crank length, toe clip interference can be overcome only by making the head tube angle shallower. A laid back tube and the resulting increase in rake will both act to lengthen the distance between the front axle and the crank axis, eliminating the interference problem. These moves may require an offsetting increase in the length of the chain stays to prevent an imbalance in weight distribution. I should also point out that if the amount of toe overlap is small you probably will not have an interference problem because, as the fork is rotated about the head tube axis, the wheel's periphery follows an arc pulling it away from the interference zone. It is beyond the scope of this text, but a true picture of the wheel's turning arc can be obtained by making a *normal view* on the drawing. Now complete the layout of the head tube by establishing its upper limit. Depending on specific lug design, the tube's end will be approximately 1⅛ inch above the intersection of the top tube and head tube center lines.

The last element to be designed is the rear triangle. The most important dimension here is chain stay length. Decide on an appropriate length based on the performance characteristics and weight distribution criteria described earlier. Place the end of your ruler on the crank axis and mark the horizontal wheel axis center line at the selected distance. This locates the rear axle. Now connect the two points with a straight line. Next draw the seat stay center line by connecting the point of intersection of the seat and top tube center lines with the rear wheel axle. In an Allen Key Fastback design, the seat stay center line is drawn to the center of the seat bolt tube. (See Figure VIII-1 for details.)

Draw the seat tube, rear tire, and rim outlines. See how much clearance exists between the tire and the edge of the seat tube. If using fenders, the rear fender outline should also be drawn. Ascertain whether there is enough clearance to pull the rear wheel forward and remove it from the drop-outs without resorting to tire deflation. If the frameset is designed for all-out sprinting, then the inconvenience of having to deflate the tire to get the wheel off may be a small price to pay for the improvement in stiffness. If you want to eliminate the problem, lengthen the chain stays, but remember, you are also changing the weight distribution.

At this time you may want to check the wheelbase to see how your design compares with contemporary custom framesets built for the same purpose. If it comes up shorter than desired use your eraser and go back over the design, increasing the chain stay length and decreasing the head tube angle until you obtain the wheelbase you want. If you aim for high performance and want a really stiff, quick-handling frameset, rework the design, experimenting with shorter chain stays and more upright head tube angles. Whatever the adjustments, try to keep them balanced to maintain proper weight distribution.

Once you are satisfied with the overall geometry and wheelbase, mark the location of the brake bridge on the seat stay center line. Its location is based on brake reach and fender considerations. Also locate the chain stay bridge, placing it so that it does not impair wheel removal or restrict the use of a fender if you are designing for touring.

The basic geometry of the frameset is now defined. An aesthetic touch is to draw in all tube, lug, drop-out, and fork outlines, rendering a true orthographic view of the assembly rather than just a one-line representation. Also, scale the tube lengths, and mark their *true* dimensions on the drawing. Record all angular dimensions as well. Finally, a Bill of Materials should be listed on the sheet showing complete specifications for tubing, lugs, drop-outs, etc. Selection of these components will be discussed in Chapter VI.

If the layout is on vellum, make several prints to use in the shop during construction. This will save wear and tear on the rather fragile original. If the drawing is made on opaque paper, purchase a can of Krylon "Workable Fixatif" from a stationer or graphic arts store, and spray three or four coats on the sheet. The protective coating it provides will give the drawing more durability and prevent smudging.

For those who may have decided not to build a frameset but instead will be serviced by a professional framebuilder, the effort put into making a first-class design drawing is *still* worthwhile. With your specifications and drawing in hand, the builder will have a much better idea of your needs, and you will have a ready means of checking his compliance with your instructions.

CHAPTER III

A PRIMER ON BRAZING
KEY TO SUCCESSFUL CONSTRUCTION

Construction of a roadworthy, home-built frameset will ultimately rest on your ability to master the rudiments of brazing. No assembly operation is more essential to guarantee its structural integrity and, unfortunately, none is quite so difficult to learn. Even if all braze-on attachments are eliminated, the frameset will require at least 22 brazed joints. Some designs may need as many as 45 or more. Each joint must be done correctly. The penalty for poor brazing is more than cosmetic; failure of a lug or blade connection can lead to a disastrous road crash.

I hope not to discourage you because, even if you have never handled a torch, brazing skills can be learned provided you are persistent and willing to make the necessary effort. It is a *hands-on* learning experience requiring much practice — you learn by *doing*. Those who already know how to braze and are familiar with brazing alloys may skip over the remainder of this chapter. For the rest of you, let's start with the subject of torches.

Torches

Most readers are probably familiar with the common handyman's propane torch. Perhaps you already own one. It is possible to braze an entire frameset using one of these. However, a propane/air torch does not develop much heat and burns with a relatively low temperature (maximum is about 3,700 F). The torch might do a passable job on most joints if a rod of high silver content were used (it melts at a lower temperature than conventional brass material), but difficulty would be encountered in heating the more massive joints to proper

temperature and holding them at that level during the brazing process. The likely result would be "cold-brazed" connections at such locations as the fork crown and bottom bracket shell, with the attendant risk of subsequent structural failure.

The following is a list of common air and oxyfuel torches with their respective flame temperatures. The hotter the flame the more BTU's available and the easier it is to bring the joint up to temperature and keep it there.

Torch Type	Maximum Flame Temperature
Propane/Air	3,700 F
Mapp Gas/Air	4,700 F
Mapp Gas/Oxygen	5,255 F
Acetylene/Oxygen	5,615 F

The best torches for frameset brazing are the last two — Mapp Gas/Oxygen and Acetylene/Oxygen. The latter combination is widely used by professional framebuilders. Unfortunately, these rigs are quite costly for a one-bike project. Unless such equipment can be rented or borrowed you will most likely have to do the job using a Mapp Gas/Air torch.

Sometimes referred to as "Supertorches," Mapp Gas/Air rigs are available at most hardware stores and the larger discount chains. The price for a complete kit containing the "Supertorch," gas cylinder, small torch head, safety glasses, igniter, and rod is about $25 at the time of this printing. Purchase an extra two cylinders of Mapp gas when you buy the torch. If you own a Propane/Air torch, it still can be put to good use in conjunction with your new Mapp Gas/Air unit, as will be explained later.

One note of caution while using Mapp gas is that the flame temperature shown in the table is possible only when the torch is equipped with its special head. The device is designed to induce a greater volume of air than conventional heads and to provide the optimum air to fuel mixture for the Mapp gas fuel.

The Brazing Process

Brazing is a process in which a joint between two metals is made by drawing a liquid, nonferrous, filler metal into the space between closely adjacent surfaces of the parts to be joined at a temperature *above* 800 F. The parts that make up the joint need not be made of similar metals, they are not heated to their melting points, and they are not of the same composition as the filler metal.

By contrast, *soldering* is a process in which the parts to be joined are heated to temperatures *below* 800 F. The term soldering should never be applied to conventional frameset construction because all contemporary filler metals used for joining bicycle tubing require heating to temperatures exceeding 800 F. In this regard, the term *silver-soldering* is an unfortunate misnomer and is frequently misused to describe what is actually a brazing process employing silver alloy filler metals (in common parlance — "silver rod"); the correct term is *silbrazing*. With these definitions in mind, let's take a closer look at the properties of filler metals.

Filler Metals — Brazing Rods

Filler metals are alloys composed of two or more elements combined in various ratios to achieve specific physical, chemical, and electrical properties in the brazed joint. Silver, copper, zinc, cadmium, phosphorus and tin are some of the more commonly used elements. Melting temperature, flowability, material strength, and corrosion resistance are some of the variables that can be controlled by formulating these and other elements in various combinations and ratios. Filler metals are manufactured in several forms. The most common shapes used for framebuilding are rods and wires.

An interesting and seemingly paradoxical characteristic obtained when combining certain metals is that the resulting alloy has a lower melting point than any of its constituents. For example, pure copper (Cu) melts at 1,881 F and pure silver (Ag) at 1,761 F. If both are combined to make a filler metal containing 50 percent silver and 50 percent copper and the alloy is heated, it will start to melt at 1,435 F, but the temperature will have to be increased an additional 140 F (to 1,575 F) before complete liquefaction is achieved. The temperature at which the alloy just starts to melt and below which it remains solid is called its *solidus*. The temperature above which the material is fully liquid is called its *liquidus*. The difference between the two temperatures is defined as the *melting range* of the alloy. In the example just given, the solidus is 1,435 F, the liquidus is 1,575 F, and the melting range is 140 F. Note that the solidus and liquidus temperatures of the alloy are lower than the melting point of either of its constituents.

Now observe what happens to an alloy made of the same constituents but with the ratio changed to 72 percent silver and 28 percent copper. The new alloy will still have to be heated to 1,435 F before melting starts, but at this temperature the alloy *completely* liquefies; the melting range has been reduced to zero. Alloys with this thermal characteristic and those with very narrow melting ranges are called *eutectics*.

By combining different elements in various ratios, brazing rod manufacturers are able to control the strength of these materials and their thermal, chemical, and electrical properties to fit specific joint applications. Rods with narrow melting ranges, or of *eutectic* composition, are very fast flowing and are best used in places where prolonged heating would be detrimental to the parts being joined. Also, for these alloys to develop their full design strength, joint clearances must be relatively small. Rods with expanded melting ranges are termed sluggish and find wide application where clearances are large or where precise joint gaps cannot be maintained. Typical applications are where large gaps must be bridged or a thick buildup of material is required, such as in joint filleting.

From a framebuilder's viewpoint, free flowing, low liquidus, eutectic-type rod would be favored for lugged connections where joint clearances can be maintained between .003-.005 inch. Conversely, joints with larger gaps and those where clearance dimensions cannot be assured require the use of rods with sluggish flow characteristics. Such fillers are usually best applied to brazing the front and rear drop-outs, the seat-stay-to-seat-lug attachment, and the bottom bracket shell/chain stay joints.

Rods used for frameset brazing are mainly general purpose alloys containing silver and copper, or brass (which is mostly copper and zinc). Commonly used *silver* rod ranges from 45 percent to 60 percent silver content, and when alloyed with zinc and certain other metals can be made to melt at around 1,100 F. It has excellent tensile strength (66,000 to 90,000 PSI range) *provided* joint clearance is held to within the recommended .003-.005 inch. It also has high flexibility and good corrosion resistance. The best applications for silbrazing are sleeved joints, such as the lugged connections in the main triangle and, in certain instances (where joint clearances don't exceed .005 inch), the fork crown joints of cast or forged units. Because of their mass, these crowns are sometimes difficult to heat using a Mapp Gas/Air torch alone. The low melting temperature of silver rod and its high flowability and strength thus permit a better joint in this application than would a rod of higher liquidus. The lower melting temperature of silver alloy also gives greater protection from possible tube damage due to overheating. Silver alloys are more expensive than brass, but for the small quantities required in a single frameset, not prohibitively so.

Filler rods containing a lower percentage of silver, and brass rods, usually have higher melting temperatures, 1,300 F to 1,700 F depending on specific composition. Extra care is needed when using these alloys to prevent tube overheating. Overheating or prolonged heating causes embrittling of the base metal and reduces tube strength. In the case of Reynolds "531" the limiting temperature is about 2,000 F before substantial loss in strength occurs. The margin of error when using silver alloy for joining "531" is thus approximately 900 F, while with brass or other hard fillers it is often as little as 300 F. Colum-

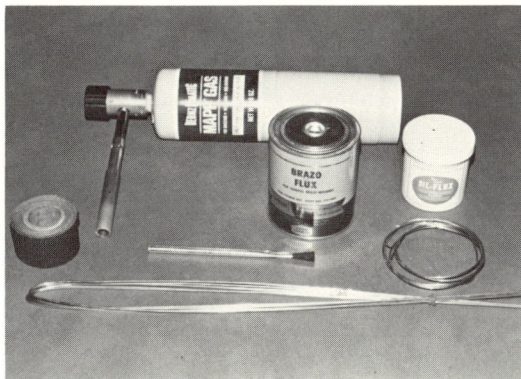

P3.1 Brazing equipment and supplies, Mapp Gas/Air "Supertorch," production cloth, flux brush, powder flux for brass rod (large can), paste flux for silver, brass rods and coil of silver alloy.

bus tubing is even more temperature sensitive and should never be heated above 700 C (1,292 F).

Good sources of quality rod and flux are professional custom framebuilders, frameset material suppliers, and local welding supply houses. The latter may sell only in lot quantities larger than what you will need. With all the different types of brazing material available at these outlets, it is possible to end up with the wrong alloy. In this regard, you are cautioned never to use rod containing even a trace of cadmium. When heated to brazing temperature, alloys containing cadmium generate toxic cadmium oxide fumes which, if inhaled, can be fatal! DON'T USE CADMIUM.

Brazing alloys used by framebuilders are sold in rod and wire form. Brass and low-silver content alloys are usually available as rods. The handiest size for frameset brazing is $\frac{1}{16}$ inch diameter or less. The more expensive high-silver content alloys are made in the form of wire coils—$\frac{1}{32}$ to $\frac{3}{32}$ inch diameter. A comparison chart and specifications covering major domestic brazing alloys is shown in Table III-2. Table III-3 contains detailed data on four cadmium-free silver brazing alloys.

When you buy rod, also purchase flux that is suitable for the particular brazing alloy and temperature range being used. Most suppliers will furnish assistance in making a specific choice. Fluxes are important because they provide a protective atmosphere which inhibits the formation of oxides—a principal source of surface contamination. Fluxes are available in powder, paste, and liquid form. Table III-4 provides application information on two proprietary brazing fluxes.

How Brazing Works

We will now focus our attention on the three fundamental principles underlying the formation of all brazed joints: capillary action, wetting, and diffusion, then discuss basic brazing techniques.

Capillary Action

You may recall from high school physics that capillary action is that phenomenon which causes liquids to rise in small bore tubes or spaces. Capillarity is caused by cohesion — that force by which atoms or molecules of dissimilar substance are held together.

In a properly brazed joint, the molten alloy must *completely* fill the space between the surfaces being joined. The smaller the space, the greater the degree of capillarity. From this explanation it may be surmised that proper fit and clearance are fundamental to successful brazing. To assure capillarity, the joint should be set up so that the clearance gap is small and uniform over its entire length, and the surfaces must be as clean as possible. The closer this ideal is approximated, the better the quality of the joint.

Wetting

Wetting is a phenomenon in which the surface tension of a liquid in contact with a solid is relatively low and the liquid spreads out to *wet* the solid. The action of brazing flux is most important here. When heated to the proper temperature, flux changes to a watery consistency, then acts as a cleaning agent clearing the joint surfaces of all oxides. The flux provides a shielding action for the molten alloy as it flows throughout the joint.

Diffusion

Diffusion is the ability of some of the atoms of the liquid brazing alloy to become an actual part of the solid surfaces being joined. Such interchange increases the strength of the joint. The process is not one of melting but is rather an exchange of atoms between both solid surfaces being joined and the brazing alloy.

Brazing Practice
The Basic Stages in Brazing a Joint

There are five basic stages in making a brazed joint:

- Cleaning the surfaces to be joined.
- Fluxing to facilitate capillarity, wetting, and diffusion.
- Assembling the joint and positioning it.
- Heating the joint to proper temperature.
- Cleaning the joint after brazing.

Cleaning the Surfaces to be Joined

From our discussion of the principles underlying the brazing process it should be evident that meticulous cleaning of the joint surfaces is essential for a strong bond. Cleaning is accomplished using emery, or, preferably, aluminum oxide production cloth. All joint surfaces must be thoroughly sanded to the bare metal. Any residual sanding dust must also be removed before going on to the next step.

Fluxing

In frameset building, a paste-type flux is generally brushed onto the joint surfaces. The flux is specially formulated for the type of rod used and the brazing temperature range. When heated, flux turns watery and provides a cleansing medium (discussed earlier) in which the processes of capillarity, wetting, and diffusion are accelerated.

Assembly

Specific joint assembly techniques and clamping are covered in detail in the chapters concerning frameset construction. The general principle is to securely hold the parts to be joined in a position that assists the flow of molten brazing material throughout the joint. The parts must also be held in a manner that promotes uniform heating. For example, vertical arrangement of a lugged joint will facilitate the flow of molten brazing material by using gravity to advantage, while fire bricks or heat reflectors can be employed to speed up and promote uniform heating.

Heating

Uniform heating to the proper temperature is very important. Prolonged heating or overheating must be avoided to prevent "cooked" joints and damaging changes to the grain structure of the base metal. The torch technique necessary to achieve these goals is learned only through much practice. As an aid in judging metal temperatures, a color-coded temperature chart for steel is contained in Table III-1. The chart is the principal means of gauging joint temperatures. A secondary indicator is flux action; when it turns watery and starts to run, the temperature is in the vicinity of 1,100 F.

Study the chart carefully, and become familiar with the temperature/color relationships, especially the dangerous colors of yellow and white. With 45 percent silver rod, the joints need only be heated to approximately 1,100 F, a dark cherry red. When using the harder rods, such as brass or those silver alloy fillers with elevated liquidus, more heat must be applied, bringing the parts up to at least 1,400 F, a full cherry red. Here is where color recognition and proper torch handling are important to prevent overheating. On heavier joints, two torches may be required to bring the joint to brazing temperature. As mentioned earlier, heat reflectors and fire bricks may also be arranged around the joint to promote uniform heating and reduce cold spots.

Joint Cleanup

After brazing, parts are allowed to cool *slowly,* then are immersed in flowing water and brush-scrubbed to remove residual flux. If left to harden, flux turns into a glass-like coating that is very difficult to remove. If the first scrub does not remove all of it, then wire brush the joint under a flow of *hot* water. Final cleanup entails finish-filing and sanding which are discussed in the chapters on construction. To minimize the amount of joint cleanup required, always wipe excess flux from around the joint *before* brazing, otherwise molten brazing alloy will follow the flux outside the immediate joint areas, creating a real mess.

Safety Precautions

When brazing, the following precautions should be taken:
- DO NOT USE ROD CONTAINING CADMIUM.
- Always wear safety glasses or goggles.
- Avoid breathing fumes given off by fluxes. Braze in a well ventilated area.

Keep a window open and use an exhaust fan, if possible.
- Wear gloves, and remember that it takes a long time for parts to cool before they can be picked up bare-handed.
- Keep a small fire extinguisher or water bucket nearby.
- When brazing parts that are held in wooden jigs, be careful not to ignite the jig.

Learning How to Braze

The best way to learn brazing is under the guidance of an experienced instructor. No book can duplicate that. Investigate the possibility of taking a formal course before trying to teach yourself. Local high schools and vocational schools usually offer adult education classes or extension programs. If courses in welding or brazing are not offered, you may still be able to get some brazing practice and instruction by enrolling in an allied course, such as auto repair, auto body, metal working, or plumbing. If none of these options is available, then you are on your own.

A variety of manuals and other sources of information on brazing are listed in Appendix Table IX. A call to your local welding supply house can bring a wealth of material at no cost. I do suggest delaying purchase of a torch or brazing supplies until *after* you have finished reading this book and have made a decision on whether to attempt construction yourself or go to a professional builder. If you do decide to proceed on your own, then borrow, rent or buy a torch, order some rod and flux, and purchase a few lugs and tubes to practice on. (Junked bikes are one source of *free* tubing.) As you practice, cut apart the completed joints and examine them to determine the degree of alloy penetration and the strength of the bond. *"Destructive testing"* is a particularly useful learning tool and is really the only way to gauge your proficiency (or lack of it).

Keep practicing until you are convinced either that you can do a passable brazing job or that brazing is simply not for you. If you come to the latter conclusion then, by all means, have a professional framebuilder construct the frameset for you. Perhaps you will make the decision to contract the work out, based on your reading of this chapter. If that is the case, the chapters on design and materials of construction, plus the up-to-date list of professional custom framebuilders con- tained in Appendix Table VIII, may be of im- mediate use to you.

COLOR/TEMPERATURE CHART FOR STEEL

Color	Temperature (Deg F)
Dark blood red, black red	990
Dark red, blood red, low red	1,050
Dark cherry red	1,175
Medium cherry red	1,250 *
Cherry, full red	1,375
Light cherry, light red	1,550
Orange, free scaling heat	1,650
Light orange	1,725
Yellow	1,825
Light yellow	1,975
White	2,000

*Close to maximum temperature for Columbus tubing. See cautionary note in Appendix Table III.

TABLE III-1

J. W. HARRIS AND COMPETITIVE BRAZING ALLOYS
SPECIFICATION TABLE

AWS NUMBERS	J.W. HARRIS CO. INC.	HANDY & HARMAN	ALL STATE	ENGELHARD	OTHER	AIRCO	UNITED WIRE	WESTINGHOUSE	Ag	Cu	Zn	Cd	Ni	Sn	OTHER	Melt	Flow
BCup-2	Stay-Silv 0	Fos-Flo 7	21+Silflo-O		180 & 800	Phos-Copper	Phoson 0	Phos-Copper		92.75					7.25 P	1310	1460
	Brayzon		23						2	92.0					7 P	1185	1450
BCup-6	Stay-Silv 2	Sil-Fos 5	Silflo-5	Silvaloy 5	1804	Arcosil No. 5	Phoson 5	Phos-Silver 2	5	91					7 P	1185	1450
BCup-3	Stay-Silv 5		29		1803		Phoson 6	Phos-Silver 5	6	88.75					6.25 P	1175	1350
BCup-4	Stay-Silv 6	Sil-Fos	Silflo-15	Silvaloy 15		Arcosil No. 15	Phoson 15	Phos-Silver 6	15	86.5					7.5 P	1185	1300
BCup-5	Stay-Silv 15							Phos-Silver 15		80					5 P		
	Stay-Silv 20	Braze ATT		Silvaloy 20	1600		Sil-20C		20	45	30	5				1140	1500
BAg-2a	Stay-Silv 30			Silvaloy 30					30	27	23	20				1125	1310
	Stay-Silv 31	Easy-Flo 35	S-135	Silvaloy 35	Flotectic 2	Arcosil 35	Sil-Bond 31		31.5	34	15.5	19				1165	1390
BAg-2	Stay-Silv 35		111	Silvaloy 40	1700		Sil-Bond 35		35	26	21	18				1125	1295
	Stay-Silv 40								40	18	15	27				1120	1205
BAg-1	Stay-Silv 41	Easy-Flo 45	S-145	Silvaloy 45	1603	Arcosil 45	Sil-Bond 45		41	17	18	24				1125	1160
BAg-3	Stay-Silv 45	Easy-Flo 3	S-150N	Silvaloy 503		Arcosil 3	Sil-Bond 50N		45	15.5	16.5	24	3			1125	1145
BAg-1a	Stay-Silv 50n	Easy-Flo	S-150	Silvaloy 50		Arcosil 50	Sil-Bond 50		50	15.5	15.5	16				1170	1270
	Stay-Silv 50								50	15.5	16.5	18		3.0		1160	1175
	Stay-Silv 60								60	20	20	10				1270	1300
BAg-18	Safety-Silv 1115	Braze 603	155	Silvaloy 60	1800	Arcosil J	Sil-60T		60	30				10.0		1115	1325
BAg-7	Safety-Silv 1200	Braze 560		Silvaloy 355			Sil-56T		56	22	17			5.0		1145	1205
	Safety-Silv 1298			Silvaloy 105					45	30	12				13 Mn	1298	1298
	Safety-Silv 1305	Braze 505		502			Sil-60		50	20	28		2			1220	1305
	Safety-Silv 1325	Braze 600		A-33	Arcosil 60		Sil-65		60	25	15					1245	1325
	Safety-Silv 1331	Braze 650		Easy					65	20	15					1235	1325
	Safety-Silv 1340	Braze 752		K-427					75	22						1300	1330
	Safety-Silv 1435U	Braze ET		A-28	1602	Arcosil G	Sil-40		57.5	28			1.8		3 Mn	1250	1340
	Safety-Silv 1345	Braze 580							40	30.5	29.5			7.0		1120	1345
	Safety-Silv 1350								55	31.5	17					1150	1300
	Safety-Silv 1355								70	20	10					1150	1355
BAg-5	Safety-Silv 1360	Braze 700		Medium			Sil-70		45	30	25					1275	1360
	Safety-Silv 1370	Braze 450		A-18			Sil-45		40	36	24					1230	1370
	Safety-Silv 1400	Braze 400		A-14			Sil-EEN		40	36					2 Li	1235	1415
BAg-8a	Safety-Silv 1400L	Lithobraze BT		AE-102					30	38	32					1400	1400
BAg-20	Safety-Silv 1410	Braze 300		A-13			Sil-30		50	34	16					1250	1410
BAg-6	Safety-Silv 1425	Braze 501		Silvaloy A-25			Sil-50		40	30	28					1250	1425
	Safety-Silv 1435	Braze 403	100	Silvaloy 250	1601 & 200	Arcosil H	Sil-40N		50	28			2			1220	1435
BAg-4	Safety-Silv 1435U	Braze 720		Silvaloy 301	1806	Arcosil E	Sil-72		40	30	3					1435	1435
BAg-8	Safety-Silv 1450	Braze 750		Hard		Arcosil M			50	22						1365	1450
	Safety-Silv 1475	Braze 630		A-49					72	28						1275	1475
BAg-21	Safety-Silv 1490	Braze 800	120	A-11	181		Sil-80 (TRON)		75	22			2.5	6.0		1345	1490
	Safety-Silv 1500	Braze 202		A-4			Sil-20		63	28.5	4					1315	1500
	Safety-Silv 1550	Braze 090		Silvaloy 54			Sil-9		80	16	35					1410	1565
BAg-13	Safety-Silv 1575	Braze 541		A-79		Arcosil L	Sil-54N		20	45	38		1			1340	1575
	Safety-Silv 1577	Braze 250	164	Silvaloy 254			Sil-25		45	53	25		5.0			1250	1575
	Safety-Silv 1580	Braze 404		Silvaloy T-50					9	40	25		5.0			1220	1580
	Safety-Silv 1600	Braze 624		S-475					54	52.5						1425	1590
BAg-19	Safety-Silv 1635	Braze 951		AE-100					25	32.5					5A1	1550	1600
BAg-13a	Safety-Silv 1640	Lithobraze 925		T-562					40	7.3			2		2 Li	1400	1635
BAg-MN	Safety-Silv 1780	Braze 559		850	1807		Sil-85M		62.5	42						1420	1640
		Braze 852							95						15 Mn	1760	1780
QQS 561d	Stay-Brite		430		157				4			83		96		430	430
	Stay-Brite 8								6			95		94		430	535
	Alsolder 500	TEC	509	H-377	155 & 192X		Sil-5C			17	17					509	509
	Alsolder 740		105						5							640	740
BAg-3*	Ag Clad 50n	Trimet 258		Silvaloy Ply-metal #5031											Refer Stay-Silv 50n for Composition		
BAg-A*	Ag Clad 1435	Trimet 201		Silvaloy Ply-metal #2501											Refer Safety-Silv #1435 for Composition		

*Alloy on both sides of copper shim.

Reprinted Courtesy of J. W. Harris Co., Inc.

TABLE III-2

silver brazing alloys-cadmium free safety-silv®1200, 1350, 1370, 1410

These non-toxic alloys completely eliminate the danger of illness or death which can result from cadmium poisoning caused by cadmium oxide fumes. Safety-Silv alloys may be used on both ferrous and nonferrous alloys.

safety-silv 1200

This high 56% silver content alloy makes first-quality brazes. It is free-flowing, with unequalled capillary attraction and deep penetration. Ductility is very high, corrosion resistance suitable for all but strong chemical applications. Offers highest elongation of silver brazing alloys. The non-toxic composition deems it suitable for use in the food processing industry even where food comes into contact with the joint area. The color is bright silver, making an excellent color match for stainless steel and silver-ware applications. Thin sections of stainless steel and nickel (often subject to stress cracking when brazed with ordinary materials) will not crack when brazed with Safety-Silv 1200.

safety-silv 1350

Ductile, free-flowing alloy offers economy, good penetration into tight fitting connections, and medium temperature. Color is silver to light yellow as associated with polished brass.

safety-silv 1370

Excellent general purpose non-toxic silver brazing alloy. Often specified in Governmental use. Good ductility and capillary flow. Color is silver to light yellow as associated with polished brass.

safety-silv 1410

This is an economy alloy which has good strength and ductility. Safety-Silv 1410 flows in a sluggish manner making it especially good for loose fit-ups. This alloy requires additional heat and good supervision to insure the best results. Brassy in color.

flux

Use Stay-Silv white brazing flux on application requiring normal heat; Stay-Silv black flux on heavy parts, oven brazing or when parts are heated over a prolonged period.

forms

1/64, 1/32, 3/64, 1/16, 3-3/32 and 1/8″ wire diameter, bare rod, flux coated rod in straight lengths, coil, strip, rings and other types of pre-forms.

packaging

1, 3, 5 and 50 Troy oz. coils

Reprinted Courtesy of
J.W. Harris Co., Inc.

TABLE III-3

31

J. W. HARRIS SILVER BRAZING ALLOYS

specifications

HARRIS ALLOY	Chemical Composition				ASTM B-260-52T & AWS 5.8-76	Federal Spec. Q.Q.B. 654	Federal QQS-561d Army 196-131-80	Military MIL-B-15395A (Ships)
	Ag% Silver	Cu% Copper	Zn% Zinc	Sn% Tin				
Safety-Silv #1200	56	22	17	5	BAg-7	----	----	----
Safety-Silv #1350	40	30.5	29.5	-	----	----	----	----
Safety-Silv #1370	45	30	25	-	BAg-5	Gr. I	Gr. I	Gr. I
Safety-Silv #1410	30	38	32	-	BAg-20	----	----	----

properties

HARRIS ALLOY	MELTING RANGE		P.S.I.	Troy oz. per cu. in.	Specific gravity	Electrical Conductivity	Elongation	Wire length in inches per T.O.			
	°F Solidus	°F Liquidus						.031 1/32 dia.	.046 3/64 dia.	.062 1/16 dia.	.093 3/32 dia.
Safety-Silv #1200	1145	1200	66,000	5.00	9.49	11.9	36%	260	116	65	29
Safety-Silv #1350	1150	1340	70,000	4.80	—	—	—	270	120	67	30
Safety-Silv #1370	1250	1370	70,000	4.82	9.15	19.0	28%	270	120	67	30
Safety-Silv #1410	1250	1410	70,000	4.78	9.08	—	—	270	110	67	30

Reprinted Courtesy of J. W. Harris Co., Inc.

TABLE III-3 (continued)

stay-silv brazing flux (white)

For use with all silver brazing alloys on all metals other than aluminum, magnesium or titanium. Effective to 1600°F. Meets Fed. Spec. OF499C, Type-B. AWS 3A, AMS 3410, MIL 51F4A.

Case Packaging

(24) 1/4 lb., (24) 1/2 lb., (24) 7 oz. brush-cap, (12) 1 lb., (6) 5 lb., 50 lb. pails.

stay-silv brazing flux (black)

Use with silver or other brazing alloys liquidus below 2200°F. Recommended for stainless, heavy parts, and whenever heating cycle is prolonged. All metals other than aluminum, magnesium, titanium. Meets Fed. Spec. OF 499, AMS 3411, AWS 3B.

Case Packaging

(24) 1/4 lb., (24) 1/2 lb., (12) 1 lb., (6) 5 lb., 50 lb. pails.

Reprinted Courtesy of J. W. Harris Co., Inc.

TABLE III-4

CHAPTER IV

TOOLING UP

It isn't necessary to make a major investment in tools to build a satisfactory frameset. Chances are you already own most of what will be needed. The one exception will probably be files. Because hand-shaping comprises such a large portion of the labor that goes into frameset construction, it will pay to purchase a good selection of quality files.

Files

Lacking the sophisticated machinery of bicycle manufacturers and the larger volume custom framebuilders, amateur builders (and many professionals) rely heavily on hand-filing for shortening and mitering tubes, dressing and fitting lugs and other components, and finishing operations. The following table may be used as a guide to determine your file requirements. It is possible to do the job with fewer than these. However, if you scrimp too much, the amount of fine detailing work that can be accomplished will be limited, and the mitering task may turn into an unnecessarily difficult job.

If the number of files must be reduced, the Swiss diemaker's files can probably be pruned from the list. Also, if you have the right type of file available, but not in the suggested size, it still may be possible to use what is on hand. Experiment. Rifflers are costly but ideal for cleaning up lug edges both before and after brazing, an all but impossible task with larger files. Instead of purchasing a complete set of rifflers, try to buy them individually. Study some of the photographs in this book to get an idea of which shapes might be appropriate.

Suggested Files and Their Applications

File Size, Type, and Cut	Application
12 inch and 14 inch Half Round Bastard	Tube shortening and mitering. Rough finishing of integral fork crown, drop-outs, seat attachment, and domes.
10 inch and 12 inch Round Bastard	Mitering seat stay ends on an Allen Key Fastback attachment, metal removal from inside lugs, contouring radii on built-up connections, fork crown finishing, and drop-out hogging.
10 inch Mill Bastard	Tube chamfering, deburring, lug thinning, removing brazing material from tubes, finish-doming operations, finish-filing flat or large convex surfaces.
8 inch Warding File (3/32 inch thick or less)	Slotting fork and stay ends and dressing the seat tube slit.
Set of Diemaker's Rifflers	Finishing all tightly contoured surfaces and drop-outs. Filing lug outlines and cut-outs, both before and after brazing.
Set of Swiss Pattern Diemaker's Files	Used on any surface during preliminary shaping or final finishing where space prohibits use of larger files.

35

Always use handles on the larger files which are made with integral tangs. Handles help achieve better control and prevent hand injuries. Rifflers have small filing surfaces cut on each end and are made to be held like pencils to obtain precise control; handles are not needed for these. Swiss Pattern files are made with integral handles and may be held like rifflers or with two hands.

File teeth can be kept cleaner longer by rubbing chalk into them prior to each use. Also, frequently cleaning your files with a file card prevents their teeth from becoming filled up with metal (called pinning). A clean file cuts better and is easier to control. Use care in handling the files and avoid bumping them together; it blunts their cutting edges, prematurely aging them. Dull files are worthless and dangerous.

Scrapers and Burnishers

Other hand tools that are file-like in operation and good to have (but not mandatory) are a machinist's scraper and a curved burnisher. The scraper is a triangular piece of hardened steel sharpened on each edge. It is used to remove burrs from the insides and outsides of tubes and lugs. You can make one yourself by grinding and sharpening the edges of an old 6 inch or 8 inch three-square (triangular cross-section) file.

The curved burnisher is a throwback to the days when precision machine tools were brought to proper tolerance by hand burnishing — the process of smoothing and polishing. The tool has the general appearance of a scraper but is made with only two edges. Its blade is curved and drawn to a very sharp point at the tip with more rounded surfaces near the handle. By regulating the position of the tip, the user can both cut and smooth with the same tool. It is an excellent device for removing scratches from tubes and lug surfaces without having to cut away excess metal. The tool is also particularly useful for cleaning up lug seams on brazed joints and smoothing imperfections on surfaces adjacent to brazed seams.

Saws and Drills

For tube cutting, a hacksaw and several blades will be required. The blades should have a pitch of 28 or 32 teeth per inch to provide a smooth cutting action on the thin-walled tubing. A ¼ inch electric hand drill and assorted twist drills will also be needed. Metric hole sizes do not really present a problem; American standard number-size or even fractional-size drills will come close enough. Just be certain the drills are made of *high-speed steel*.

Brushes

You will need an old paint brush for cleaning the tubes with solvent and a stiff wire brush for removing flux.

Layout Tools

Suggested tools and sundries for layout and marking are as follows:

- Scriber
- Center punch
- Six-foot steel tape graduated in inches or centimeters
- Two steel straight-edges about three feet long
- Metal yardstick (may also be used as a straight-edge)
- Machinist's square
- Protractor
- Small can of Dye-Kem or similar type layout fluid

Layout and Clamping Aids

Ideally, all layout and construction work should be done on a rigid work bench equipped with a machinist's vise. You will also need at least nine 4 inch or 6 inch C-clamps. Special jigs and clamping blocks are required to hold the parts while they are being worked on. These last items are fabricated from wood and will be built by you. Their construction is covered in Chapter V.

Sanding Supplies

Aluminum oxide production cloth is the preferred abrasive for shaping and cleaning joints prior to fluxing and for surface preparation in general. The cloth is costly when purchased in small quantities. Contact a tool supply house and try to purchase through them. The most useful grades of cloth are 8 and 120 open grit. Avoid cheap emery cloth. It loads up quickly, is dusty, and does a poor job when compared to the fast cutting production cloth. If you must limit yourself to one grade choose the No. 120 open grit cloth in inch-wide roll form. In a pinch, the 120 grit may be used for both lug thinning and tube cleaning. Very fine grit cloth and papers will be required when painting the frameset. Details concerning these abrasives will be explained in Chapter XI.

Special Bike-Related Tools

You probably will not own any of these, and I do not recommend their purchase because they are too costly for a one-frameset project. Either rent them from a bike shop or professional builder, or pay to have the operations requiring their use done for you. The following special tools will definitely be used.

- Bottom bracket taps and facing tool
- Head tube reamer and facing cutter
- Fork crown race cutter

The following tools may also be needed, but you probably can get by without them.

- Steering tube threading die
- Headset cup setting tool
- Fork crown race setting tool

Part II
FRAMESET CONSTRUCTION

CHAPTER V

JIGS AND MISCELLANEOUS AIDS

Building a frameset that will meet reasonable alignment tolerances requires some means of holding the tubes in exact position while they are brazed together. This is best accomplished through the use of jigs. Mass production builders employ a variety of precision metal jigs to hold practically all frameset components during assembly and brazing operations. Unfortunately, such tooling is costly and beyond the reach of most amateur builders.

However, by substituting wood for metal it is possible to build some simple and inexpensive jigs that will do a passable job. It is neither practical nor necessary to make more than two — one for holding the fork components, the other to secure the main triangle tubes. In fact, you may get by with only one — the fork jig. The main and rear triangles can be completely brazed using C-clamps and clamping plates alone. I have done it that way, and luckily, alignment came out fine with practically no cold setting required. I urge you not to rely on *luck*. Save yourself the likelihood of a distorted assembly by spending the short time required to build the simple main triangle jig described later in this chapter.

Miscellaneous Aids

In addition to the two jigs, additional aids must be built before starting frameset contruction. Full details for making most of these items are shown in Figure V-1. Also, if your vise is not fitted with soft jaw covers, make a pair from sheet copper or aluminum; even wood will do. Jaw covers prevent marring of frameset components when they are vised.

Vise setups involving tubing require the use of special tubing blocks. These are absolutely essential to prevent the tubes from being crushed by the compressive force of the vise jaws. Build two sets of blocks in accordance with Figure V-1, one with a 1⅛ inch diameter hole, the other with a 1 inch bore. To make the concave surfaces, drill through the blocks using a wood bit, then cut them lengthwise removing about ⅛ inch of material from each cut-surface.

Make up four clamping plates using ⅜ inch thick scrap plywood or pine. A handy size is 4 x 8 inches. While you are at it, scrounge some scrap pieces of ⅛ inch thick fiberboard and cut two wedges to the shape shown in the figure. The plates are used in conjunction with C-clamps to hold certain tubes in alignment during brazing. The wedges are inserted into the bottom bracket shell to prevent tubes from slipping into its interior during stay-mitering and brazing operations.

Another helpful item is a fork cutting board (not illustrated). It is a piece of 12 x 18 x ¾ inch thick plywood, or particle board, upon which a full scale side view of the fork is laid out showing all principal center lines and part locations. The device is used by placing the drop-out and crown on the board, setting them up to conform to the pictorial representation. Next, the fork blade is aligned until it is in a position that will meet the required rake and designed curvature. The blade ends are then marked for cutting.

41

Building the Fork Jig

Figure V-2 furnishes plans for building the fork jig. The jig backboard is cut from ¾ inch thick unwarped plywood or particle board. The steering tube block is a length of 2 x 2 inch pine stud, and the axle block is a piece of 2 x 4 inch stud. The jig must be rigid, the surfaces true. Overall dimensions are not critical provided the fork assembly can be locked securely in place and held true in all planes. If you don't have a spare front axle and skewer then simply use a ⁵⁄₁₆ inch diameter threaded rod in its place. Washers and nuts may be used to clamp the drop-outs at the proper spacing, normally 100 mm. Use a front wheel hub to double check the distance. It is easier to get the jig parts aligned and assembled by gluing them together first. (P5.1) After the glue has dried, drill through the backboard, and an-chor the axle and steering tube blocks using flat head wood screws.

Building the Main Triangle Jig

The main triangle jig illustrated in Figure V-3 is used to hold the head, top, down, and seat tubes during brazing operations. All other frame tubes are held in place with C-clamps and the wood clamping plates discussed earlier. Construction is similar to the fork jig. Use at least ¾ inch thick plywood or particle board for the backboard and position the tube blocks using Elmer's glue or contact cement *before* reinforcing the jig with wood screws. Detailed instructions for setting up the jigs and using the miscellaneous aids discussed earlier will be given in Chapters VII, VIII and IX.

P5.1 Building the fork jig.

MISCELLANEOUS AIDS

(Not to Scale)

$\frac{1}{4}$"

2"

2"

2 $\frac{1}{2}$"

1" Bore

1 1/8"Bore

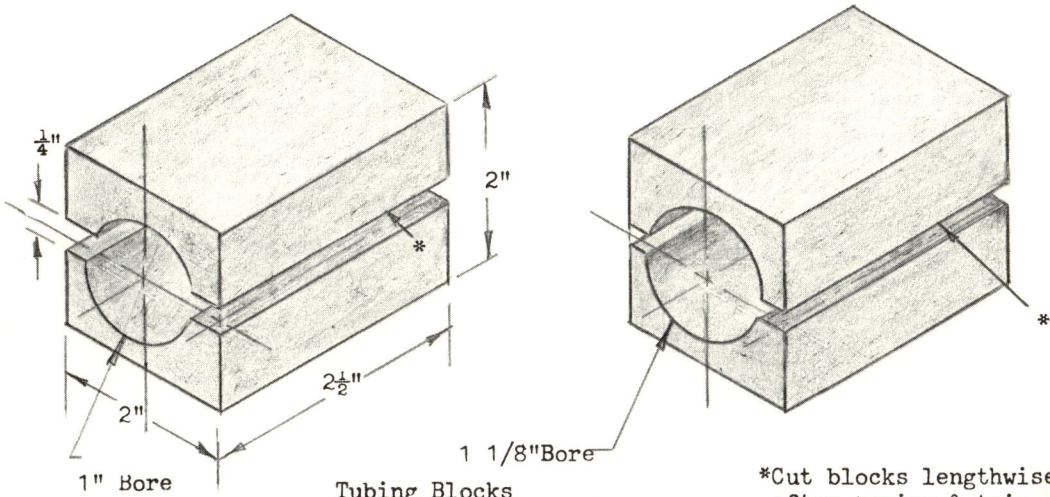

Tubing Blocks
(Make 1 of each size)
Hard pine

*Cut blocks lengthwise
after boring & trim each
surface 1/8".

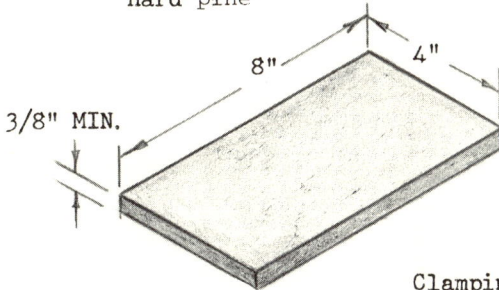

8"

4"

3/8" MIN.

Clamping Plate

(4 required)
Use plywood or hard pine

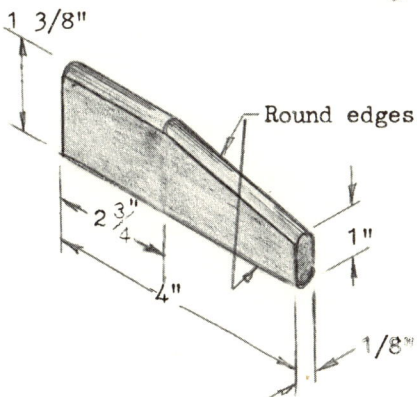

1 3/8"

Round edges

2 $\frac{3}{4}$"

1"

4"

1/8"

Wedge

(2 required)
Use fiberboard.

FIGURE V-1

FORK JIG

(Not to Scale)

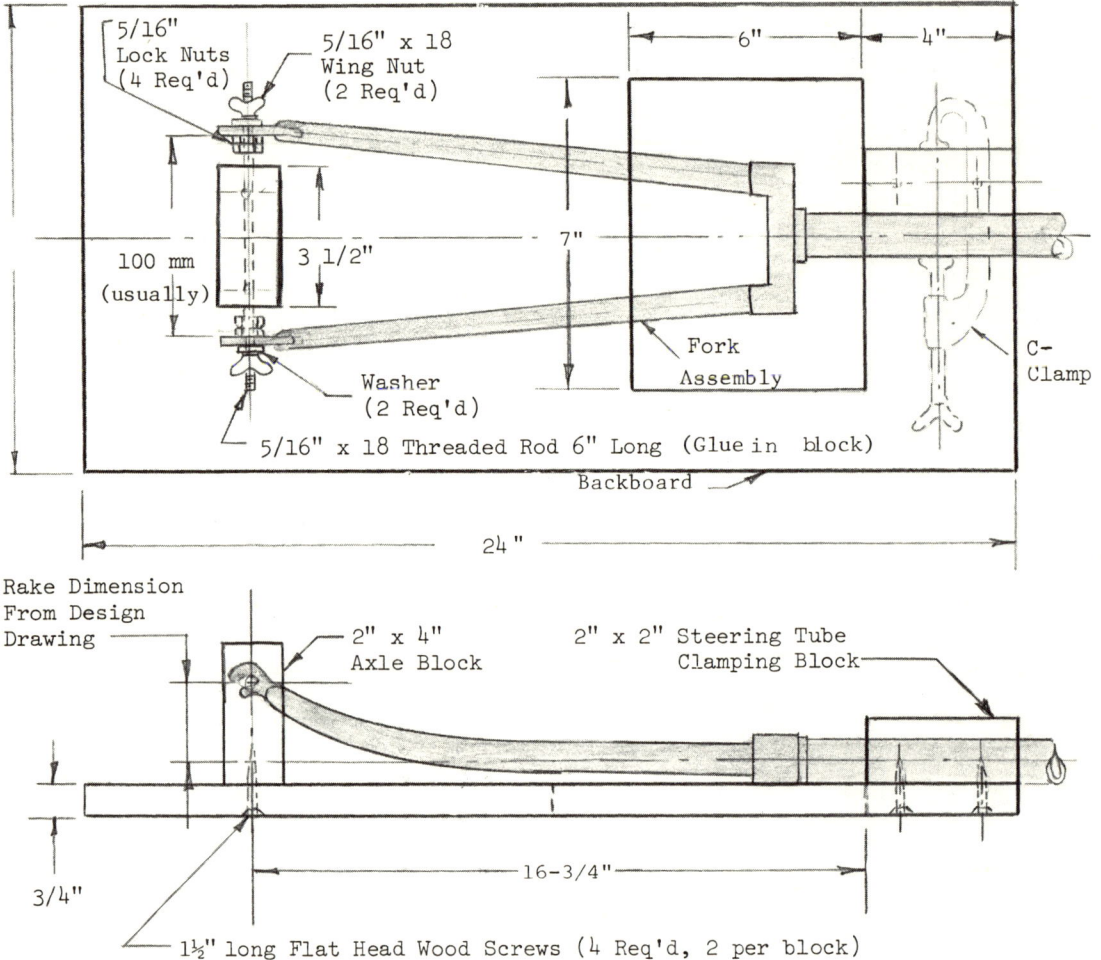

5/16" Lock Nuts (4 Req'd)

5/16" x 18 Wing Nut (2 Req'd)

6"

4"

100 mm (usually)

3 1/2"

7"

Fork Assembly

C-Clamp

Washer (2 Req'd)

5/16" x 18 Threaded Rod 6" Long (Glue in block)

Backboard

24"

Rake Dimension From Design Drawing

2" x 4" Axle Block

2" x 2" Steering Tube Clamping Block

3/4"

16-3/4"

1½" long Flat Head Wood Screws (4 Req'd, 2 per block)

Construction Notes :

1. Use unwarped piece of 3/4" particle board or plywood for backboard.

2. Make axle and steering tube clamping blocks from scrap pine stud stock.

3. Use fork parts and C-clamp to align blocks on backboard before gluing them in place. Use contact cement or wood glue. Double check dimensions and alignment in all planes then allow 24 hours drying time before installing wood screws.

4. If available, front hub axle assembly and skewer may be substituted for 5/16" x 18 threaded rod, nuts, and washers illustrated.

FIGURE V-2

MAIN TRIANGLE JIG

(Not to Scale)

Use sheet of 3/4" particle board or
plywood for jig backboard. Size
determined by main triangle.

Cut away to suit.

* Note: On
small size
frames, head
tube clamping
block may have
to be eliminated.

Cut away to suit.

2" x 2" clamping block
(typical for four)

Final out-
line of jig
backboard.

Typical tube
clamping arrange-
ment using C-
clamps.

2" x 2"
clamping
block (typ)
*

Cut away
to suit.

Cut away
to suit.

Section A-A

No shim required.

Section B-B

1/16" thick, sheet metal shim
strip. Drill near edges and secure
to backboard with brads.

Section C-C and
Section D-D

1/8" thick continuous
fiberboard shim. Nail
to backboard.

1 1/4" diam head tube

1/8" diam down tube

1" diam top or seat tube

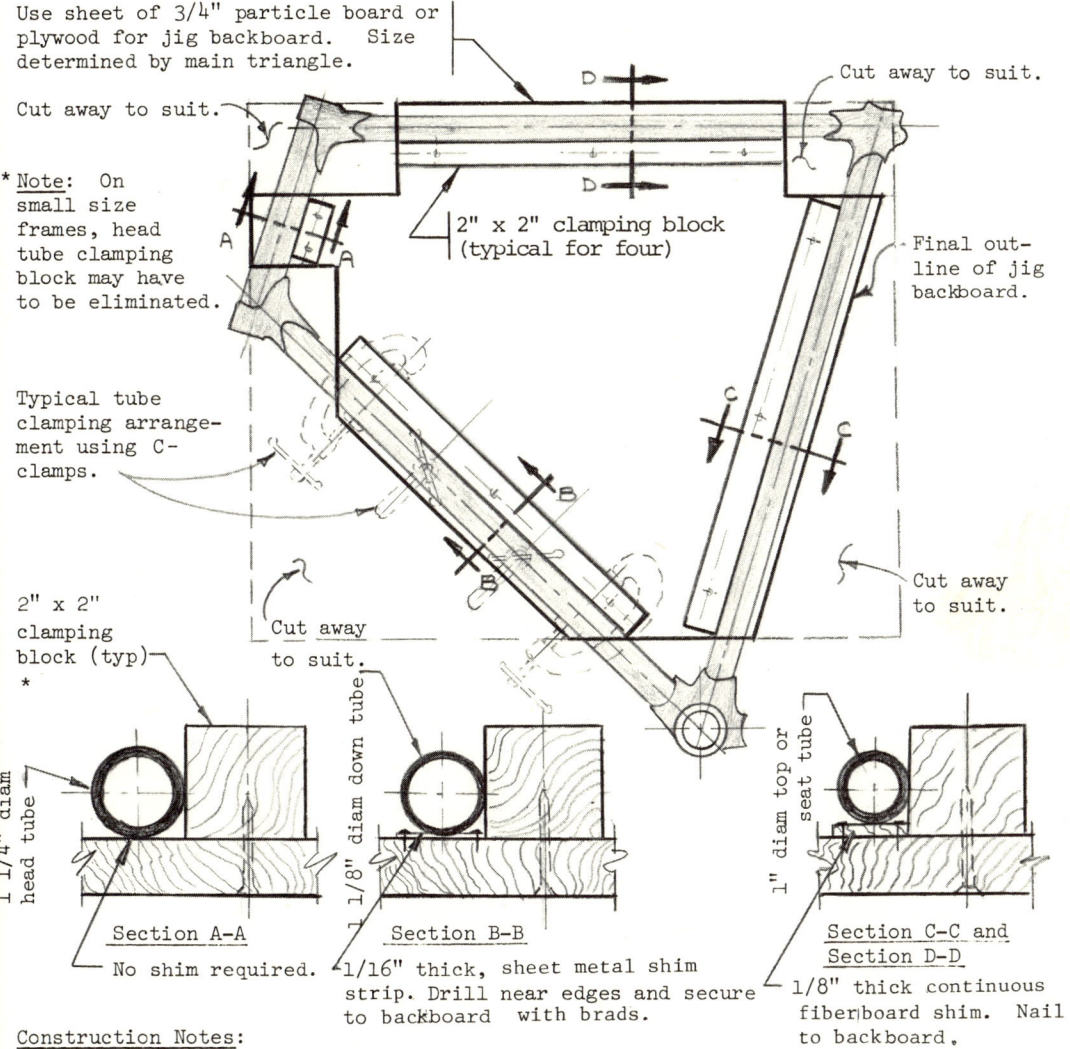

Construction Notes:

1. Lay out main triangle full size on jig backboard , then cut away areas indicated
   to permit clamping and clearance for brazing.
2. All clamping blocks cut from 2" x 2" pine stud stock, glued in place, then secured
   with 1 1/2" long flat head wood screws.

FIGURE V-3

45

CHAPTER VI

SELECTING FRAMESET MATERIALS

Chapters I and II laid a foundation for designing the geometry of your frameset, taking into account anatomical factors and the primary use of the bicycle. Materials of construction — tubes, lugs, crown, etc. — also affect bicycle performance and are an important consideration in attempting to achieve an energy-efficient design. First-time builders are advised to base the selection of these materials on practical aspects rather than on what is theoretically possible. Structural safety, ease of assembly, and your mechanical aptitude should be the paramount concerns. Professional builders have little difficulty constructing quality framesets using superlight tubing, radically cut-out lugs, and other lightweight elements because they possess skills that only time and experience can provide. Lacking such experience, a novice would be foolish to expect to duplicate the performance of these experienced craftsmen on his first attempt.

The discussion and recommendations that follow are thus heavily biased in favor of conservatism and practicality. The objective here is to give the novice a wide margin for error before the structural integrity of the frameset is compromised. As in any new undertaking, mistakes are inevitable, but through conservative selection of materials, their effects can be minimized.

Tubing

The well known Reynolds "531" butted steel tubing, manufactured by T.I. Reynolds, Ltd., of Birmingham, England, is widely used in constructing quality framesets. Other respected tubing manufacturers are A.L. Co-

lombo of Milan, Italy, makers of the high quality Columbus tubing; the French manufacturer Ateliers de la Rive, with its Durifort, Vitus and Super Vitus tubing; and two Japanese firms, Isiwata and Tange. Reynolds "531" is available from many retail mail order bike suppliers and most custom builders, while the other brands are not quite so accessible. Appendix Table VI contains a partial listing of retail suppliers who normally stock tubing in addition to lugs, crowns, bottom bracket shells, and other frameset materials.

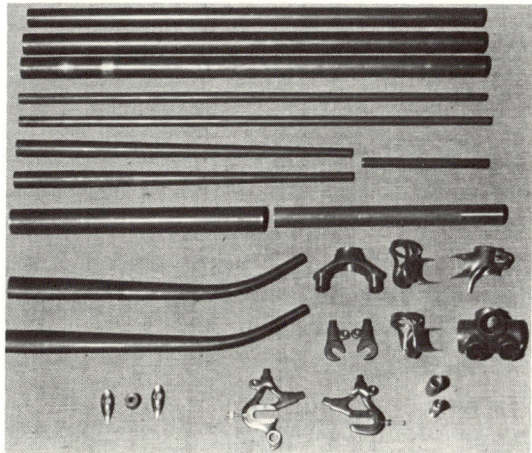

P6.1 Frameset materials. 12 piece Reynolds "531" butted, standard weight tube set, Cinelli integral crown, Prugnat S₄ lugs, Gargatte bottom bracket shell, brake bridge reinforcing diamonds with slip-on reinforcement, Sun Tour GS road drops, seat bolt tube and Allen-type seat bolt.

Bicycle tubing manufacturers offer their products in a variety of sizes, weights, and

47

butting configurations to meet a range of performance requirements. Some tubes can be supplied already preshaped at the factory, such as fork blades bent to specific rakes, indented or round-oval-round chain stays, and blades and stays with semi-finished ends. Even tubes of different alloy compositions, within a given manufacturer's line, are marketed for special applications. The recently introduced Reynolds "753" tubing is a case in point.

Most high-grade steel bicycle tubing is made from either chrome molybdenum or manganese molybdenum alloy steel and is butted, a process whereby the walls at the end(s) of the tube are made thicker than those of the remainder of the tube. Tubes may be single-butted (thicker walled only at one end), double-butted (thicker walled at both ends), straight gauge (constant wall thickness), or taper gauge (gradually thickened over most of the length of the tube).When butted, the thicker walled end(s) of the tube are made stronger and are thus better able to withstand the added stress at the frameset's joints.

Two corollary benefits accrue from butting. First, the extra thickness of the butt aids in offsetting loss of strength in the metal itself caused by heating during the lug brazing process, and secondly, the heavier wall allows for some unavoidable thinning which occurs when the completed joint is filed and sanded. Overall weight is reduced by thinning the walls in those areas of the tube where the stress is less and where little or no heating occurs. Also, only a minor amount of metal must be removed from these sections during finishing operations; hence, there is no need for extra thickness on that account.

Double butted, single butted, straight gauge, and taper gauge tubes may all be combined in a single frameset, the mix being dictated by specific tube function and duty requirements of the bicycle. Straight gauge tubing is used mostly for head tubes and bridges. It is also frequently employed for down tube service where extra strength is needed in larger size framesets or where the bicycle may be exposed to extreme loads. Because of the variety of tube brands, alloy compositions, butting configurations, and gauges available, custom builders will sometimes combine a mixture of tubes from different manufacturers to meet certain design objectives and to achieve the best balance between tube strength, weight, and resilience.

To simplify the discussion on tube selection, the following comments are confined to Reynolds "531". It is the tubing I used to build my first frameset. What is said for Reynolds has rough parallels in the other manufacturers' tube products, although metallurgical composition, gauge thicknesses, butting configurations, and sizes will vary among them.

Reynolds "531" Tubing

Reynolds "531" is high quality, precision made, seamless tubing manufactured from manganese molybdenum alloy steel. The manufacturer claims it is superior to chrome molybdenum for two reasons: first, it is said to possess superior mechanical properties; and secondly, the tubes are said to retain a greater percentage of those properties after brazing. The resultant benefit is claimed to be a frameset that can be made stronger than the same weight of chrome molybdenum, or lighter for the same strength. (At one time the "531" identified the ratio of various elements used in the metal, but now the number has no significance other than that of a trademark.) The present metallurgical composition of "531" is as follows:

Element	Percentage
Carbon	.23 - .29
Manganese	1.25 - 1.45
Molybdenum	.15 - .25
Silicon	.15 - .35
Sulfur	.045 max
Phosphorus	.045 max

Reynolds states its "531" has the following physical properties:

	As Drawn	After Brazing
Yield Stress	90,000 psi	80,000 psi
Tensile Strength	100,000 psi	90,000 psi

With its excellent strength and high fatigue resistance, "531" builds into a light, strong, and responsive frameset when properly handled. It may be heated to all normal brazing temperatures without excessive loss of tensile strength. Reynolds recommends brazing alloys with a melting point of 1,560 F; this is compatible with the brazing materials discussed in Chapter III.

Within the "531" line, the company manufactures heavy gauge, standard gauge, and a very light gauge tube known as "531 S/L" (Special Lightweight). We will be concerned mostly with standard gauge tubing as that is the minimum weight recommended for your first attempt. Reynolds "531" tubes are available double butted, single butted, straight gauge and taper gauge in lengths sufficient to build up to a 25½ inch frameset. A supplier's catalog will usually show the "531" butting configurations, shapes, gauges, lengths and sizes available. Illustrated catalogs may be obtained from several of the suppliers listed in Appendix Table VI or by writing directly to T.I. Reynolds, Ltd.

"531" Butting Configurations

Down tubes and top tubes of "531" are usually double butted. Head tubes are straight gauge. The steering tube is single butted. It is the heaviest gauge tube, is butted only on its crown end and is straight gauge on its threaded end. Single butted tube is used where bicycle components mate with the tube and provide supplemental reinforcement for it. Two such cases are the seat tube and steering tube. The butted end of the seat tube is brazed into the bottom bracket shell to provide extra strength at that point, while its upper unbutted end accepts the seat post, which furnishes supplemental reinforcing. In the case of the steering tube, its butted end is brazed into the fork where extra strength is needed; the unbutted end receives the handlebar stem which acts to stiffen the thinner walls at that end of the tube.

Taper gauge tubing displays a long gradual change in wall thickness along its entire length. Fork blades and stays represent this *special* kind of wall cross section. Reynolds "531" taper gauge fork blades are a unique case. If a tube of uniform diameter and wall thickness is compressed along its entire length to form a long taper towards one end (characteristic shape of blades and stays), a natural result will be a gradual thickening of the tube wall at the smaller end of the taper. The thick-

ened wall reduces resiliency at the smaller end of the tube and creates a stiff, unyielding, structural element. These are undesirable characteristics, especially in fork blades which must be flexible enough to even out road shocks, yet possess stiffness and strength at the same time. To prevent the problems associated with wall-thickening, special steps are taken in the manufacture of "531" fork blades.

The blade starts out as a single butted tube, the butt being formed on what will be the crown end. Butting provides the necessary stiffness and strength required at the highly stressed crown joint. The remaining, unbutted, tube wall is then gradually thinned out, diminishing in thickness toward the drop-out end. The blade is next worked into its final cross-sectional shape by compressing its unbutted length into a gradual taper in the direction of the drop-out end. This last forming process causes the wall thickness to increase as the tip is approached. The previously tapered wall thus returns to a state of near uniform thickness over its entire length. The butted crown-end is unaffected. When bent to the proper rake, the fork blade possesses the desired degree of resilience for absorbing shocks while retaining necessary strength and stiffness at its crown-end.

To become familiar with what a "531" butted standard weight tube set for a typical road frameset might consist of, refer to Table VI-1. It is a compilation of the tubes used on my first "home-built," a 23⁷⁄₁₆ inch road frameset. Comments on the listed tubes are contained in the table's notes. Figure VI-2 shows cross-sectional views of Reynolds "531" double and single butted tubes. You may want to select heavier gauge tube depending on the size frameset being built, your weight, or any unusual conditions that would impose additional loads. All tube dimensions in the table conform to Imperial (English) sizing as it is the most common. Continental (Metric) sizes are available, but they are far less popular in the U.S., and unless there is a compelling reason for doing otherwise, it is best to use Imperial sizes. Appendix Tables I and II contain a complete listing of the Reynolds "531" and "531 S/L" product line while Appendix Table III provides similar data for Columbus tubing.

Selecting Tubing

There are several factors to consider when ordering tubing or tube sets. First, the frame size should be specified so the supplier will ship tubes of the proper length. Also note, the *lower* the gauge number, the *thicker* the tube wall. A table of English legal standard wire gauge sizes, abbreviated SWG, and their equivalent thicknesses in inches and millimeters is contained in Appendix Table IV. Use this table and Appendix Tables I, II and III as a guide in deciding on the gauge of tubing to use. If you are heavy for your height, or if the bike is going to be subjected to rough treatment, then consider heavy gauge, especially for the down tube. If the frameset is larger than 24 inches, heavy gauge tubes should be considered regardless of your weight.

Lastly, it is important not to order tubing that is too long. For instance, if the steering tube length is excessive, you may end up cutting away too much of its butted end when trimming the tube to size. With the unbutted (thinner) section left to absorb the additional stress at the joint connection, the fork could be seriously weakened.

Selecting Fork Blades

Reynolds "531" fork blades are available in three cross sections: a 22 mm round, and two oval shapes. Oval cross sections include the new Continental oval measuring 27.5 x 20 mm and the traditional oval measuring 28.5 x 16.5 mm. *The oval blade dimensions must be matched to the specific fork crown being used.* Round blades are normally used only on track framesets. Blades are available in different rake configurations with ends domed, slotted, or simply plain cut. The plain cut is recommended to allow maximum flexibility in custom finishing the ends to your own design.

When ordering fork blades specify the rake and blade curvature, the cross section dimensions, and include a full-size outline drawing of the blade with your order. Some suppliers stock blades in five or more rake patterns; a drawing of your particular design will aid in getting a better match-up (also necessary if blades are ordered custom bent).

Selecting Lugs and a Bottom Bracket Shell

The selection of lugs and a bottom bracket shell is not as critical or involved as the purchase of tubing. However, lugs do perform several important functions. In the completed frameset their principal task is to distribute stresses through the joints and onto adjacent tube members; this spreads the load over as large an area as possible and results in a stronger overall structure. By using lugs with cut-outs or windows and carefully tapering and thinning their edges, the builder also ensures that the joint will flex. Flexing is necessary to prevent abrupt changes in load distribution, a principal cause of joint failure. During frame assembly the lugs also act as jigs, helping to hold the tubes in proper alignment while they are brazed together. Finally, lugs add aesthetic appeal, lending balance and beauty to the assembled frameset. You may even cut your own window designs and outlines to add a personal touch. For the novice, lug finishing can be the most satisfying of all construction operations; it is an art form in itself.

Your tubing supplier will probably have a fair selection of lugs and bottom bracket shells available. Lug ID's must, of course, be compatible with the OD of the tubing being used, i.e. Imperial or Continental. If you have remained in the English "camp" there will be little problem; lugs sized for Imperial tube diameters are widely available. Thread dimensions and width of the bottom bracket shell must also be specified. Again, English threading is the most common, but French and Italian are available.

Lug Specifics (Figure VI-3)

The more popular lugs are manufactured in two ways. The most common and least expensive method is that in which the lugs are cut from sheet steel, rolled and pressed into final shape, then welded at their seams. Many manufacturers use this method. For the most part, the process is entirely suitable; however, the lugs may look a bit crude before being worked into final shape.(P6.6) They also sometimes split along their welded seams while the joints are being brazed, a particularly aggravating circumstance that means a lot of extra work for the builder. To minimize

his possibility dress the lugs' edges prior to
brazing, but save the last bit of thinning work
until afterwards.

A second and newer lug manufacturing
process is investment casting. While more
costly than the cut-form-weld method, investment, or lost wax casting as it is sometimes
called, has many advantages over other
manufacturing methods. It produces a dense,
high quality, precision part requiring little or
no finishing work. Castings may be produced
with extremely thin or intricate cross sections
while maintaining close dimensional control.
Because of these advantages, investment
casting is becoming more widespread, not
only in making lugs, but in the manufacture
of precision fork crowns, bottom bracket
shells and drop-outs.

The process has two variations — flask
casting and shell casting — but these differ
only in the way the molds are made. Shell
casting will be outlined here. The process
begins with the making of a precision,
reuseable metal die. The die is a two piece
form in which a cavity has been made for producing a heat disposable pattern of the part to
be cast. The pattern is formed by injecting
molten wax or plastic into the die where it is
left to solidify.(P6.2)

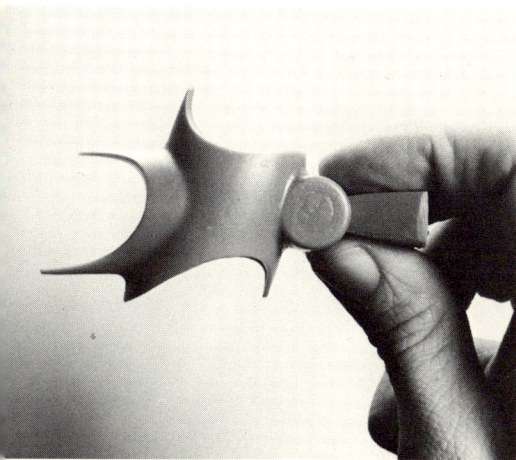

*P6.3 Front view of a Henry James investment cast
steel seat lug. Note integrally cast shoulder against
which the seat tube will rest. Top of the lug is
already contoured to final shape.*
Photo courtesy Henry James Bicycles, Inc.
Redondo Beach, California

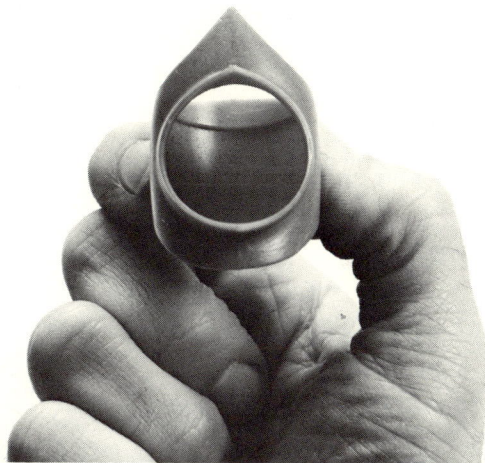

*6.2 "Wax" for a Henry James seat lug. It is being
held by its gate (where the molten steel will enter the
mold). This wax replica has all the detail of the final
lug — including pre-tapered walls.*
Photo courtesy Henry James Bicycles, Inc.
Redondo Beach, California

The die is then opened and the pattern, a
perfect replica of the part to be cast, is removed and dipped in a ceramic slurry, then
stuccoed with several layers of refractory ma-
terial to build a coating $\frac{3}{16}$ to $\frac{1}{2}$ inch thick. The
assembly is allowed to thoroughly dry, then is
placed in an oven and fired to 1800-2000 F.
The heat disposable wax, or plastic, melts and
flows out of the mold through a previously
provided opening. The high temperature fir-
ing turns the shell into a ceramic material.

Immediately after the shell is removed from
the furnace (the shell has now become a mold)
it is filled with molten metal by gravity, pressure, vacuum or centrifugal force. The
permeability of the shell allows gasses and air
to escape as it is filled, permitting the molten
metal to completely fill the mold. This assures
a metallurgically sound casting with close
dimensional tolerances. Also, during the fir-
ing, the ceramic formed produces a smooth
porcelain finish on the mold's inner surfaces
and creates a casting having a similar surface
texture. When cool, the mold is destroyed,
and the finished part is removed.(P6.3)

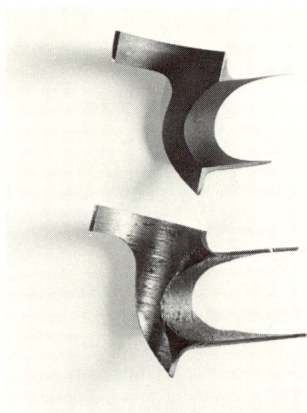

P6.4 Cut-away sections of Henry James investment cast head tube top lug (upper) and typical stamped lug (bottom). Note differences in surface finish and lack of voids in the investment cast part.
Photo courtesy Henry James Bicycles, Inc.
Redondo Beach, California

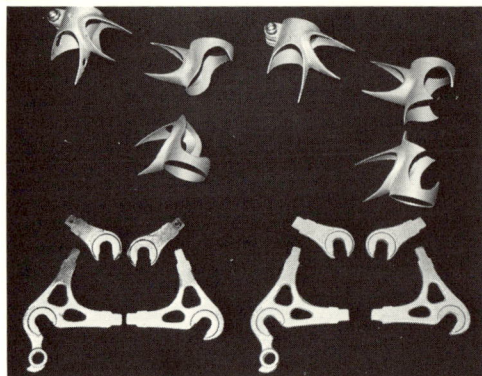

P6.5 George P. Wilson investment cast lugs and drop-outs. Material is 14PH stainless steel.
L to R Top: SUPER PRO and STANDARD lugs.
Bottom: ULTRA-LIGHT and STANDARD drops.
Photo courtesy George P. Wilson
Hemet, California

Investment cast lugs are available in various outlines and are made with holes to match a variety of frame angles. This is because investment castings are quite rigid and cannot be as easily bent as their pressed steel counterparts. Investment cast lugs are currently not marketed as extensively as other types, but with the addition of three new American manufacturers they soon should become more readily available to amateur builders.

Some of the more popular European lug manufacturers are Prugnat, Bocama, Haden Nervex and Cinelli, with the latter making investment cast lugs that enjoy a good reputation among professional builders. George P. Wilson, an American manufacturer and professional framebuilder, makes a fine set of investment cast stainless steel lugs that are now available to amateur builders. (P6.5)

Henry James Bicycles, Inc. is another domestic manufacturer that will soon be producing and marketing the "Cleanline" brand of investment cast lugs. The addresses of the American manufacturers are contained in Appendix Table VI. Lugs of foreign manufacturers may be obtained through the bicycle parts retailers, also listed in the table.

Due to their availability, Prugnat lugs are popular among novice builders. The company makes a wide variety of pressed steel lugs to meet almost every type of design. Shapes include the familiar model S_4 with its fancy cutouts and various scroll and long-point designs. Prugnat also makes plain lugs for those who want to create their own designs or

P6.6 Front view of a typical stamped seat lug.
Photo courtesy Henry James Bicycles, Inc.
Redondo Beach, California

52

who simply like the Spartan look. Prugnat's road lugs are made to accommodate a tube angle of 73 degrees, their track model — 75 degrees. Do not despair if your tube angles differ from these. The company states angles may be builder-altered ± 2 degrees. That gives a range of 71 through 75 degrees for road lugs and 73 through 77 degrees for the track lugs.

Bottom Bracket Shells (Figure VI-3)

Gargatte manufactures a bulge-formed, steel bottom bracket shell that is popular and readily available to amateur builders. Shells may be purchased with special cutouts, but I do not recommend them. They open up the crank bearings to moisture and dirt unless a sleeve is used. More importantly, cut-outs can also weaken the shell. The spigots that are an integral part of the shell are another matter, and they may be barbered to any contour you desire. When ordering a shell be sure to specify desired threading, width, and the size tubing being used — Imperial or Continental.

If you desire a European-made investment cast shell, Roto and Cinelli are both popular among domestic builders. In this country, the "Cleanline" investment cast shell manufactured by the previously mentioned Henry James Bicycles, Inc. also enjoys a good reputation among top professional builders. (P6.7)

6.7 Henry James CLEANLINE investment cast bottom bracket shell.
Photo courtesy Henry James Bicycles, Inc.
Redondo Beach, California

The Fork Crown (Figure VI-3)

The fork assembly, and the crown in particular, are the most severely stressed components in the frameset. This is one area where compromising strength for weight can lead to dire consequences. An ancillary consideration, perhaps more important for the novice, is that of using a crown design that is inherently safe, even in the event of a less-than-perfect brazing job.

Steel crowns are made by forging, investment casting, conventional casting, or stamping. There are two basic designs — a shell type where the fork blades fit into holes in the crown and an integral type where the crown is made with tangs that fit inside the fork blades. Further divisions in each type can be made according to the shape of the crown's shoulders.

There are pros and cons for each type of crown. Shell designs are generally lighter than integral ones and, if investment cast, are made to very close tolerances requiring little finish work. The blade sockets of investment cast designs are a close fit with the mating blades, permitting the use of silver brazing rod. When properly brazed, the joint is very strong and results in a fork assembly that yields an ideal combination of strength and lightness. We are speaking of a *perfectly* brazed joint; a novice may braze in a manner far less exacting than the accomplished brazer and problems can develop. The sockets of shell crowns are sometimes shallow. In addition, their sides may be cut away, leaving fancy shapes but little material to resist side loads. A high quality brazing job is required.

By contrast, integral crowns like the Cinelli type or similar designs have tangs that fit deep inside the blades; there are no cut-outs. Because of these features a faultily brazed integral crown joint should have less severe consequences on the road than a poorly made shell crown joint. Forces tending to bend the blades sideways would be better resisted by the deeper ears of the integral crown than the shallow shell-socket sides which, in some cases, have less wall bearing area. You will have to be the final judge on which type to use. If a forged or conventionally cast integral crown is employed, be prepared for some extensive filing work. These parts are quite hefty in their unfinished state.

Several European companies manufacture crowns that are popular in the U.S. and are available to amateur builders. Cinelli offers two forged integral crown models, one with shallow sloping shoulders, the other fully sloped. The company also manufactures a high quality investment cast unit used by many professional builders. Vagner makes a variety of light, strong, forged-steel shell crowns; one of their most popular is a flat-shouldered diamond top model. Frejus, Haden and Bocama are other quality crown manufacturers.

In the U.S., quality investment cast crowns are currently being manufactured and sold by Proteus Design. (P6.8) Their address may be found in Appendix Table VI. The previously mentioned Henry James Bicycles, Inc. also manufactures an investment cast unit.

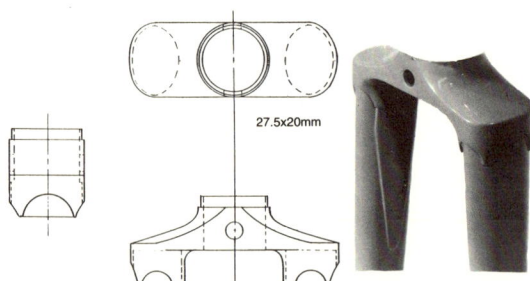

P6.8 Proteus investment cast semi-sloping fork crown.
Photo courtesy Proteus Design
College Park, Maryland

Drop-Outs (Figure VI-3)

Campagnolo, Sun Tour, and Zeus are but a few of the many foreign manufacturers making road, track, and vertical forged drop-outs for the American market. American-made investment cast drops are manufactured by both George P. Wilson and Henry James Bicycles, Inc. (P6.5) A good feature on the Sun Tour GS road model and on similar designs is that the drop-outs are *offset* to simplify alignment and to minimize the amount of cold-setting after brazing. A French manufacturer, Huret, makes rear drop-outs that have an integral derailleur conduit stop, a clever feature that will save you one brazed connection.

Road drops come with axle adjuster screws and are made with or without eyelets for mounting fenders and carriers. Vertical drops are currently in vogue, but I do not advocate their use by novice builders because they require a precision brazing jig to achieve perfect rear wheel alignment. Use adjustable road or track drops to save yourself a lot of aggravation. Vertical drops became popular on professionally built racing framesets because of the modern trend toward shorter wheelbases and ultrashort chain stays. If your design incorporates short stays, it is still possible to use adjustable road dropouts, but they must be modified. This will be covered in Chapter IX.

Braze-Ons

My personal preference is to keep the frameset as clean as possible and free of all but a few basic items, such as pre-threaded water bottle nuts, down tube shifter stop, and a rear derailleur cable housing stop. This is done to minimize the number of brazed joints. Actually, for a derailleur-equipped machine with down tube mounted shifters you can get by with but one braze-on, a small tab attached to the down tube to keep band-mounted shift levers from sliding along the tube.

At the other extreme, the frameset can be built with all conceivable kinds of paraphernalia. The more commonly used braze-ons one might consider, other than those already mentioned, are derailleur control bosses, left and right derailleur cable guides, brake cable housing tunnel guides, bridge reinforcing diamonds, reinforcing tabs, carrier anchorages, generator and light brackets, pump pegs, etc. Figure VI-3 illustrates many of the popular braze-ons, in addition to lugs and other framebuilding materials available from one retail mail order supplier.

This completes our discussion of frameset materials. More detailed data can be found in specification sheets and catalogs which may be obtained by writing directly to manufacturers and distributors. For a partial listing see Appendix Table VI.

The remaining chapters deal with the actual frameset construction process. Some of the

54

assembly setups discussed will be quite complex. I urge you to pay particular attention to the captioned construction photographs that accompany the text. It is easy to change a design mistake on paper, but once you are locked into a cutting and brazing setup, the rectification of errors can be a horrendously time consuming and costly task.

REYNOLDS 531 — STANDARD WEIGHT, BUTTED TUBE SET

Used for 23 7/16 inch Road Frame
Imperial Tube Sizes

Tube	Type of Butting	Wall Thicknesses SWG	Wall Thicknesses Inches	OD Inches	Notes[3]
Steering Tube	Single	13/16	.092/.064	1[1]	Butted on crown end, available in various lengths.
Head Tube	Straight Gauge	19	.040	1 1/4	Available in extra long lengths.
Top Tube	Double	21/24	.032/.022	1	Also available in 19/22 DB and extra long lengths.
Down Tube	Double	20/23	.036/.023	1 1/8	Also available in 19/22 DB and extra long lengths.
Seat Tube	Single	21/24	.032/.022	1	Also available in 19/22 SB and extra long lengths.
Seat Stays	Single	20	.036	(13 mm)	Also available in 16 mm OD and extra long lengths.
Chain Stays	Single	21	.032	(22 mm)	Also available in extra long lengths.
Brake Bridge	Straight Gauge				
Chain Stay Bridge	Straight Gauge				
Fork Blades	Taper Gauge	18/21	.048/.032	Oval Size[2] 28.5 x 16.5 mm	Can be furnished in five rakes.

(1) English thread, 25.4 mm x 24 T.P.I.

(2) To fit Cinelli fully sloping integral crown.

(3) For complete listing of "531" butted tubes available, refer to Tables I and II in Appendix.

Data Courtesy of T.I. Reynolds Limited, Birmingham, England.

TABLE VI-1

CROSS SECTION VIEWS OF DOUBLE AND SINGLE BUTTED TUBES

(Not to Scale)

3" Short Butt	2" Taper	11" Parallel	2" Taper	6" Butt
75 mm	51 mm	200 mm	51 mm	152 mm

25.4 mm 1"

Stamped identification
mark on this end.
Reynolds 531 D/Butted 21/24

24"
610 mm

All shortening
must be done
on this end.

REYNOLDS 531 DOUBLE BUTTED TOP TUBE

28.6 mm

1 1/8"

*

Stamped identification
on this end.

*Butted end dimensions same as
short butted end of top tube.

REYNOLDS 531 SINGLE BUTTED SEAT TUBE

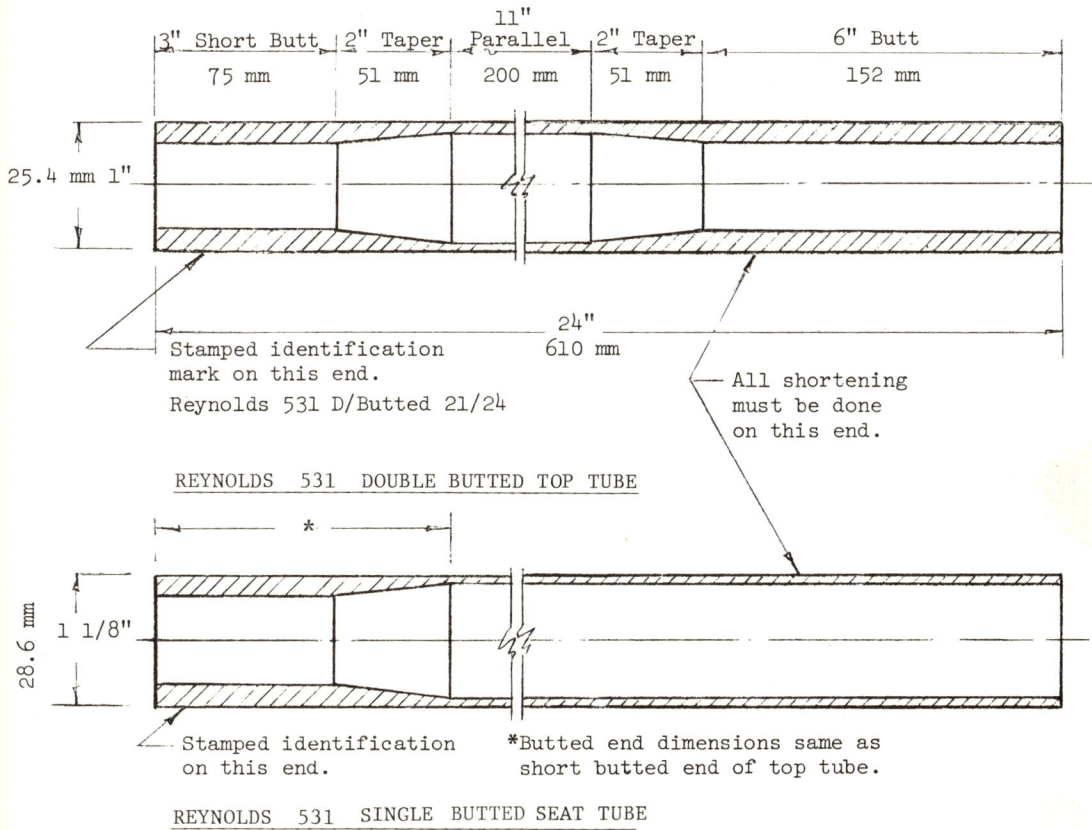

Data Courtesy of T. I. Reynolds Limited, Birmingham, England.

FIGURE VI-2

57

BRAZE-ONS AND OTHER FRAMEBUILDING MATERIALS

frame kits

Reprinted Courtesy of Bike Warehouse
A Division of Nashbar
Associates, Inc.
New Middletown, Ohio

practice frame kit, includes:
one lug, one Reynold tube, one drop-out, one stay or blade, 3 sticks of brass,

braze·ons

1. Seat stay reinforcement
2. TA Star pre-threaded bottle cade mtds. and allen key attaching bolts
3. Top eyes for English wrap around
4. Brake bridge reinforcement
5. Fork tab reinforcement
6. Brake/Transmission Guide(3)
7. Brake cable stop
8. Gear cable stop
9. Campy controls 1013/5 /6.
10. Allen fast back for seat cluster, uses Campy 10MM seat post bolt.
11. Campy Allen seat post bolt, 1010. 10MM
12. B.B. tunnel guides.
13. Campy chain stay eye, 621.
14. Campy derailleur control bosses for down tube, 660

CINELLI BRAZE-ONS

15. Brake bridge
16. Brake tunnel
17. Allen key bolt
18. Chain stay bridge reinforcement,Pr.
19. Brake bridge reinforcement,Pr.
20. Seat lug conjunctions,Pr.
21. Allen key bolt for front brake
22. Shifter boss w/washer,Pr.
23. Brake/Transmission guide(3)
24. Front der. cable runner
25. Rear der. cable runner
26. Bottle braze-on
27. Chain stay eye

Frame kit, includes everything you need but the flux. Reynolds double butted tubing (large enough for a 25½" frame), with threaded steering column. Tubing is 21/24 guage, English threads and diameters. Reynolds stickers, Prugnat Italian long point lugs (for 72° to 75° frame), gargatte bottom bracket shell - 68MM wide-English threads, Cinelli full sloping crown, Campy Road 1010 dropouts with adjusters (racing drop-outs are without eyelets) seat stay reinforcements, top eyes for wrap around, brake bridge reinforcement and 5 sticks of Proteus brazing rod (1450° F)

Options:
1. Long (touring) or short (racing) fork rake.
2. Vagner diamond top flat crown.
3. Suntour road dropouts, off-set.
4. Campy vertical dropouts

Extras: (or changes)
1. Silver brazing rod (1150° F)
2. Extra long tubes for up to 29" frame
3. Columbus "SL" or "SP" tubing
4. Semi-sloping crown

tubing

Complete set of Reynolds 531 D.B.
Top tube, down tube or seat tube
Chain stays or seat stays, pr.
Fork blades (specify rake)
Head tube
Steering column, normal length-eng
Reynolds bridge tube - 12"
Columbus "SL" tube set
Columbus "SP" tube set

29" chrome moly seat tube
14" 13G steering column

crowns

1. Cinelli full sloping for Reynolds
2. Finely finished Cinelli for Colum.
3. Vagner flat diamond top for Reyn.

drop·outs

Suntour con cave for road
Suntour vertical dropouts
Campy Road w/ or w/out eyelets
Campy Road Fork
Campy Track
Campy Vertical
Campy small road w/out eyelets

5. Cinelli Seat Lug
6. Cinelli Bottom Head Lug
7. Cinelli Top Head Lug

lugs

Lugs: (sets of 3)
1. Prugnat Italian long point "S"
2. Prugnat - "S4" series (cut out)
3. Prugnat "D" series
4. Nervex Lugs (Paramount type)
Gargatte B.B. shell, English, 68MM

FIGURE VI-3

Chapter VII

PREPARING THE TUBES AND BUILDING THE FORK

Cleaning the Tubes

Tubing is supplied with a factory-applied layer of metal preservative. This viscous coating must be completely removed before commencing layout and cutting work. Gather together some kerosene or other nontoxic solvent, a plastic pail, rags, a small paint brush, and two three-foot lengths of wood doweling — ⅛ inch diameter and ¼ inch diameter.

Pour solvent into the bucket and scrub each tube separately, inside and out, using brush and rags.(P7.1) Clean the inner surfaces of the tubes by pushing solvent-saturated rags through their bores. Use the dowels as ramrods. Be careful not to bump or drop the tubes; their unbutted walls are only a few hundredths of an inch thick and are easily dented. See SWG gauge dimensions in Appendix Table IV.

Wipe each tube dry inside and out and carefully inspect for dents and other imperfections. Dented tubes should be scrapped; a small crease can severely compromise the overall strength of the frameset and lead to a buckling failure under stress.

Assuming you have purchased Reynolds "531" butted tubing, note that with the exception of the seat stays and bridges, each tube is stamped on one end with the gauge number and the Reynolds name. The numbers indicate wall thickness of the butted and unbutted sections in SWG. The stamp also serves to identify the tube end with the short butt. This end is only long enough to accommodate the minor amount of filing associated with mitering. The unmarked tube end has the longer butt that is shortened when cutting the

P7.1 Removing metal preservative with solvent.

tube to length. Refer to Chapter VI, Figure VI-2 for butt dimensions and marking details.

To prevent future cutting mistakes, wrap masking tape around the unmarked end of each tube right after it is cleaned. When you shorten the tubes later, it will be the taped ends that will undergo any major shortening. Exceptions to this general cutting rule are the fork blades and, to some extent, the stays. These tubes have ample wall thickness to be cut at either end to accommodate a particular fork rake or stay length. After cleaning, prepare all tubes for marking by painting a coat of layout fluid on their ends, then store them where they will be safe from damage or corrosion. (P7.2)

P7.2 Painting tube ends with layout fluid.

slips easily through the hole, the two parts must be pinned together before brazing.

Pinning keeps the crown in position while the joint is brazed, preventing linear and rotational movement. It is an easy operation that consists of drilling a small hole through the crown and tube at the future brake hole location and inserting a tight-fitting nail or steel pin to hold the two parts together. After brazing, when the brake hole is made, the pin will be completely drilled away.

If the tube will not fit into the crown hole, lightly file its butted end all around the circumference for a distance equal to the crown hole's depth. The hole can be filed also but this is not recommended because of the difficulty in maintaining concentricity. Use a mill file for reducing the tube's OD. (P7.3) Alter-

Building the Fork

A logical place to start construction is the fork assembly. It has fewer components than the frame, is easier to build, and less costly to replace should you make a mistake. The first step is to cut the steering tube to length. Normally, it should only be cut on its unthreaded end at this time (that is the butted section on this tube). Add ⅛ inch to the length shown on your drawing, scribe a mark on the tube at that distance from its threaded end, then cut it with a hacksaw. Use tube blocks when you vise the tube.

Cutting the tube in this manner now should eliminate the need for threading operations later, when the completed fork is assembled to the frame. You should only have to shorten the threaded end at that time, bringing it to exact length, then hand-cut the necessary keyway to match the headset. I caution that if you are building a very small frameset it may be necessary to cut a bit off the threaded end of the tube also. This is to prevent removing too much of the butt (possibly all of it on designs which require extremely short steering tubes) and thus weakening the fork assembly.

Next, take the crown, which I assume is an integral-type (not the shell-type for reasons covered previously), and see if you can fit the unthreaded end of the steering tube into its machined hole. Chances are it will not fit, or it will just enter the hole if forced. If the tube

P7.3 Filing the steering tube OD to fit the crown hole. Note tube blocks.

nate the filing with sanding operations using long, inch-wide strips of No. 80 grit production cloth. Hold the cloth at both ends, and briskly draw it back and forth, working your way around the tube end using a shoe-shining motion. (P7.4)

The tube should be vised either horizontally or vertically while doing this work, using whichever position gives you the best control. Be careful not to crush the tube's threaded end. Use those tube blocks. Careless metal removal leads to egg-shaped cross sections, sloppy fits, and an unsatisfactory joint. Keep

P7.4 Sanding helps maintain concentricity.

this in mind during future filing operations involving lugs and tubes as well.

Check progress by frequently trial-fitting the tube into the crown. When it will enter the full depth of the crown hole, using hand pressure alone, it is ready to be brazed in place. It is no problem if a little bit of the tube, ¼₆ inch or so, protrudes beyond the underside of the crown. This can be filed off later during finishing operations. If you have reduced the tube's diameter too much, it may slip farther into the crown than the required amount. In that case pin the joint as described earlier.

To set the parts up for brazing, place tube blocks around the tube and hold it in a vise with the butted end pointed up. Give the mating surfaces of both parts a final cleanup, sanding joint surfaces until they are bright. Remove all traces of sanding grit, apply a thin coat of flux to the parts, and assemble the joint so that the crown's tangs point upwards. Wipe away any excess flux which may have squeezed out of the joint onto adjacent surfaces, and you are ready to braze. With the parts so arranged, gravity will assist the flow of molten brazing material down into the joint.

Integral crowns are fairly massive and require substantial heating to bring them up to brazing temperature. I brazed mine using a single Mapp Gas/air torch, but it helps to use a second torch, even if it is a propane/air unit. Two torches make it easier to heat the joint and maintain a more uniform temperature. Of course, if you have an acetylene/oxygen rig or

Mapp Gas/oxygen torch then you won't have this problem. It also helps to partially finish the crown *before* brazing it. Thin the part as much as possible by filing away all excess metal, thus reducing the amount of material to be heated. A further aid is to silbraze the joint *provided you have a good fit.* Another is to arrange some firebricks or heat reflectors around the assembly.

When brazing, play the torch flame on the outside of the thickest part of the crown and around its periphery. As the crown comes up to temperature watch for color changes, comparing them to those in the color/temperature chart in Table III-1. Also observe flux action; when it begins to turn watery the joint is close to brazing temperature.

When the correct temperature is reached feed rod into the top of the joint. Sweep the torch flame downward, working it back and forth around one half of the crown. You should shortly observe a thin line of brazing material flowing out of the bottom of the joint around the crown boss. This indicates full penetration of the brazing alloy. Continue the flame-sweeping action around to the other side of the crown. Feed in more rod and look for the emergence of molten brazing material at the bottom of the joint on that side also. Once you are sure full penetration has been achieved leave the assembly in the vise and let it cool slowly while you go on to the next step, cutting the fork blades.

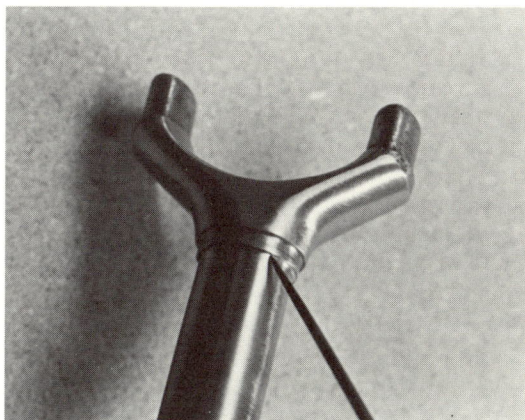

P7.5 Crown/steering tube joint after brazing and finishing. Integral crown was semi-finished before brazing.

61

Fork Blade Shaping Operations

• Cutting

Accurate blade cutting is aided by using the fork cutting board described in Chapter V. The board layout is made using dimensions from your drawing. Just be sure to factor in any adjustments to account for possible dimensional differences between your drops, blades and crown *as designed*, and the actual components you are building with. By the way, I am assuming your blades (and stays) are not pre-domed by the manufacturer and such work will be done by you. In figuring blade lengths, make them long enough to permit ample penetration of the drop-out tangs into what will be the slotted end of the blades. In the finished assembly the blade domes must extend at least $\frac{7}{16}$ inch down the sides of the drop-outs to provide sufficient brazing surface. See Figure VII-1.

Now place each blade on the cutting board, aligning it as closely as possible to the curve you need to get the proper rake. Scribe a line at the drop-out end of the blade allowing $\frac{1}{8}$ inch extra for doming. The crown ends of the blades are not marked until after the drop-outs have been brazed in place.

• Slotting and Doming

The blade ends must now be slotted and domed to receive the drop-outs. Again, I am assuming you will want a domed end. If a different end shape is desired, such as a bevel type, the job will be easier than the doming process that follows. Refer to Figure VII-1 for various end-designs. What will be discussed here for finishing the blade ends is also applicable in preparing the drop-out ends of the seat and chain stays.

Using a hacksaw, cut the drop-out ends of the blades at the marked locations. Clamp one of the blades in your vise (use jaw covers) and commence slotting by carefully making a $\frac{1}{2}$ inch deep slit in the blade tip. Keep the slit parallel to the major axis of the blade's oval cross section, or if you are using round blades, keep it parallel to the plane of the rake curve. The slot is cut using a hacksaw with two blades mounted side by side in its frame.

Now take an 8 x $\frac{3}{32}$ inch warding file and carefully file the slot to the required depth and width so it fits snugly over the drop-out tang. Insert the slotted tip into a vise, and applying pressure, squeeze the slot closed. (P7.6)

Again, saw the slot open to its former width and open it up with the warding file. This time start to shape the ends of the blade to form an

P7.6 Doming. Slot is squeezed closed.

ellipse or semicircle (P7.7, P7.8) Continue the opening-squeezing-shaping operation until you achieve the desired shape with a slot width that firmly grips the drop-out. Do the same to the other blade tip. Frequently check to make sure parallelism is maintained between the blade's major axis and the sides of the drops

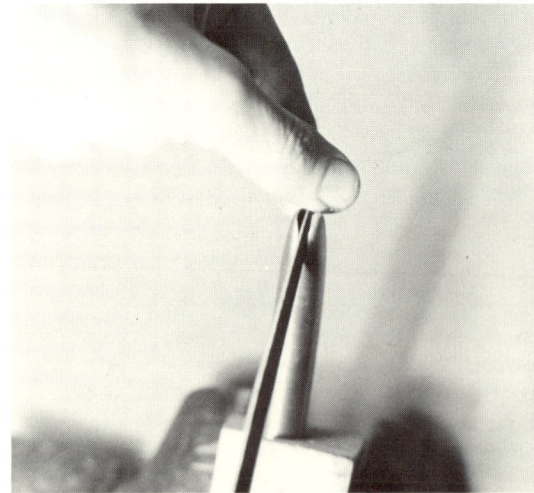

P7.7 Reopening the slot with a warding file.

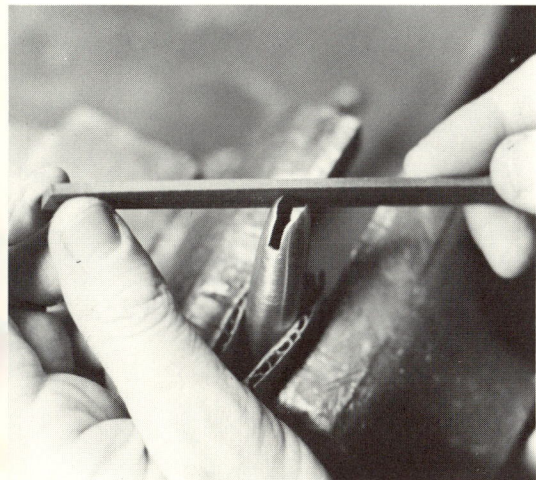

P7.8 Rounding a tip.

P7.10 Checking drop-out fit.

lest they skew out of alignment. Go slowly; it is not an operation you can rush. When the contour is close to perfect, bring it to final shape by sanding. (P7.9) Check both

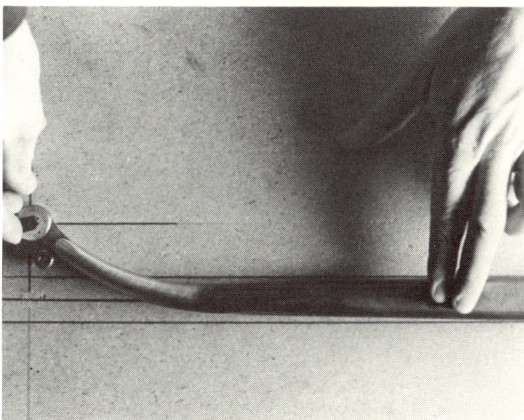

P7.11 Checking blade rake on the fork cutting board.

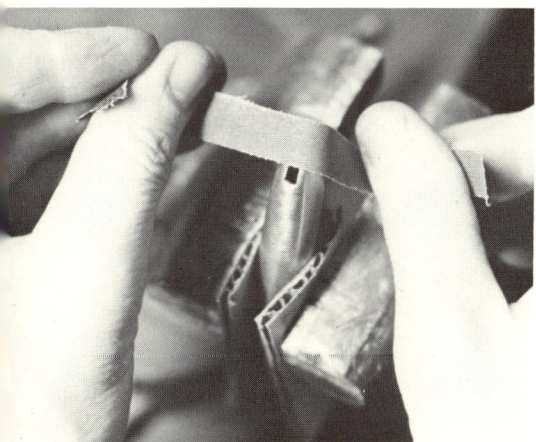

P7.9 Final shaping with production cloth.

assemblies by holding the drop-outs in the blade slots and comparing them to the full-sized fork layout on the fork cutting board. (P7.10, P7.11, P7.12, P7.13)

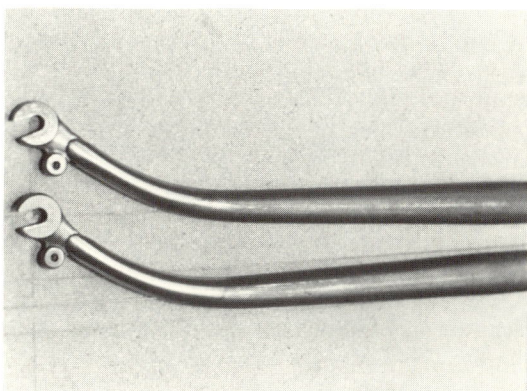

P7.12 Blade assemblies ready for brazing.

63

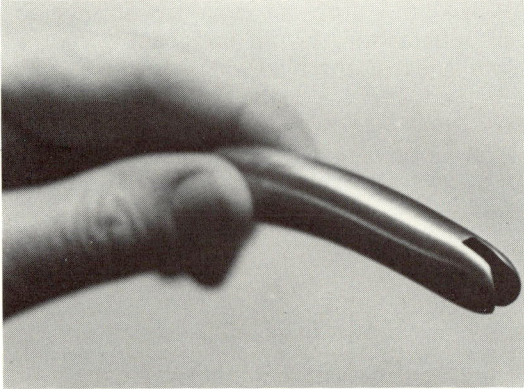
P7.13 The finished blade tip.

P7.14 Brazing a drop-out.

Brazing the Drop-Outs to the Blades

Give the slot interiors and drop-out surfaces a thorough, final sanding. A small die-maker's file or sandpaper stick works well for getting inside the blade tips. Blow the parts clean; apply flux to the joint surfaces and slip the drop-outs into the slots. The assemblies are brazed while the blades are held vertically in a vise. If a slot is a bit wide and the drop-out will not stay in place, squeeze the sides of the tip together until there is enough friction to hold the drop-out in position. It is also possible to do some preliminary finishing work on the drop-outs before brazing, but generally it is better to wait until afterwards. Once joined to the blades, the drop-outs are much easier to work on.

Brass or filler rod is used for brazing all drop-outs (front and rear) because of the need to bridge the rather large gaps that will exist at the blade slots. These clearances are simply too large to permit the use of silver rod. When brazing, concentrate the torch flame on the drop-out rather than on the domed blade. This will guard against overheating the thin tube walls. When the joint is sufficiently heated, flow the rod into and across the slot. (P7.14) Do one slot side at a time, then reposition the assembly in the vise and braze the other side. Flow plenty of brazing material into the joint. Excess blobs can be filed off easily later. Let the blade assemblies cool slowly; wirebrush them under flowing water to remove flux; then go to work on the joints with rifflers and production cloth to shape up the tips, and feather out the drop-out eyes (or remove them completely) as desired. (P7.15, P7.16, P7.17, P7.18)

P7.15 Excess brazing material is filed away.

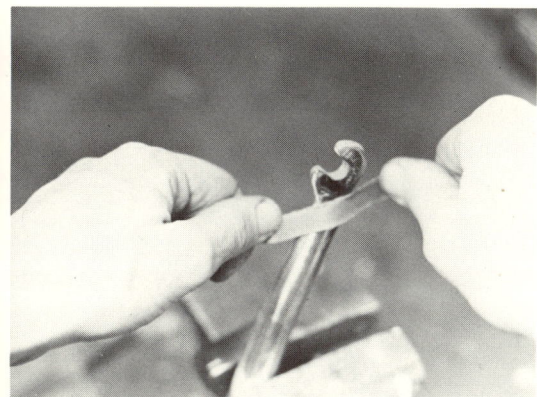

P7.16 *The joint is finished with production cloth.*

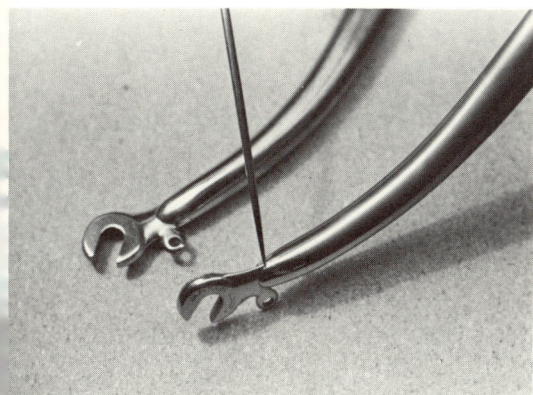

P7.17 *Completed joints. Note domed blade ends and thinned drop-outs and eyes.*

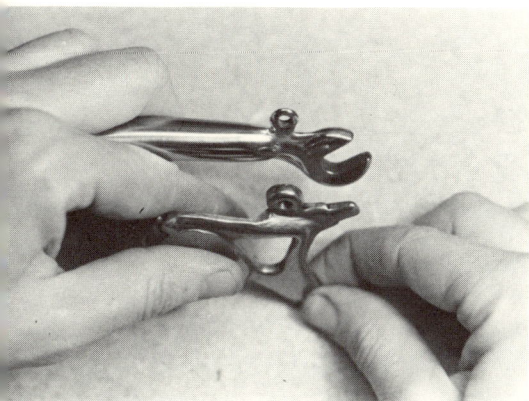

P7.18 *Comparison of "thinned" drop-out and eye (top) with typical drop-out "as purchased."*

When both drop-out ends are finished to your satisfaction, layout and cutting of the crown ends of the blades can be done. Lay each blade on the fork cutting board, and mark the crown ends for cutting, leaving $\frac{1}{16}$ inch extra for final fit-up. (P7.19) Now cut the blades. (P7.20)

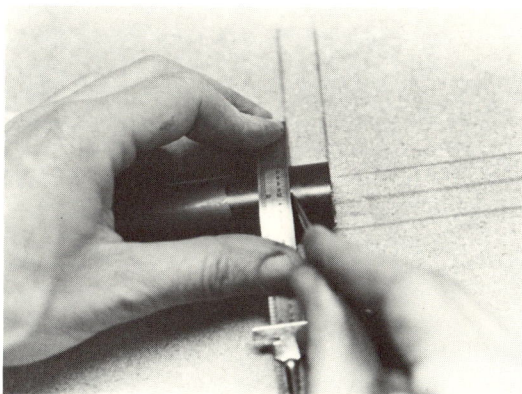

P7.19 *Marking the blade's crown end.*

P7.20 *Cutting the fork blade to final length.*

Assuming an integral crown is used, push the blades onto the crown tangs. You must carefully file the elliptically shaped tangs so that each blade slips fully over its respective tang using light hand-pressure. (P7.21) One note of caution: if offset drop-outs are used, such as the Sun Tour Model GS, they have already been bent slightly, so their sides will be parallel in the assembled fork. *Be sure you have each blade assembly matched to its corresponding crown tang.* Examining the blade tips will clearly show which is the right and which is the left. Limit filing to the crown tangs only. *Do not file the insides of the fork blades.* Also, file the tangs so the drop-out ends are parallel to each other.

When each blade will slip fully onto its respective tang and their lengths are identical to that of the full-size fork layout, the vents may be made. This is done by drilling a $\frac{1}{32}$ inch diameter hole on the inside of each blade two inches from its crown end. (P7.22) The holes will permit gasses to escape from the blade interiors when the assemblies are brazed to the crown. Without vents, heated gasses would force their way through the joint, ruining it. When brazing dead-ended tubes, a pathway for the escape of gasses must *always* be provided.

Brazing the Blade Assemblies to the Crown

Now you are ready to braze the blade assemblies to the crown. The fork jig described in Chapter V will be needed. First make a trial setup of the fork components in the jig. (P7.23) Slip the blade assemblies onto the crown making certain that the left and right blades are on the correct tangs (the vent holes should be on the inside of each blade, facing each other). The blades are farther apart at the axle end than at the crown so you may have to pry them apart slightly to achieve the correct angularity. Clamp the fork assembly in the jig using a C-clamp at the steering tube end and the axle skewer or nuts at the drop-out end. See Figure V-2.

With a machinist's square, measure up from the jig backboard to the center line of each blade at the crown. Keep adjusting the steering tube until the distance from the board to the center line is the same for each blade. Now, check the mating of the blade ends at

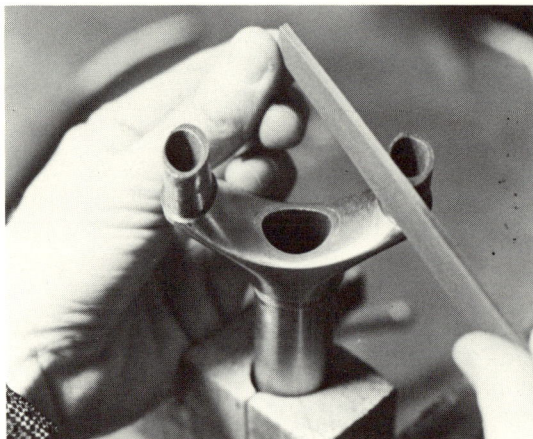

P7.21 Integral crown tangs are filed for blade fit-up.

P7.22 Drilling the blade vent holes.

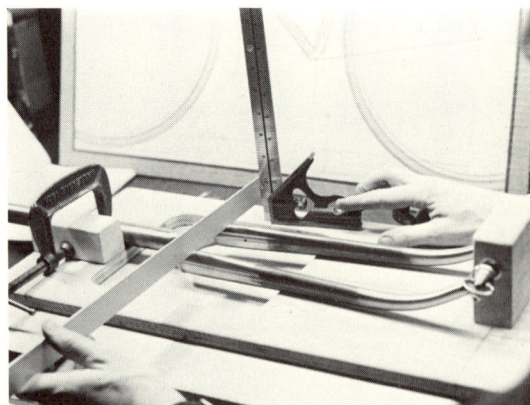

P7.23 Trial set-up of the fork assembly in its jig.

he crown. There may be a slight gap between he blade ends and the crown's mating suraces, especially at the inside surfaces of the rown's tangs. This is caused by the angularity ituation mentioned earlier. The gap must ow be completely eliminated by filing the lade ends on an angle. Remove only enough netal to achieve a perfect mating of the two urfaces. Recall that an extra $\frac{1}{16}$ inch was llowed for this purpose when the blade ssemblies were originally laid out.

Once filing work has been completed, eassemble the fork and set it up in the jig, naking a final alignment check. Now dissemble the parts, and sand all mating suraces clean. A thorough sanding job on the inide surfaces of the blades may be achieved by sing wood dowels wrapped with production loth. (P7.24) Wipe away sanding grit and aply flux to both joints. (P7.25) Slip the blades nto the crown's tangs; set the whole assemly up in the jig, making the alignment neasurements with the machinist's square as efore; then, clamp the parts in place. (P7.26) Vipe away any excess flux.

P7.25 Fluxing the crown/blade joints.

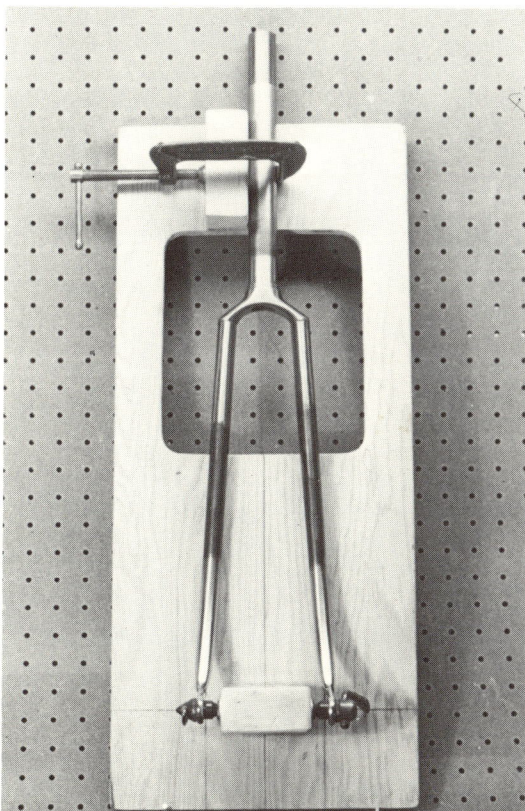

7.24 Sanding blade interiors in preparation for razing. Production cloth glued to a dowel helps ere.

If the blades are a close fit with the tangs, hen the joints may be silbrazed. If too much naterial has been removed from the tangs and oint clearances are larger than .005 inch, use rass or an appropriate filler rod. Position the g in the vise so the fork is vertical with the hreaded end of the steering tube uppermost. his will put gravity to work for you.

P7.26 Fork assembly set up in the jig and ready for brazing.

Thoroughly heat the joint to proper temperature (you may need two torches plus some heat reflectors), and feed rod into the joint crevice. (P7.27) Braze one blade at a time starting at its outside surface and finishing on the inside. A final caution: the jig is combustible so do not be careless with the torch. The jig will be of little use if you incinerate it on your first pass (I almost did). (P7.28) After brazing, set the fork assembly aside in a draft-free area, and let it cool while it is still clamped in the jig.

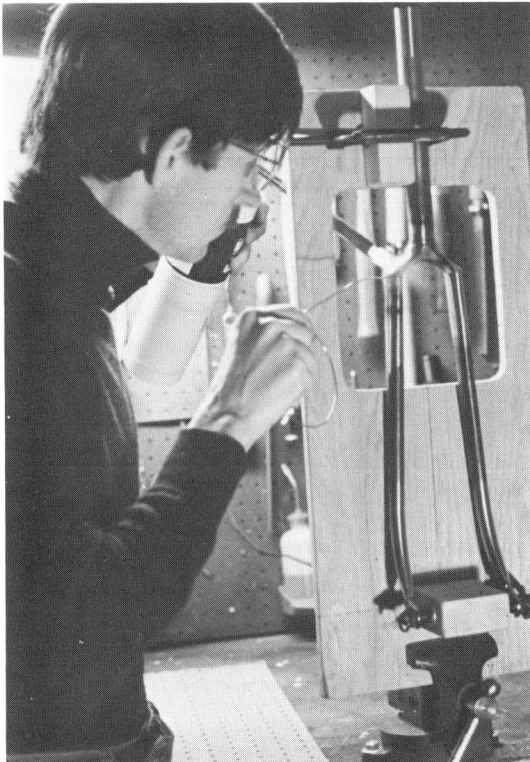

P7.28 The assembly is set aside to cool slowly while still clamped in its jig. (Note scorched jig.)

justments to the blade spacing are accomplished by bending them by hand (cold-setting). Slight bending is permissible, but if the drop-outs are badly skewed, they should be heated before attempting major corrections. As a final check mount a perfectly trued front wheel in the fork, and measure the distance between the inside of the blades and the wheel rim. (P7.29)

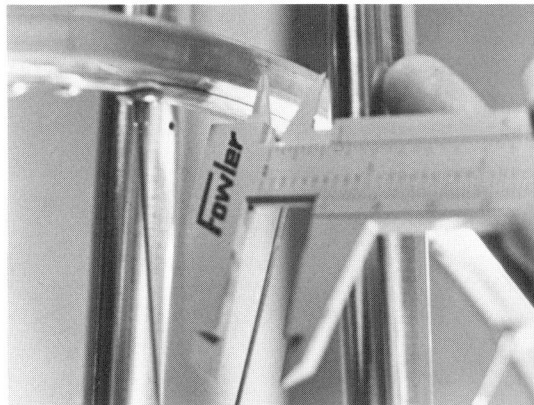

P7.27 Brazing the crown/blade joints.

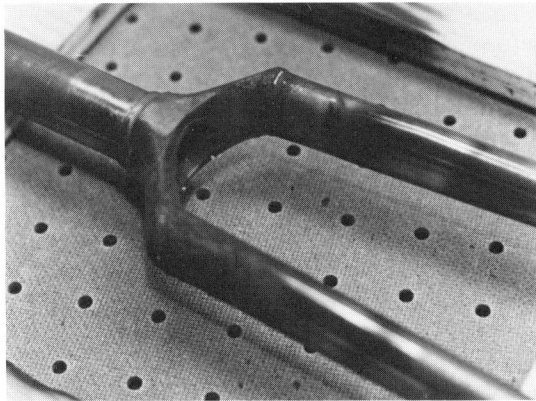

P7.29 Using a trued wheel to check rim-to-blade clearance and wheel centering.

Aligning and Finishing the Fork

When the fork has cooled, remove it from the jig, clean off flux, and check blade alignment. It may be necessary to adjust the fork ends slightly so they fit the front axle perfectly. The inside surfaces of both drop-outs must be parallel to each other. Minor ad-

The next step is to drill the brake bolt hole. Before you do, verify its location using dimensions taken from the brakes that will actually be used on the completed bicycle. When that has been done, center-punch the front and rear of the crown at the proper brake bolt hole location. (P7.30) Drill the hole in two stages, first through the front half of the crown, then through the rear. This will reduce the chance of an off-center hole which can ruin the fork. Each hole is drilled in two stages — first with a $\frac{1}{16}$ inch pilot drill, then with the full size clearance drill. (P7.31) Deburr the hole with a machinist's scraper, then smooth the entire fork assembly into final shape.

Start with the crown's shoulders, filing them so they flare smoothly into the blades. If the crown was partially finished before brazing there should only be a minor amount of metal removal required. (P7.32) Finish by sanding the entire assembly first with No. 80 then No. 120 grit production cloth. When properly done, it should be nearly impossible to notice the seam formed by the juncture of the blades and the crown — the fork will appear as one piece. Now mount the front wheel and brake, and double check the wheel centering and brake pad reach.(P7.33)

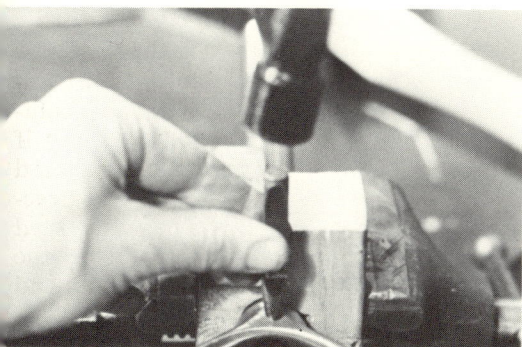

7.30 Center punching the brake pivot-bolt hole location.

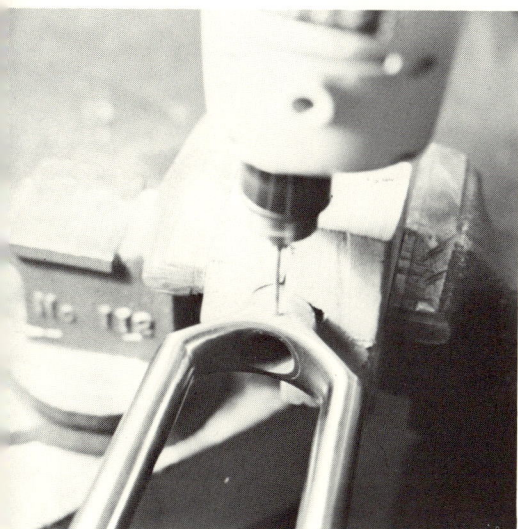

P7.32 Crown joints are cleaned up with a file.

7.31 Pilot-drilling the brake pivot-bolt hole.

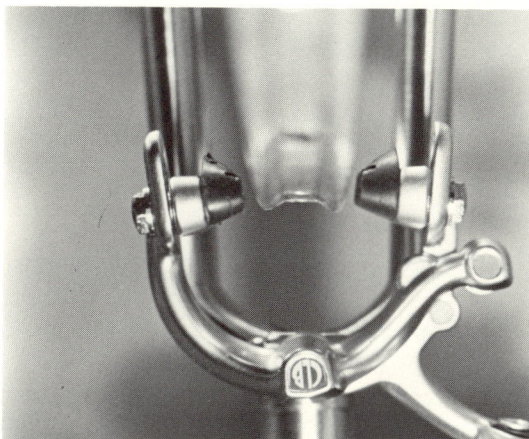

P7.33 Checking pad reach.

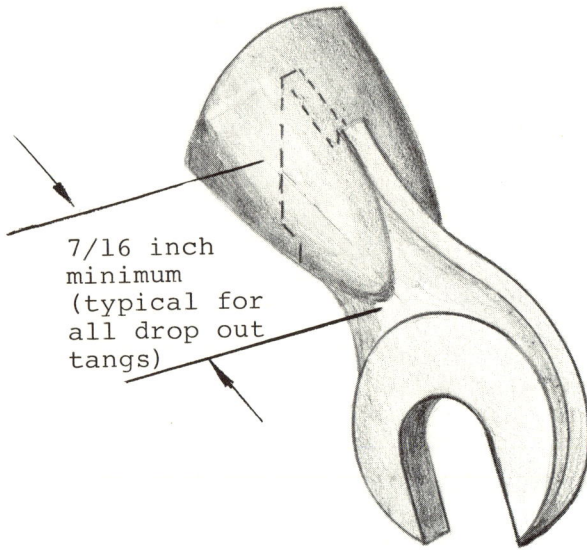

7/16 inch
minimum
(typical for
all drop out
tangs)

Domed

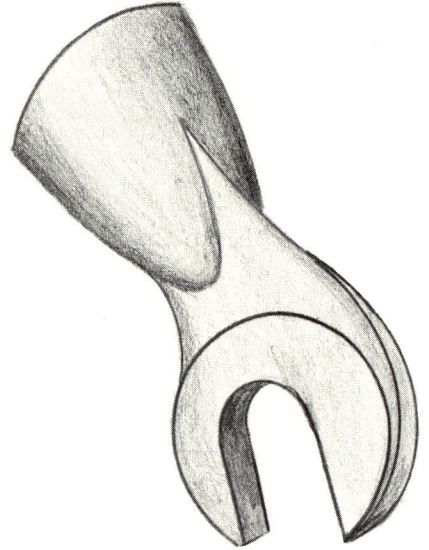

Domed with Thinned Drop

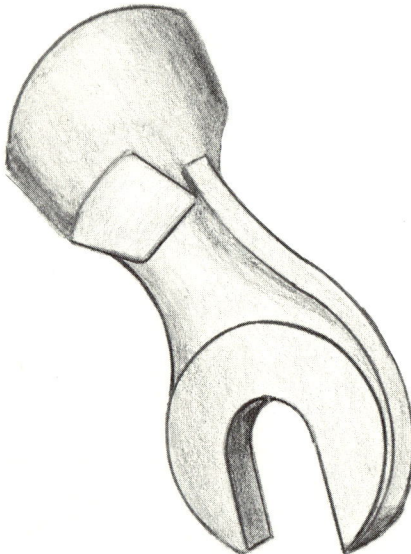

Bevel Type - Stay and blade ends
may be cut on bevel, at right angles,
or curved (sometimes called "Masi"
style).

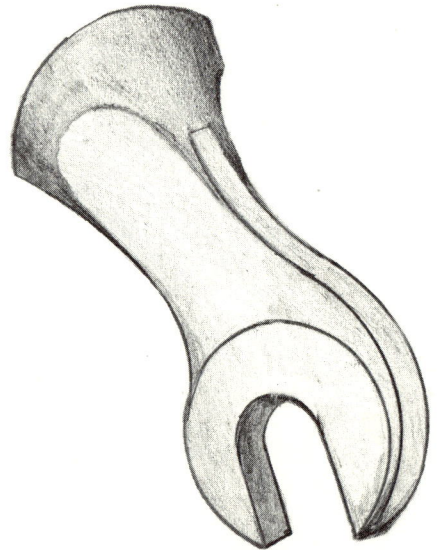

Flared

FIGURE VII-1

CHAPTER VIII

BUILDING THE MAIN TRIANGLE
AND SEAT STAY ATTACHMENT

Building the Main Triangle

With the fork completed, construction of the main triangle may begin. *Triangle* is somewhat of a misnomer. The structure is really not a *triangle* at all but a *quadrilateral* in almost all cases (very small frames may come close to true triangles because of their short head tubes). The assembly consists of four tubes — head, top, down, seat — lugs which hold the tubes together, and any braze-on attachments that may be used. The assembly may be built without the use of jig-ging, but the simple wooden jig described in Chapter V and illustrated in Figure V-3 is strongly recommended to simplify the brazing job and minimize the amount of cold-setting afterwards.

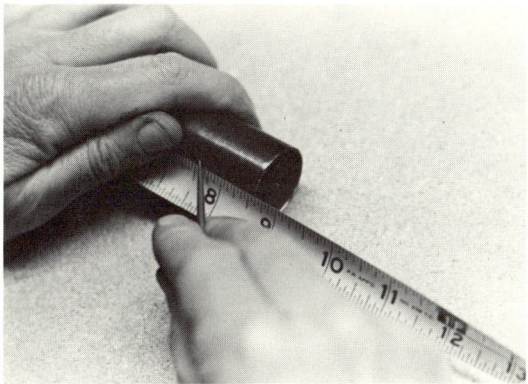

P8.1 Laying out the head tube.

Tube Mitering

All main triangle tubes are cut and mitered *before* preparing the lugs or doing any brazing work. Start by cutting the head tube to length. I assume all tubes have been painted with layout fluid. Take the head tube and, using your drawing as a guide, mark and cut it to length allowing at least ¼ inch extra for final finishing (⅛ inch per end).(P8.1) The head tube is straight gauge so it may be shortened on either end. (P8.2)

Next, miter the top tube so it fits against the head tube at the angle corresponding to your particular design. The miter is cut on the stamped end of the top tube; that is the end with the short butt. The opposite end should have that piece of masking tape wrapped around it, reminding you it has the long butt.

P8.2 Head tube cutting. (Note tube blocks.)

Slip the head tube top lug over the end of the top tube then scribe the outline of the lug's head tube hole onto the end of the top tube. (P8.3) This will leave a pattern to follow when filing the miter. (Use the same procedure when mitering the head tube end of the down tube and the seat tube end of the top tube.)

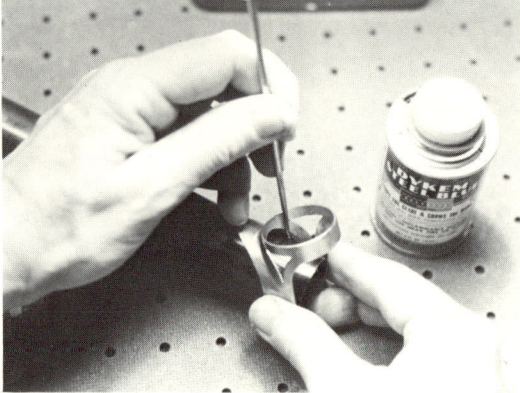

P8.3 Using the head tube top lug as a template.

Using tube blocks, grasp the tube in a vise so it is held in place in the vertical position. (By now you know that tube blocks must always be used when clamping the tubes so I shall not repeat it again.) Take a 14 inch half-round bastard file and start filing the end of the tube at an angle that approximates the one shown on your drawing. (P8.4) Use the

scribed line as a guide. (P8.5) As the file works deeper into the tube's end check the progress of your work by frequently trial-fitting the top tube against the head tube, holding them together over the drawing to verify the angle. (P8.6) Make any necessary corrections in the filing angle, and keep removing metal until you obtain the best fit possible while matching the drawing angle. Holding the tubes together over a bright light source aids in checking for joint gaps when you are nearing completion of the miter. The closer the fit, the stronger the joint. The head

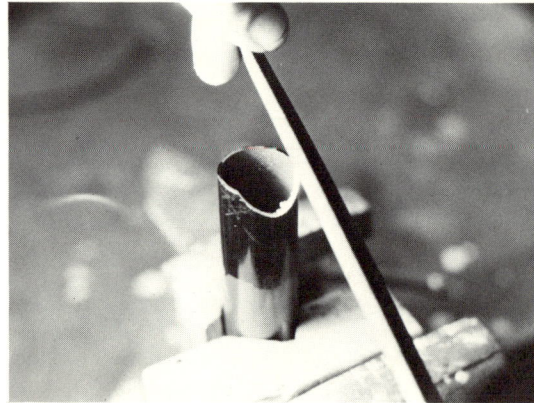

P8.5 Filing progress should be frequently checked.

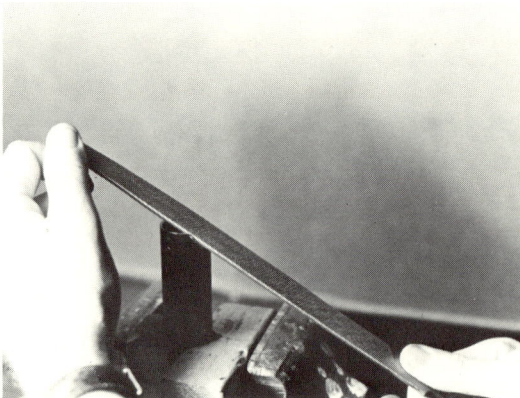

P8.4 Top tube is mitered with a 14-inch half-round bastard file.

P8.6 Head tube angle and top tube miter are checked using the design drawing as a guide.

tube end of the down tube is next mitered using the same procedure just described. (P8.7)

When both tubes have been mitered they may be marked, then cut close to their final lengths. Tube lengths are taken from the drawing. When marking the top tube take into account the extra length needed to allow for its angular intersection with the head and seat tubes, then add ½ inch to provide some margin for filing error. Lay out the top tube, then cut it to rough length using a hacksaw. The bottom-bracket-shell end of the down tube does not have to be mitered now. When you lay out its length just be sure it is long enough to penetrate the full depth of the shell's spigot. Allow an extra ¼ inch beyond that point, and cut that tube also.

P8.8 Checking seat tube angle and fit.

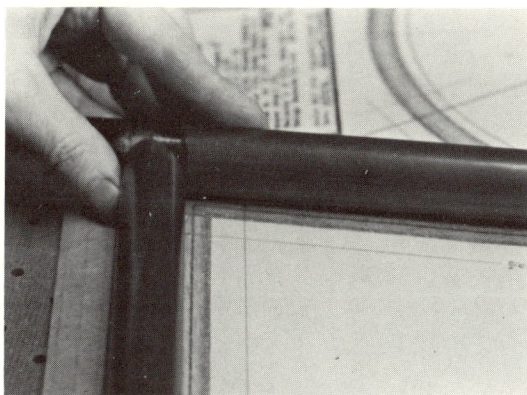

P8.7 Checking head tube/down tube angle and fit.

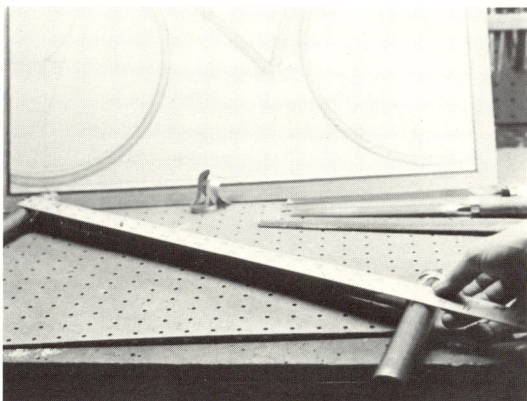

P8.9 Measuring top tube length.

The third miter to be made is on the seat tube end of the top tube. The procedure is the same as that described for the first two miters, but work *slowly* because you will be mitering and shortening the tube to *exact* length simultaneously. There is no room for error here. Frequently interrupt the filing and monitor your progress.(P8.8) Check the top tube length by holding the head and seat tubes firmly against its ends while aligning a metal yardstick along its center line. The measurement is taken from the head tube center line to the seat tube center line. (P8.9) The seat tube angle is checked by holding the top tube and seat tube together over the drawing and comparing angles. In addition to obtaining the correct center line length and seat tube angle, you must also be certain the head and seat tubes are parallel to and in line with each other when viewed edgewise, i.e. as if you were standing in front of the completed frameset and looking at the head tube.

Set the completed top tube aside, and slip the down tube into the bottom bracket shell. Hold the mitered end of the tube in firm contact with the head tube, and position the shell so that the distance between the crank axis and the intersection of the head tube and down tube center lines is the same as that shown on your drawing. The longitudinal crank axle center line must also be at right angles to the head tube center line. When the assembly is correctly aligned, reach inside the shell and scribe a line around the circumference of the down tube where it meets the inside of the shell. (P8.10) If the down tube is too long to obtain the correct center line distance, simply shorten it slightly and try lining up the assembly as before.

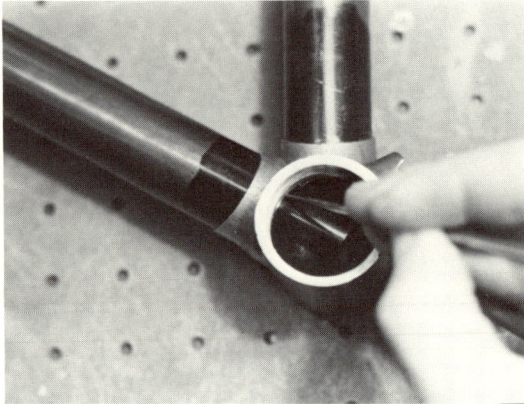

P8.10 Scribing the bottom bracket shell outline on the down tube.

On the other hand, if the tube's *entire* circumference will not reach the inside surface of the shell when the correct center line distance is established, the down tube should not be used. This problem is usually caused by attempting to use standard length tubes to build a large size frameset (over 24 inches). Another contributing factor can be unusually long upper torso dimensions (long top tube) combined with a shallow head tube angle. *If your down tube is too short do not try to use it; order a longer one.* The shell and its adjoining tubes are subjected to heavy torsion, tension, compression and thrust loads. *Full penetration* into the spigot is necessary to develop maximum strength at this important joint.

Assuming the down tube *is* the correct length, carefully file its shell end to match the line just scribed. Use a 14 inch half-round file. Insert the tube back into the shell, and double check your work. If all is well, poke your scriber into the shell's seat tube hole, and with the crank axle longitudinal center line arranged at right angles to the head tube center line, mark the outline of the seat tube hole on the end of the down tube. Remove the down tube from the shell and file away all tube

material up to the scribed line.(P8.11) The result is a double-mitered down tube.

P8.11 Double-mitering the down tube.

Next, insert the *butted* end of the seat tube fully into its bottom bracket shell spigot. Scribe a line around the tube's circumference where it meets the inside surface of the shell. Clamp the tube in a vise and contour its butted end with a 14 inch half-round file to match the scribed line just drawn. (P8.12) The upper (unbutted) end of the tube need not be cut to length until after the seat lug connection is brazed.

P8.12 Close up view of down tube and seat tube intersection. Note double miter and full penetration of both tubes into their respective spigots.

Assemble all the main triangle tubes making a final check of center line dimensions and tube angles. If the down tube and top tube are the correct length and have been properly mitered, then the seat tube length and angle should be as shown on your drawing. Check it now. Center line lengths should fall within ± $\frac{1}{16}$ inch and frame angles within ± $\frac{1}{4}$ degree of the dimensions shown on the drawing. (P8.13)

P8.13 Final fit-up of the main triangle components. Note protruding seat and head tubes which will be trimmed to final length after brazing.

Lug Preparation

With the tubes mitered, lug preparation may begin. If you are using stamped and welded type lugs give them a close inspection now, especially along their welded seams. A faulty weld can split apart under normal brazing temperatures, ruining the joint and all preparatory work done thus far. If a seam looks less than perfect, scrap the lug and get a replacement. The lug's windows and points may also be out of alignment, but this is a minor problem that can be corrected by hand-filing or grinding. (P8.14)

Be as creative as you like filing the lug windows and outlines; make your own unique designs. The bottom bracket shell's spigots may be similarly filed at this time. Just keep in mind that lugs and spigots are structural members of the frame and can be weakened if too much material is removed.

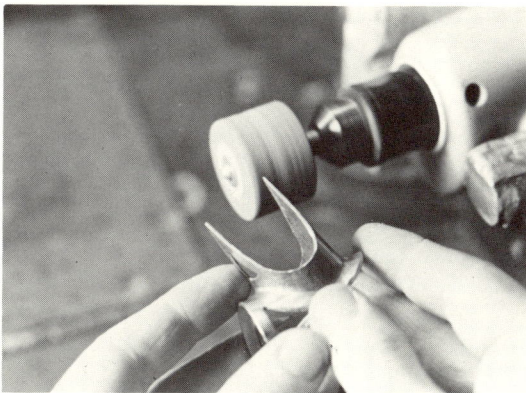

P8.14 "Pointing" lugs using a small grinding wheel.

A classic customizing detail you might like to try is to cut your initial, or other figure, into the sides of the seat tube lug. This works best with an Allen Key Fastback or Brampton Victor type design. Custom cutout work is done by painting the lug with layout fluid and then scribing an outline of the desired letter or figure on its surface. A small bit is used to drill away as much material as possible from inside the outline, then the design is finish-cut to final shape using rifflers or diemaker's files. (P8.15)

P8.15 Using a riffler to file a custom cut-out in the seat lug. Lug is clamped between wood blocks for added support.

The lugs should slip firmly over the tubes without using excessive force. If they won't, increase their inside diameters by using half-round or round files, or production cloth. *Do not file the outside diameters of the tubes.* A handy tool for sanding lug interiors is a piece of doweling to which a length of No. 80 production cloth has been glued. (P8.16) Lug points are easily bent, so file and sand carefully. Lugs may be lightly clamped in a vise or held in a gloved hand while they are being worked on. A hand-held grinder with assorted grinding heads simplifies these finishing operations, but hand-filing will do as good a job.

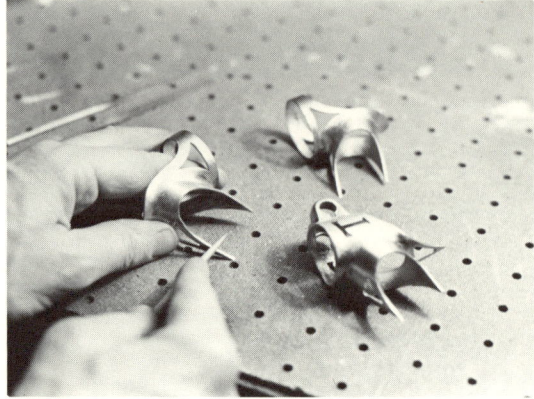

P8.17 Rifflers are used to shape lug outlines and windows.

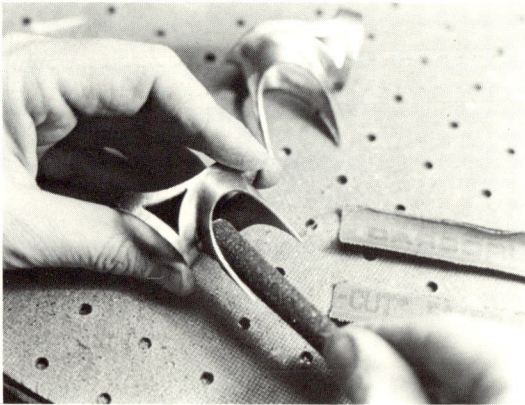

P8.16 Sanding lug interiors.

Brazing the Main Triangle

Once the lugs and shell are finished to your satisfaction, the main triangle may be brazed. Do the top tube/head tube connection first. Slip the two tubes into the head tube top lug and recheck the angle. Now, disassemble the joint and drill a 1/8 inch vent hole in the head tube at the center of where the top tube joins it. (P8.18) Meticulously clean the inside of the lug and the ends of the tubes with production cloth. (P8.19) Wipe away sanding dust and apply a thin coat of flux to all mating surfaces. (P8.20)

Also, unless the lugs are built to the exact angles of your frame, they will have to be heat-formed or filed to match your particular design. Only a small amount of bending or metal removal is required to meet all but the most extreme frame angles. Lug fit is important, but the mitered tube ends set the frame's angles. Shape the edges of the lugs and spigots so they are perpendicular to the tube surfaces and present a neat appearance. (P8.17) Some preliminary lug smoothing and thinning may also be done at this time, but save the final thickness-tapering until after the lugs have been brazed in place.

P8.18 Drilling the head tube vent hole.

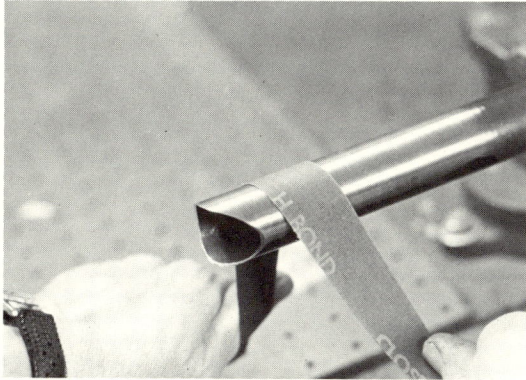

P8.19 Thorough surface cleaning is necessary for a strong bond. The top tube gets a good cleaning with production cloth.

P8.21 Clamping arrangement for brazing the joint when a main triangle jig is not used (risky). Down tube shown to illustrate miter.

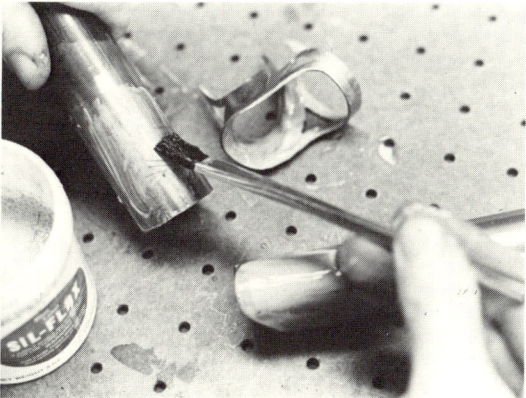

P8.20 Fluxing the head tube/top tube joint which will be silbrazed.

P8.22 Brazing the joint. Note projection of head tube beyond lug end. This will be faced off later using a special cutter.

Set the assembly up, preferably in the main triangle jig you have built. If you are not using a jig, clamp the assembly together with a C-clamp, arranging it in a vise so the top tube is vertical. (P8.21) If using this arrangement, make sure the correct head tube angle is maintained and does not shift during brazing.

Wipe away any excess flux with a rag, and braze the joint using either silver rod or brass filler depending on the amount of clearance. (P8.22) The joint will heat up quite rapidly due to the thinness of the tube and lug walls; so be on guard against overheating. Feed rod into the uppermost crevice of the joint while sweeping the torch flame down around its sides. This will help the combined forces of

gravity and capillarity achieve good penetration.

If the lugs have cut-outs you should be able to observe the flow of brazing alloy quite easily. Try to braze the whole joint in one operation, sweeping the flame around to the unbrazed side as soon as you see a thin line of brazing material flowing out the bottom of the joint. When finished, leave the joint set up in its jig, or the vise, letting it cool slowly.

Now, braze the head tube/down tube joint, a tricky operation if done without a jig because the tubes can easily skew out of alignment. To prevent this from happening braze the joint while both tubes are firmly clamped to a table top or similar flat surface (use $1/16$

77

inch shims under the top tube). When using this method make certain the tubes are clamped at the proper angle.

The next joints to be brazed are the seat tube and down tube connections at the bottom bracket shell, followed by the seat tube/top tube connection. Prepare the three connections for brazing by cleaning and fluxing all joint surfaces. Assemble the triangle and set it up in its jig, or clamp it to a table top. It is also possible (but risky) to hold the triangle in a vise while doing the brazing. If you choose the latter arrangement, grip the triangle by its down tube or by the sides of its shell. You may also have to insert some wedges into the shell to keep the tube ends flush with the shell's ID.

The bottom bracket shell joints are brazed first, then the seat tube/top tube joint. Before brazing, be sure the bottom bracket shell's longitudinal axis (same as crank axis) is aligned in both the horizontal and vertical planes. If the shell is brazed out of alignment it will have an adverse effect on pedaling motion and may even cause the ends of the crank arms to come in contact with the chain stays. There are several ways to get fairly accurate alignment, but probably the easiest is the following, which is illustrated in P8.23.

Obtain a pair of old bottom bracket cups (or inexpensive new ones) and screw them into the shell. Thread them in several turns, until they are snug. Now, with the aid of two long straight-edges held against the machined sides of the cups, check the shell's alignment in two planes. This is done by measuring the gap between the ends of the straight-edges and the sides of the seat and down tubes. By twisting the shell you can achieve a fairly accurate alignment. Adjust the shell back and forth until you have obtained the best degree of parallelism you can between the straight-edges and the tubes. Some compromising will probably be required. Just come as close as you can, splitting any alignment differences to keep the error as small as possible.

When the shell is aligned, braze the seat and down tubes into it using brass or an appropriate filler rod. There are bound to be some large gaps within the spigot joints due to the alignment process. Play the torch flame on the shell, bringing the tube connections up to temperature last. (P8.24) Like the fork crown joint, the operation is easier with two torches.

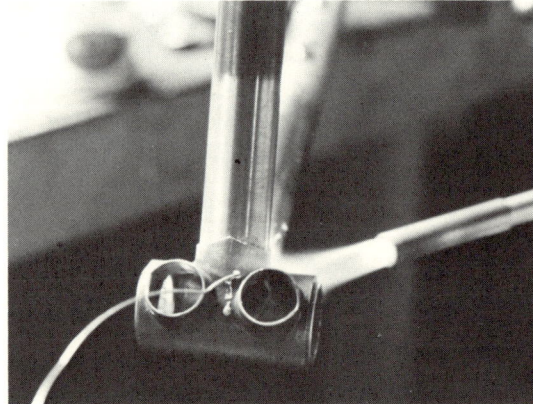

P8.24 Brazing the shell to the main triangle tubes. Heat is concentrated on the shell.

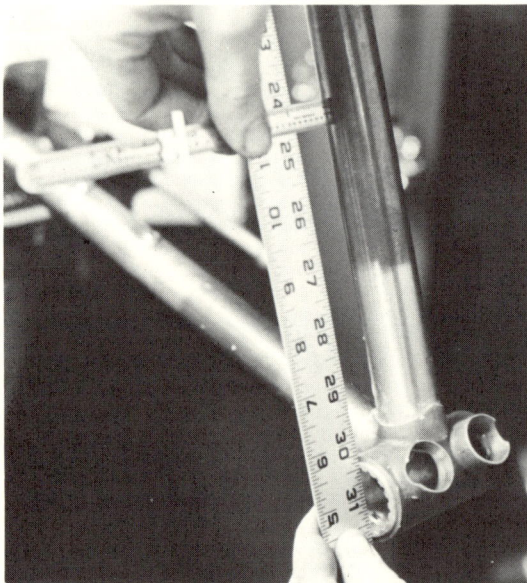

P8.23 Aligning the bottom bracket shell. Note cup (Phil Wood retaining ring).

Leave the cups in place while the joint is brazed. If you try to remove them beforehand the shell may twist out of alignment. Feed rod into the joints at the points where the tubes enter the shell spigots. Look inside the shell and check for the emergence of molten brazing alloy around the ends of each tube. Be sure to heat the shell to proper temperature so full penetration is achieved. When the shell joints are done, braze the seat tube/top tube joint.

After the triangle has cooled use the straight-edges to check for any shift in shell alignment before removing the cups. Inspect the entire triangle for alignment in all planes, especially to see if the head tube is parallel to the seat tube. If a jig has been used, tube alignment may be rough-checked by simply observing if the triangle can be rocked in it once the C-clamps have been removed. A more precise check is to lay the triangle on a coffee table which has a thick glass top. Slip $\frac{1}{16}$ inch shims under the top tube. Let the shell and lugs hang over the table's edge. Sight along the edge of the table top and assure yourself that all tubes are parallel to it. (Note: It may be necessary to braze the tube connections from inside the shell also, to achieve proper strength.)

If the triangle is found to be twisted, it will have to be bent back into alignment by the process of cold-setting. This is done by inserting a length of steel pipe through the head tube, then twisting it while the seat tube end of the assembly is firmly clamped to a rigid surface. It takes a fair amount of leverage to cold-set and it must be done bit by bit, constantly checking progress, rather than attempting to yank the triangle into alignment in a single operation.

Clean all carbon and solidified flux from the joints by scrubbing them with a wire brush under a continuous flow of hot water. (P8.25)

If you have a deep sink, set the triangle in it while doing the clean-up operation. When you have done the best you can with the wire brush, dry the triangle thoroughly and continue cleaning up the assembly using files and production cloth. (P8.26) First file away all

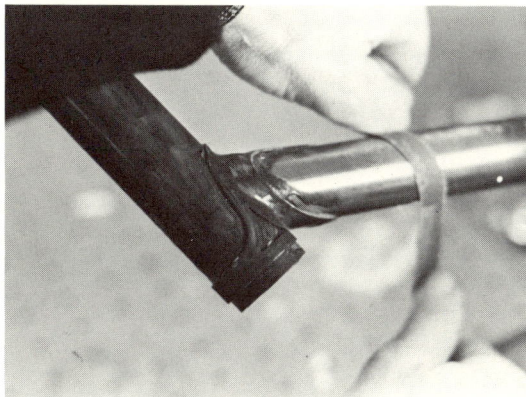

P8.26 Surfaces are then cleaned up with production cloth.

brazing material that may be stuck to the outside surfaces of the tubes and lugs. A 10-inch mill file works well for this operation. The tube walls are thin so try not to cut into them. Rifflers are helpful for cleaning up joint seams and will sharply define the lug outlines. (P8.27) When the excess brazing material has been cleaned away, start to taper and thin the

P8.25 After brazing, carbon deposits and residual flux are removed by wire brushing.

P8.27 Lug seams are best finished using rifflers.

79

lugs taking care not to file their points completely away. There should be a discernible lug line clearly defining the lug/tube demarcation point. (P8.28) While thinning with the file take care to keep it from slipping off the lugs and onto the adjacent tube surfaces. This can cause very deep gouges.

P8.28 Lug seams should be sharply defined. This view shows main triangle joints at bottom bracket shell.

At this time you may uncover some places where brazing material did not flow all the way to the lug edges. These openings can be filled in by heating only those specific areas and feeding more brazing rod into the gaps. However, if the openings are small or few in number it is best not to attempt rebrazing — you may do more harm than good. A better solution under these circumstances is to fill the gaps with auto putty or epoxy as will be explained in Chapter XI. Now let's discuss the seat stay attachment which is treated as a separate step.

Building the Seat Stay Attachment

Probably the easiest attachments to make are the so-called wrap-arounds, Italian types, and the Brampton Victor; all require less exacting preparation and are more forgiving of builder error than the Allen Key Fastback design described here. Figure VIII-1 illustrates construction details for the various designs. If you are not building an Allen-type attachment, no additional filing of the seat lug is required at this time. Simply select an appropriate design from among those illustrated

in the figure and braze the joint as shown when the "V" assemblies are joined to the main triangle. This assembly step is covered in Chapter IX.

The Allen Key Fastback Seat Stay Attachment

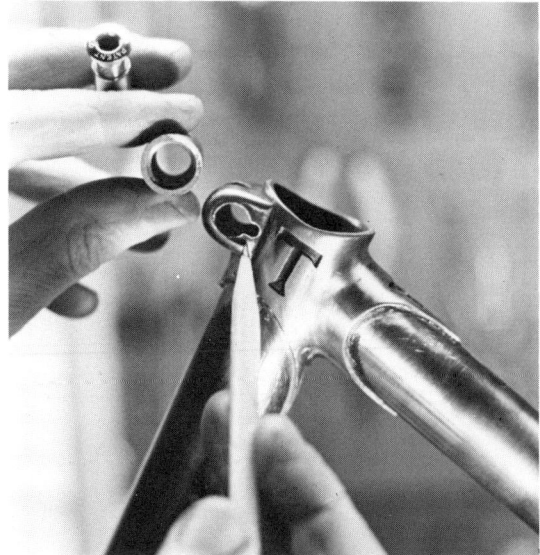

P8.29 Components used for making an Allen Key Fastback attachment. Top to bottom: Allen type seat bolt, seat bolt tube and seat lug ears which must be removed.

If you are making an Allen-type attachment then the first step is to remove the seat bolt ears that protrude from the back of the seat lug. Use a coarse bastard file to hog off half of the ears, then take a round file, equal in diameter or slightly smaller than the OD of the seat bolt tube, and file a semi-circular slot into what is left of the ears. (P8.30) File deep enough so the ears will fit about halfway around the tube. It will probably be necessary to file deep into the seat tube itself and even to remove some material from the bolt tube to obtain the correct depth. (P8.31, P8.32)

Once this is done, clean and flux the parts then braze the tube into the slot using brass or filler rod. (P8.33, P8.34) Layer on an ample amount of brazing material; the joint must be substantially built up and filleted to develop the required strength and to provide enough metal to achieve the proper contours. When the joint has cooled, remove all carbon and solidified flux by wire brushing the assembly under a flow of hot water. Now rough-shape the attachment to a smooth contour using diemaker's files and rifflers. (P8.35) Narrow strips of coarse production cloth may also be used. (P8.36) Also, cut off any excess seat tube at this time, and file the top of the seat lug to the desired shape. Now put the main triangle aside, and we will tackle construction of the rear triangle.

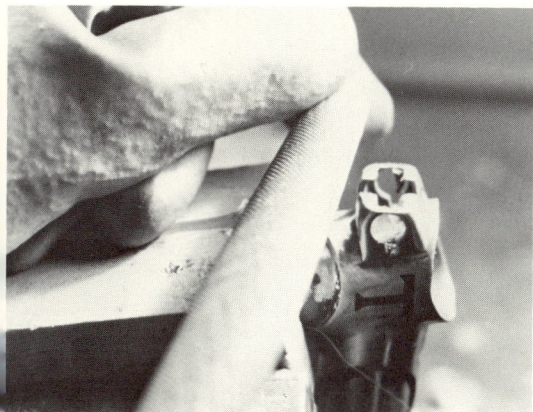
P8.32 Checking bolt tube fit.

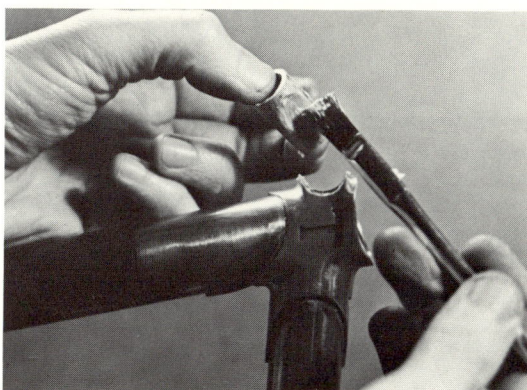
P8.30 Hogging off the lug ears.

P8.33 Fluxing the bolt tube.

P8.31 Lug with ears partially removed. Concave slots have also been filed into the bolt tube and seat tube to provide proper fit.

P8.34 Brazing the bolt tube to the seat lug. The joint must be heavily filleted.

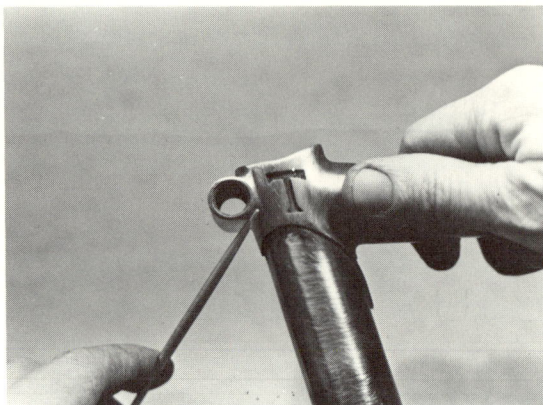

P8.35 Shaping the joint contours with a diemaker's file.

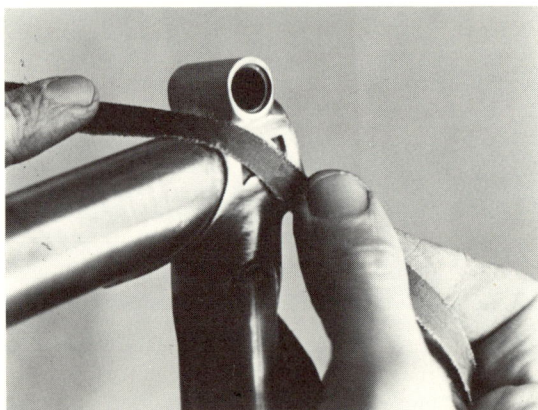

P8.36 Contours are finished with narrow strips of production cloth.

SEAT STAY ATTACHMENT DESIGNS
(Not to Scale)

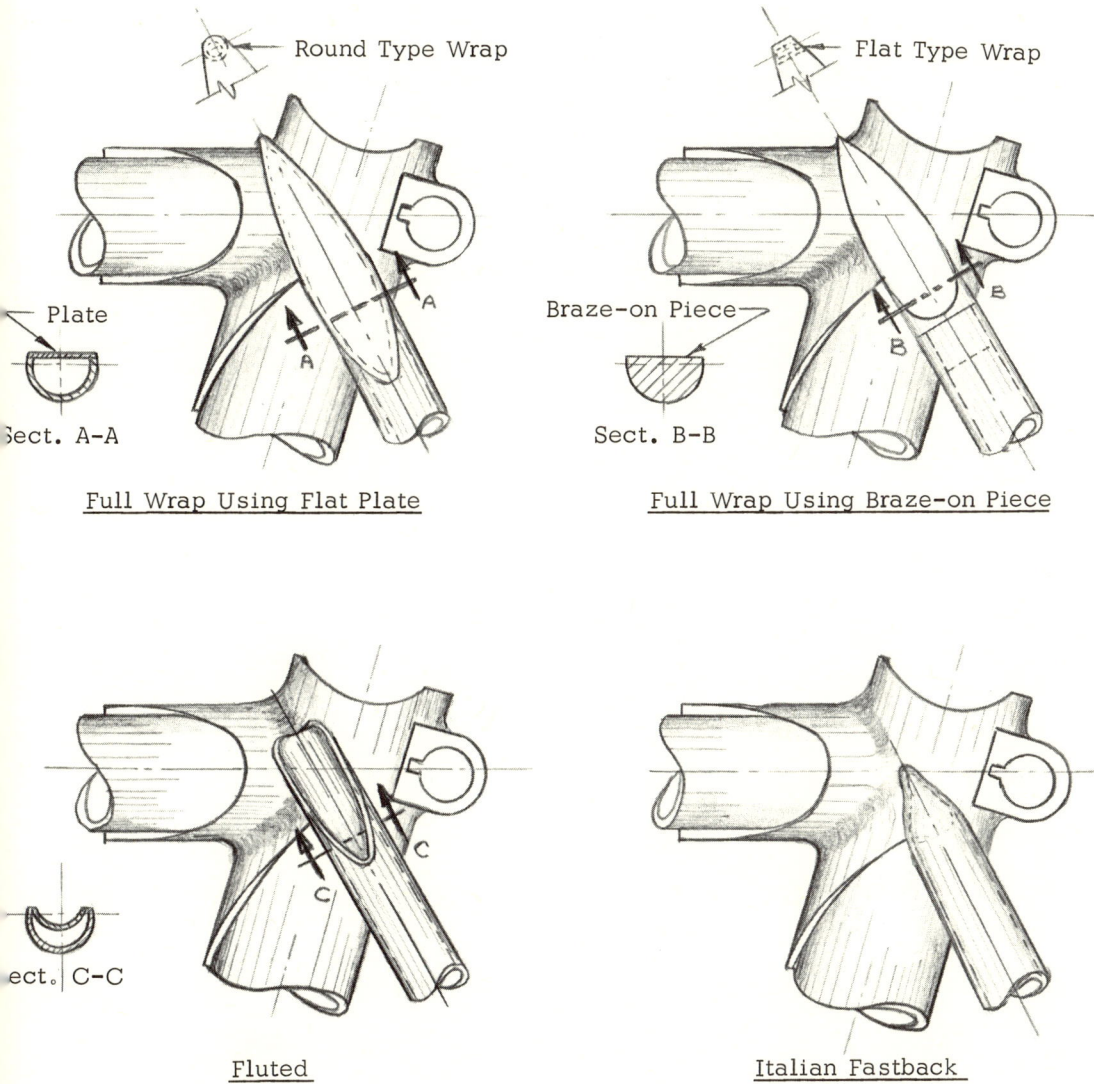

Round Type Wrap

Flat Type Wrap

Plate

Sect. A-A

Full Wrap Using Flat Plate

Braze-on Piece

Sect. B-B

Full Wrap Using Braze-on Piece

ect. C-C

Fluted

Italian Fastback

FIGURE VIII-1

SEAT STAY ATTACHMENT DESIGNS

(Not to Scale)

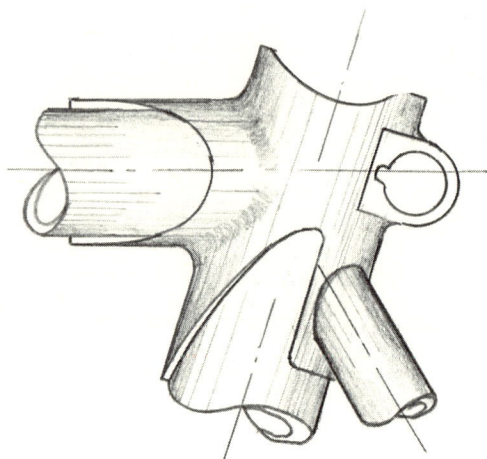

Brampton Victor

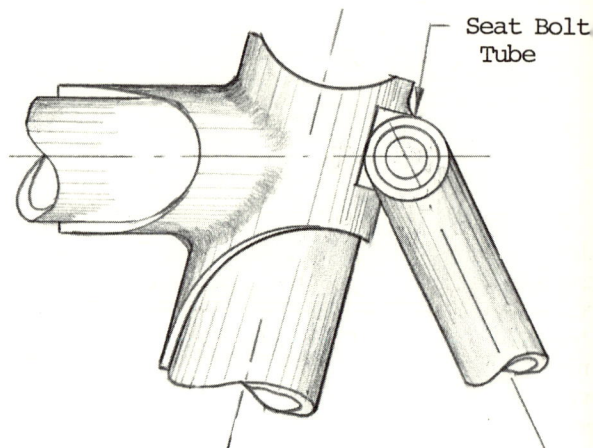

Allen Key Fastback

Seat Bolt Tube

CONSTRUCTION NOTES

Partial Wrap and Full Wrap Around Designs (Only full wrap is illustrated.)

Either design may be fabricated by beveling the stay ends, then brazing on flat plates. A popular and much   easier method is to purchase prefinished, beveled, braze-on pieces, then braze them to straight cut stay ends. In the full wrap around design, beveled ends are left extra long, heated, then tapped with a hammer to form an overlap on top of the lug. When stays are brazed to the lug, extra brazing material is used to build up the overlap, and it is then filed to either a round or flat shape. For partial wrap designs, bevel can be made any length desired.

Fluted Design

Seat ends of stays are cut on a bevel, and piece removed is reversed and braze back into the gap. Filler rod is used, as necessary, to achieve a smooth, concave shape.

Allen Key Fastback Design

See text.

All Designs: Refer to Figure VI-3 for seat stay attachment braze-ons.

FIGURE VIII-1 (continued)

CHAPTER IX

BUILDING THE REAR TRIANGLE
BRAZE-ONS — SPECIAL DESIGNS

Perhaps one of the most difficult construction steps for a novice builder is the rear triangle. It is going to test your patience and resolve, so reread the foreword to this book; "psych" yourself into the right frame of mind. The rear triangle (actually two triangles which share a common side — the seat tube) consists of the chain stays, seat stays, drop-outs, chain stay and seat stay bridges, plus any braze-ons, such as the rear derailleur conduit stop, brake bridge reinforcement, or reinforcing diamonds. There are three important points to cover before you get started.

First, when taking stay dimensions from your drawing remember that the rear triangles are angled outwards as they leave the seat tube. They are thus a trifle longer than the scaled-up dimensions obtained from the side view of your two-dimensional layout. Of course, if you have made an orthographic drawing of the frameset and drawn a *normal view* of the stays, the drawing dimensions will be exact.

Secondly, I hope you have heeded the advice given in Chapter VI regarding vertical versus road drop-outs and are using the latter (or track drops). It is also advantageous to use offset drops to simplify your work. Straight drops must be heated and bent to the proper angle while the offset types eliminate this extra step.

Thirdly, if the design features short chain stays and you are using road drops, it may be necessary to file away part of the lower axle slot tang on each drop so the rear wheel can be dismounted without having to deflate a tire. With these three points in mind, go to work on the rear drop-outs, filing away all excess

metal and shaping them as desired. You may wish to thin the drop-out eyes, or even remove them completely if you do not intend to mount fenders or a carrier. Use diemaker's files and rifflers to work on the interior drop-out contours. (P9.1) Finish with thin strips of production cloth, sanding all surfaces to a smooth pit-free contour.

P9.1 Cleaning up a rear drop-out. Note thinned eye.

Chain Stay Slotting and Doming

Once the drop-outs are shaped, slot and dome the drop-out ends of the chain stays using the same method employed earlier for the fork blades. (P9.2, P9.3, P9.4) Review Chapter VII if you need to refresh your memory. Before doming them, cut the stays to approximate length leaving ¼ inch extra on each end for final fitup. It is possible to exer-

P9.2 Slotting a chain stay.

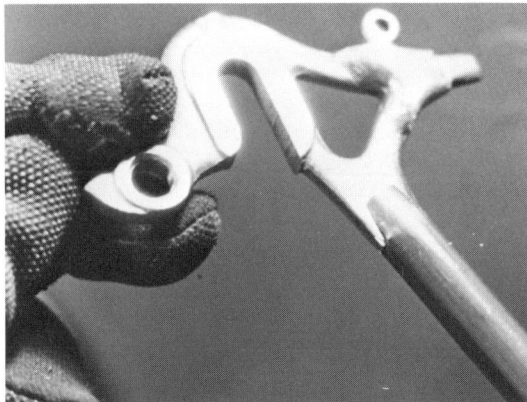

P9.3 Checking drop-out fit. Note partially domed stay end. (Lower axle slot tang has also been shortened to permit wheel removal.)

cise some control over the rear triangle's stiffness when performing the cutting operation. For example, by cutting more material away from the smaller diameter ends of the stays (as opposed to their larger [shell] ends), stiffness in the assembled triangle is increased. Taking more material from the larger ends of the stays decreases stiffness. Beware of cutting too much from the large ends. They are of uniform diameter for only a short distance,

P9.4 Finishing up a stay end with production cloth.

then steeply taper towards their tips. Overshortening the large ends can cause the tapers to rest partially inside the bottom bracket shell's spigots. This creates large annular clearances which will have to be filled in with brazing material. Strength of the resulting joints could be compromised.

Seat Stay Slotting and Doming

After the chain stays have been cut, slotted and domed, do the same to the seat stays but do not remove any material from their larger ends yet. The bores of the drop-out ends of the stays are rather small, so when mating the drop-outs to the stays, the drop-out tangs may have to be filed before they will fit. As was the case with the fork blades, it is important that the domed sides of each stay extend at least ⅞₁₆ inch over the tangs to provide sufficient brazing surface for a strong joint. Refer to Figure VII-1.

Making the Chain Stay Assemblies

When all stays have been slotted and domed, clean and flux the slotted ends of the chain stays and their mating tangs on the drop-outs. (P9.5) Vise the chain stays in a vertical position, and set the tangs into the slots so that gravity holds the drop-outs in place. Position them exactly as shown on your drawing. Braze the drop-outs to the stays using brass or filler rod. Concentrate the torch flame on the solid drop-outs to prevent

86

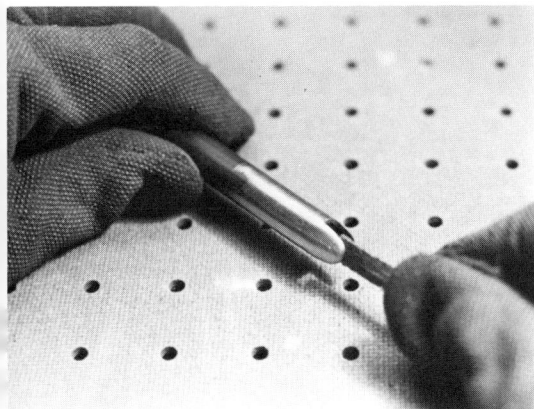

P9.5 Cleaning slot interiors.

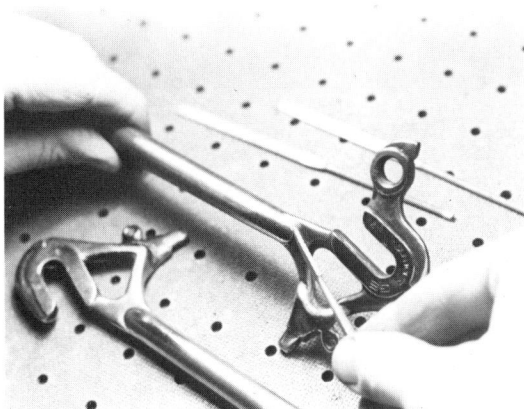

P9.7 Cleaning up the chain stay assembly joint seams with a riffler.

overheating the stay ends. Flow filler alloy into the stay slots, completely filling in any gaps. (P9.6)

P9.6 Brazing a drop-out to a chain stay.

When the joints have cooled, double check the alignment of both assemblies by laying one on top of the other. They should be mirror images and match the drawing. Give the joints the wire brush and hot water treatment to remove flux and carbon deposits, then file and sand them into shape. Carefully define the seams where the domed stay ends meet the sides of the drop-outs, and blend the tops and bottoms of the drop-outs smoothly back into the stays. (P9.7) Some designs also require a depression in the right stay to provide clearance for the inner chain ring. If yours does, make it now by crimping the tube.

Final Stay Shortening and Mitering

Now we begin a more difficult task — final fitup and mitering of the chain stay assemblies just brazed and the seat stays. In the following discussion, it is assumed that an Allen Key Fastback attachment is used. If your design is a wrap-around or other type, the construction procedure is generally the same except for the seat lug ends of the seat stays. Refer to Figure VIII-1 for particulars if this is the case.

Chain Stay Mitering

Vise the main triangle as shown in Figure IX-1. Grip it at the sides of its bottom bracket shell or hold it by the down tube. The seat tube must be vertical. Insert the chain stay assemblies into the shell's spigots. If they do not fit, file the spigot bores until the tubes will slip into them. Sometimes the stays can be wiggled to and fro slightly and they will then slip into the spigots. Be sure you have the right and left chain stay assemblies matched to the correct spigots. The right chain stay assembly has the drop-out with the derailleur hanger boss (road designs) and chain ring depression (if used).

Next, clamp a perfectly trued and dished rear wheel between the drop-outs using its axle skewer or nuts. Center the axle in the drop-out slots, and make certain you use the correct

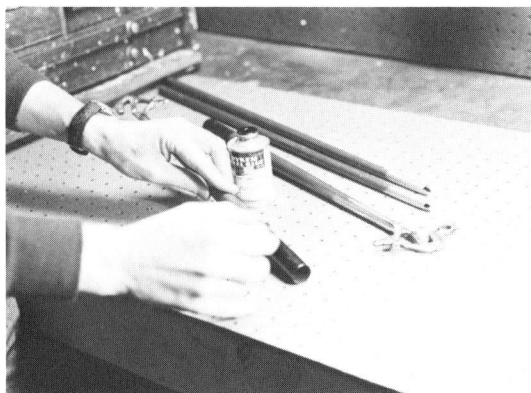

P9.8 Preparing the shell-ends of the chain stays for marking. Note slotted and domed seat stays in background.

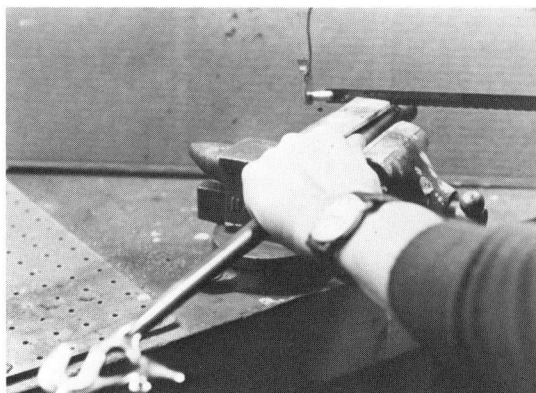

P9.9 After marking, the chain stays are cut with a hacksaw.

axle length as called for in your design, i.e., five speed or six speed. Position the wheel so that it is in line with and parallel to the seat tube. At the same time, slip the chain stays forward or backward in their spigots until the distance between the rear axle and the crank axis is equal to that shown on your drawing.

A helpful device to assist alignment of the assembly is a piece of string wrapped around the head tube and pulled tightly back against the outside edges of the rear drop-out axle slots. By measuring the gap between the string and the sides of the seat tube you can readily determine if the stays are aligned when viewed from above. Sight along the wheel from the rear to make sure it is still lined up with the seat tube. When everything is aligned in each of these planes, with the correct rear axle to crank axis distance, reach inside the bottom bracket shell and scribe a line around the circumference of both stay ends where they meet the inside surface of the shell. Release the wheel, remove the chain stay assemblies, then cut and file the stay ends to match the scribed lines. (P9.9, P9.10)

P9.10 Stay ends are contoured to fit the bottom bracket shell's ID.

Mitering the Seat Stays and Making the "V" Assemblies

The next step is to shorten and miter the seat stays. They will then be brazed to the chain stay assemblies to form two "V" shaped structures. I assume you have already cut the seat stays to approximate length and have slotted and domed their ends. The setup

P9.11 Set-up for preliminary shortening of the seat stays.

88

you will now be faced with is complex; study Figure IX-2 closely. (P9.11, P9.12)

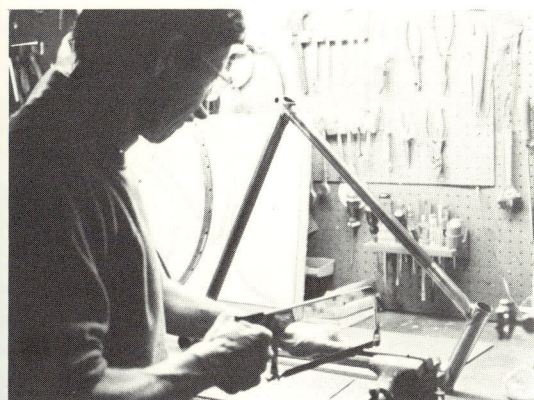

P9.13 Wedges prevent chain stays from slipping into the shell interior.

P9.12 Shortening a seat stay. Leave extra length for final mitering.

Take the main triangle and clamp it in a vise, gripping it by the seat tube. Arrange it so the seat tube is horizontal and the head tube is pointing down. Next, drive the wedges you have made into the bottom bracket shell. They will prevent the ends of the chain stays from slipping beyond the inside surface of the shell. With the main triangle set up in this manner it will be possible to prop up the chain stay assemblies and the seat stays, letting gravity hold them in place. Insert the chain stays into the spigots, making certain the wedges are properly placed and holding the stay ends flush with the shell's ID. (P9.13) Also, be sure the left and right stays are inserted into their proper spigots. Clamp the rear wheel in place and arrange the string around the head tube, tying it back tightly against the outer surfaces of the drop-outs. (P9.14)

Now, start the rather tedious process of shortening the seat stays to their final length. Select a round file, approximately the same diameter as the seat bolt tube, and begin to shape the large end of each seat stay to fit the bolt tube. (P9.15) Do this in stages, removing only a little material at a time. Check the fit frequently, going through the string and wheel set-up described above. You are mitering at an angle and shortening the stays *simultaneously*. It is a demanding operation, so go slowly.

P9.14 Assembly set-up for final mitering and shortening seat stays. Vertical arrangement of parts simplifies the work.

P9.15 Mitering seat stay ends to fit the bolt tube.

Strive for a snug fit between the bolt tube and stays. (P9.16, P9.17)

The job is done when *all* of the following conditions have been achieved: (a) the distance from the rear axle to the center line of the seat bolt tube is exactly as shown on the drawing (or intersection of seat and top tube center lines for non-Allen type designs), (b) the rear wheel is aligned in both horizontal and vertical planes, and (c) the distance from the string to the seat tube is equal on both sides of the seat tube. Congratulations! As a last step, make the seat stay vent holes. This is done by drilling a $\frac{1}{32}$ inch hole on the inside of each stay two inches down from the point where it joins the seat bolt tube (or seat lug in the case of one of the other attachment designs). (P9.18)

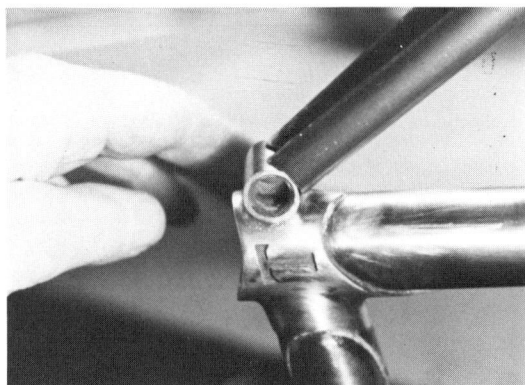

P9.16 Checking stay fit around the bolt tube.

P9.18 Drilling the seat stay vent holes.

P9.17 Finishing touches are best done with diemaker's files.

Everything should now be in order for brazing the seat stays to the chain stay assemblies (making the two "V" assemblies). (P9.19) Remove the rear wheel and the string; disassemble both "V" assemblies from atop the main triangle. Clean and flux the insides of the seat stay slots and their corresponding drop-out tangs on the chain stay assemblies. Reassemble the stays, wheel, and string as before and go through the alignment process again. When the assemblies are properly lined up, clamp the seat stays in position using the wood clamping plates and C-clamps. Wipe excess flux from the joints, and, *with great care,* remove the rear wheel without disturbing the

P9.19 Mitering and shortening completed. Joint ready for brazing.

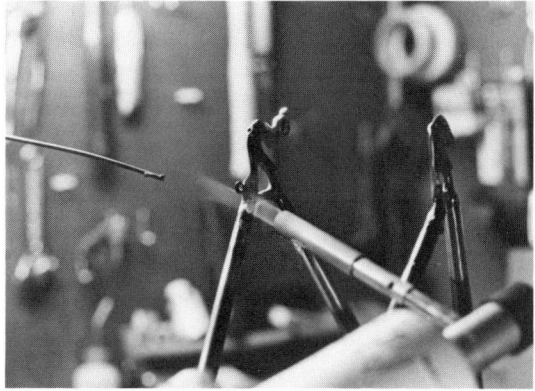

P9.20 Seat stays are brazed to dropouts to make the "V" assemblies.

setup. Double check the string measurements; then, braze the seat stays to the drop-outs using brass or filler rod. (P9.20) Allow the "V" assemblies to cool slowly; then, unclamp them and remove flux. Clean up the joints just brazed, finishing them in the same manner as those of the chain stay assemblies. (P9.21, P9.22) Use care in handling the "V" assemblies. They are fragile, and, in their present state, it is very easy to break a joint.

Joining the "V" Assemblies to the Main Triangle

With the previous work completed, the worst is over. The next step is to braze both "V" assemblies to the main triangle. You will have to go through the previous setup procedure (wheel, string, etc.) once again, only this time, before you do, clean and flux the insides of the bottom bracket shell's spigots, the seat bolt tube, and the ends of the four stays. Be thorough; the preparatory work is especially important for good adhesion. Get plenty of flux onto the seat bolt tube and the shell spigots. Set the "V" assemblies up on the main triangle and align as before, using the wheel and string.

Clamp the assemblies in position using C-clamps and clamping plates as illustrated on Figure IX-2. Keep the wood plates as far away from the joints as possible. I did not do so on my first attempt and had to contend with a fire while trying to complete the brazing

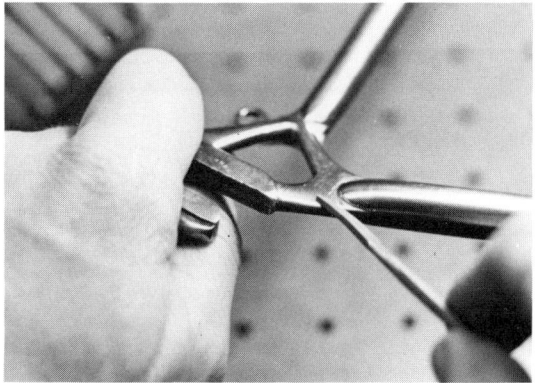

P9.21 Cleaning up a drop-out joint with a riffler.

P9.22 Finished "V" assemblies. Note thinned eyes, and shortened lower axle slot tang to permit wheel removal (necessary in a "short" chain stay design).

91

operation. It was nearly catastrophic! When the assemblies are lined up, *carefully* remove the rear wheel without disturbing the setup. Leave the string in place as a means of further checking the alignment. If you have an extra rear hub or axle, it may be clamped between the drop-outs to gain more stability. Just be sure to get everything aligned and rigidly clamped *before* you start brazing.

Brass or hard filler rod is recommended for brazing all four joints. Much filleting will be required. Braze the chain stays to the bottom bracket shell first, using two torches if necessary. Concentrate the flame mainly on the shell's spigots — less on the stays. Check for alloy penetration by inspecting the joint ends inside the shell. Feed rod into the joints at the outer spigot seams. It requires a lot of alloy to fill the rather large gaps usually present. It is also necessary to braze *inside* the shell, applying rod around the full circumference of each stay end at that location (*after* first brazing *both* outer spigot seams). Heat the outboard sides of the spigots first, then swing the torch around to their inboard sides.

Next, braze the seat stays to the seat bolt tube, building up filler material all around the joint. It takes a lot of brazing alloy to obtain the correct contour. The joint must be substantially filleted and layered. Any excess material may be filed off later during final shaping. After brazing, the "V" assemblies should be left clamped and permitted to cool in a completely draft-free area.

Bridges

The last tubes to be cut and brazed are the seat and chain stay bridges. First, check alignment of the "V" assemblies just brazed. Trial-fit the rear wheel several times to see that it slips on and off the drop-outs easily. Bend the assemblies apart or together as necessary; then, lock the rear wheel in place. Using your drawing as a guide, mark the bridge locations on the stays. Figure IX-3 illustrates various brake bridge designs. The bridge may be fabricated with or without reinforcements. Brake hole drilling and reinforcing are usually done prior to brazing the brake bridge to the seat stays. The hole can then serve as a vent. The chain stay bridge also requires a single hole for this purpose.

Start work by cutting both bridge tubes to approximate length. Then, using a round file, miter their ends to match the curvature of their respective stays. (P9.23) If reinforcing diamonds are used in conjunction with the bridges, insert them now, *before* you trial-fit the tubes between the stays. After the brake bridge has been mitered, mark its center and center-punch it on both sides to prepare it for drilling. Also mark the center of the chain stay bridge (on one side only) and center punch it.

With a $\frac{1}{32}$ inch bit, drill a hole through one side of the chain stay bridge (serves as a vent on this tube) and both sides of the brake bridge. Next, with a drill bit slightly larger in diameter than that of your rear brake pivot bolt (the bolt should fit tightly), drill through the brake bridge, one side at a time. This lessens the chance of skewing the hole and ruining the bridge tube.

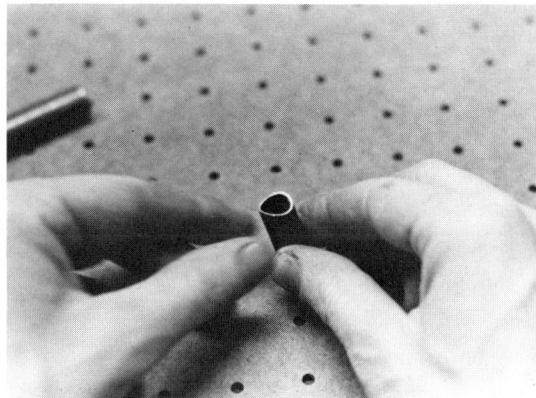

P9.23 A mitered bridge tube.

Make a final check of the fit by inserting both bridges between their respective stays and clamping them in position. With the rear wheel still installed, mount the rear brake you plan to use and check to see if its pads contact the wheel rim when the brake is operated. Ideally, the pads should come to rest on the rim when the brake blocks are positioned in the center of the brake arm slots. This permits optimum pad adjustment to allow for differences in rim diameters that may be used in the future.

If the bridge is found to sit too low, then remove it and file more material from its ends so it will slip farther up the stays. If the pads will not fully contact the rim, even when the brake blocks are in their lowest position in the brake arm slots, then the bridge is too short. In that event, fabricate a longer bridge. Also make a final check of the chain stay bridge location to be sure it will not interfere with wheel removal (if that is what you have designed for).

Assuming the fit of both bridges is good, clean the parts for brazing by sanding the stays, the bridge ends, and, if using them, any reinforcing diamonds or hole reinforcements. Bridge joints may be brazed using brass or silver alloy filler, depending on the specific design and joint clearance situation. If using a brake bolt hole reinforcement of the *slip-on* or *annulus* type (Figure IX-3), then braze it into place *prior* to brazing the bridge to the stays. Now, flux the remaining bridge parts, clamp both bridges between the stays, and braze them in place. (P9.24, P9.25)

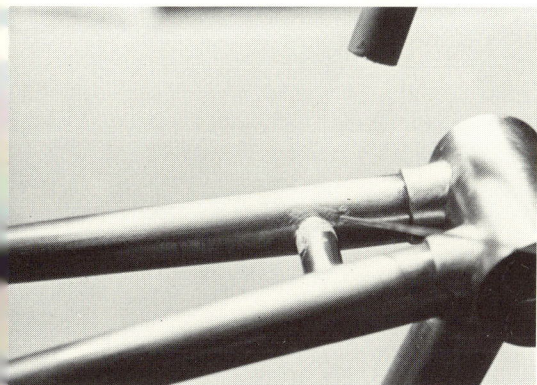

P9.25 Brazing the brake bridge assembly in place. Plain bridge illustrated. Note reinforcing diamonds.

P9.26 Checking rear brake reach.

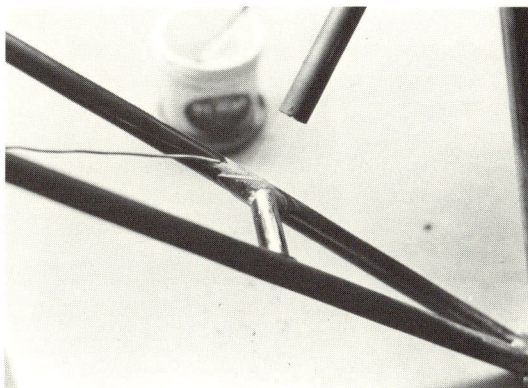

P9.24 Brazing the chain stay bridge in place.

joints just brazed may now be defluxed, then final-shaped using rifflers, a mill file, and production cloth. (P9.27, P9.28, P9.29)

Check wheel fit and stay alignment when the assembly is cool. The bridge brazing operation usually causes some distortion of the rear triangles, reducing the spacing between the drop-outs. These may be pried back into proper adjustment by gentle bending. Also check the rear brake reach. (P9.26) All

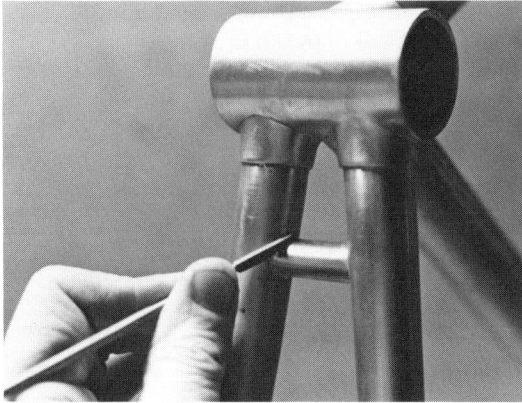
P9.27 Cleaning up the bridge joints with a riffler.

P9.30 Cleaning up the rear brake pivot bolt hole. Brake bolt should be a tight fit.

P9.28 Cleaning up and thinning the bridge reinforcing diamonds after brazing.

Braze-Ons — Special Designs (See Figure VI - 3)

Braze-ons, such as bottle nuts, cable guides, stops, etc., may be brazed in place at this time. (P9.31, P9.32, P9.33, P9.34) What to use depends upon the function of the bicycle and your personal preferences. You may want to try something unique, like concealing cabling or conduit within certain frame tubes.

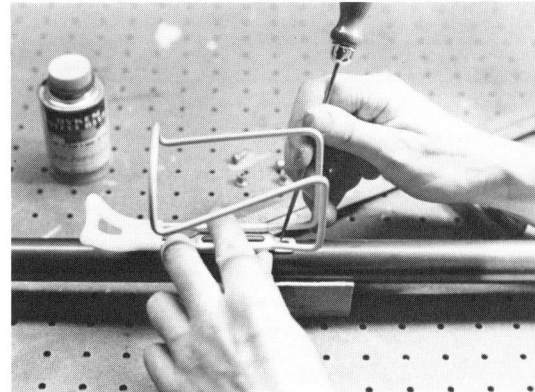
P9.31 Adding braze-ons. Bottle cage nut locations are marked on the down tube.

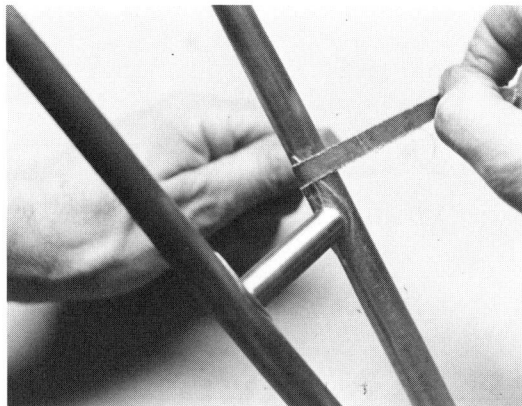
P9.29 Final thinning is done using production cloth. Similar process is used to thin the lugs.

94

P9.32 Drilling cage nut holes. Note use of tube blocks for support.

P9.33 Silbrazing the cage nuts in place. Small torch head is used for this low-heat operation.

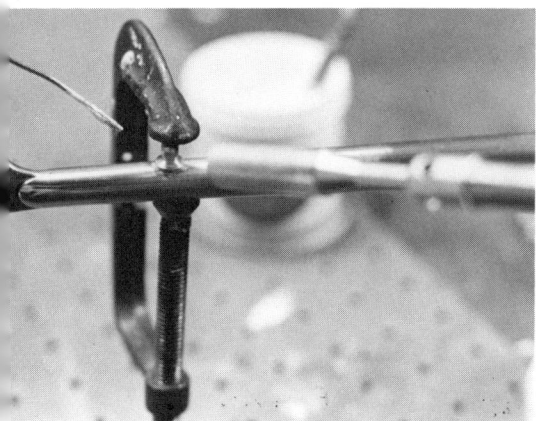

P9.34 Brazing the rear derailleur-conduit stop.

For example, I designed and built a *concealed* rear brake conduit arrangement. In this type of design the conduit is run inside the top tube. A reinforcing plate was first brazed to the top tube, then an angled hole, large enough to receive the brake cable conduit, was drilled through the plate and tube wall. (P9.35, P9.36, P9.37) The seat tube was also slotted at its interface with the top tube, and a conduit clearance hole was provided at the base of the seat tube slit. (P10.5, P10.6) The brake conduit runs inside the top tube, through the seat post (which must also be slotted), and emerges from the base of the seat tube slit.

It is a very clean design that eliminates the need for cable clamps — those bothersome little devices that always seem to leave ugly rusty rings on the top tube. With a bit of ingenuity this philosophy could be extended to the derailleur control cables — running them inside the down tube and stays. Lighting system wires could also be handled in a similar fashion. But *please* — if you are unsure about how to do the necessary reinforcing — seek the guidance of a professional builder *before* attempting anything quite so radical.

P9.35 Making a top tube reinforcing plate. Special design, used for concealed brake conduit.

P9.36 Brazing the reinforcing plate to the top tube.

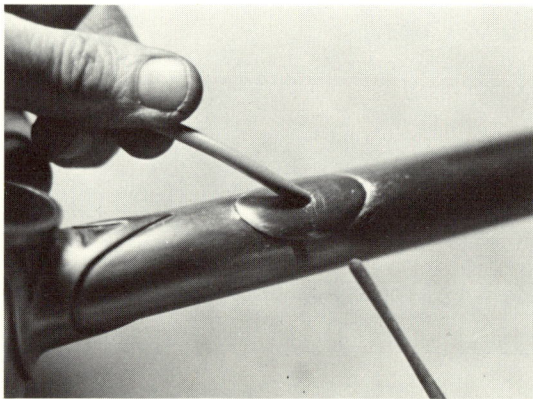

P9.37 Conduit hole has been finished with a round riffler (on right). Hole size is checked using a length of brake conduit.

SET-UP FOR MARKING AND MITERING THE CHAIN STAYS

(Not to Scale)

Perfectly trued and dished
rear wheel

Top Tube Axis

Seat Tube Axis

String

Center axle in
rear drop out
slot

Shell

Chain
Stays

Scribe chain stay
ends here
at inside
surface of
shell (2)

This dimension taken
from design
drawing

String

Seat
Tube

$A1^{(1)}$ $A2^{(1)}$

Chain
Stays

Jaw Covers

Bottom
Bracket
Shell

PARTIAL END VIEW

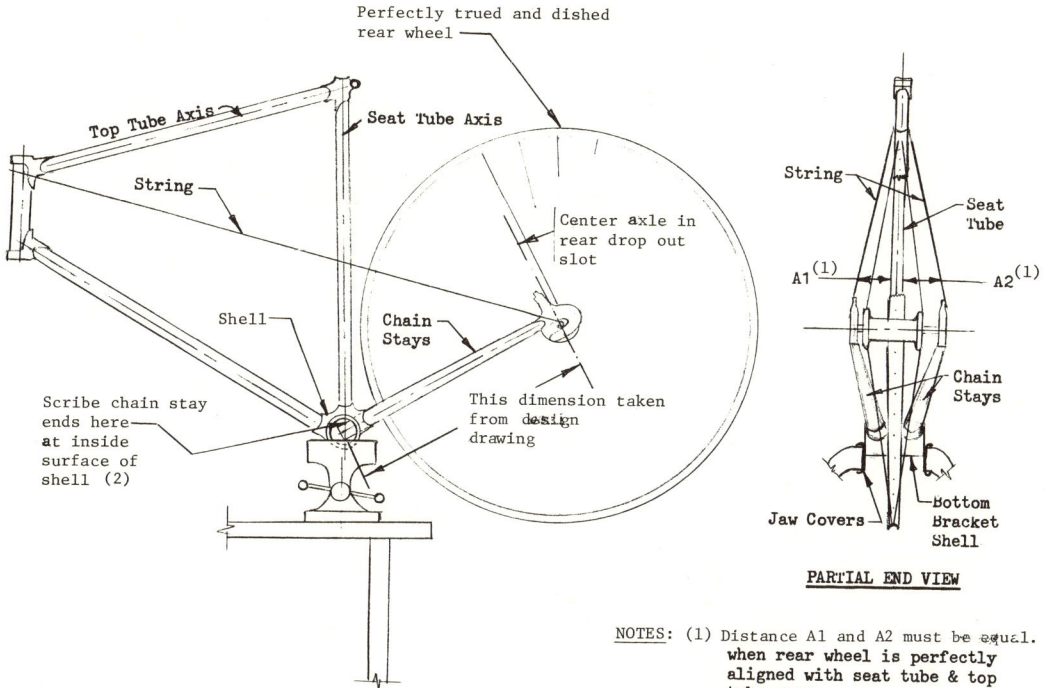

NOTES: (1) Distance A1 and A2 must be equal.
when rear wheel is perfectly
aligned with seat tube & top
tube axes.

(2) Stays project into bottom
bracket shell prior to marking
and mitering operations.

FIGURE IX-1

97

SET-UP FOR MITERING AND SHORTENING THE SEAT STAYS

(Not to Scale)

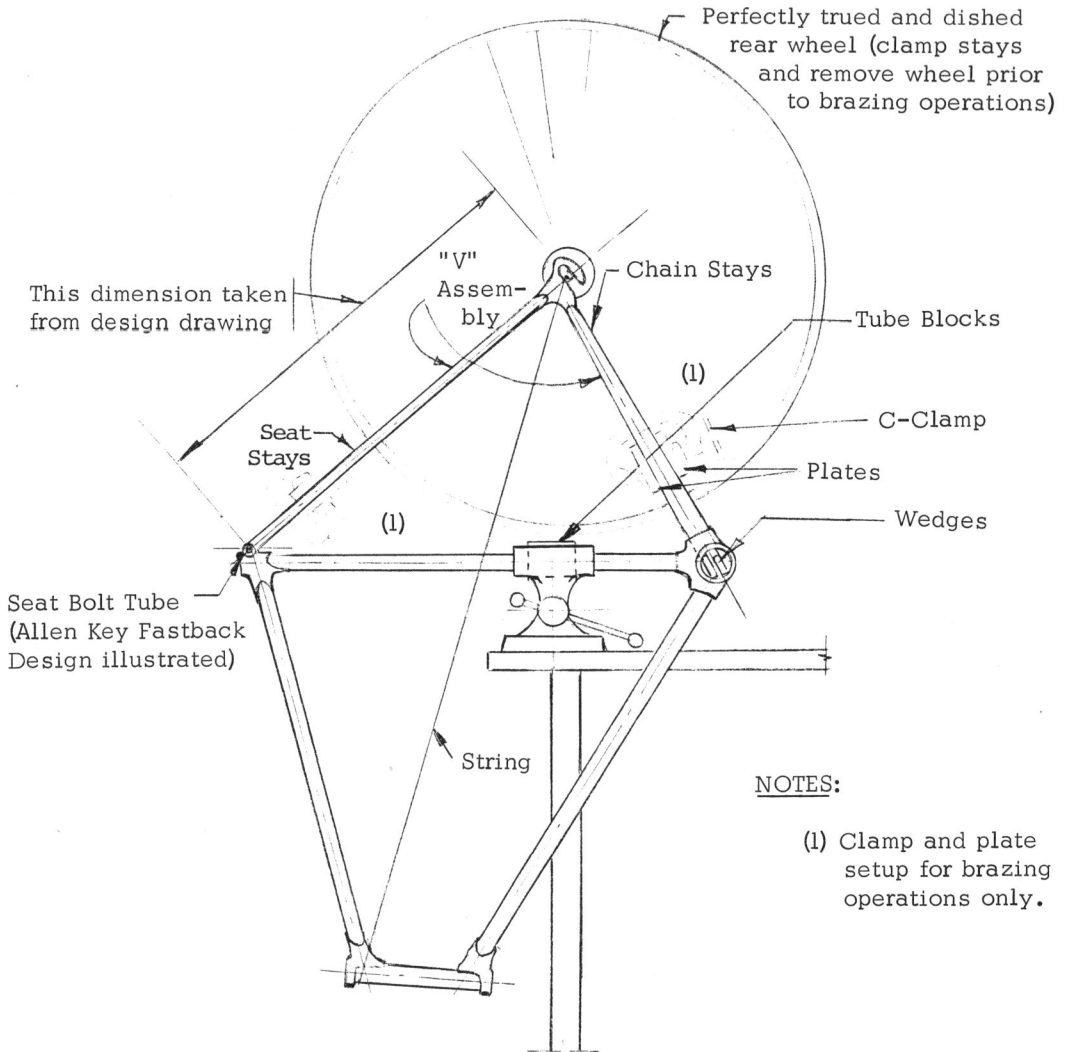

Perfectly trued and dished
rear wheel (clamp stays
and remove wheel prior
to brazing operations)

"V" Assem-bly

Chain Stays

Tube Blocks

(1)

C-Clamp

Plates

Wedges

This dimension taken
from design drawing

Seat Stays

(1)

Seat Bolt Tube
(Allen Key Fastback
Design illustrated)

String

NOTES:

(1) Clamp and plate
setup for brazing
operations only.

FIGURE IX-2

TYPICAL BRAKE BRIDGES AND REINFORCEMENTS

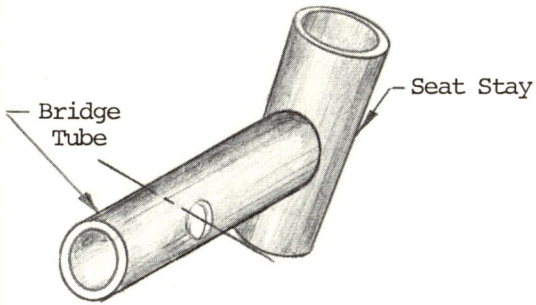

Bridge Tube

Seat Stay

Plain

Slip-On Reinforcement

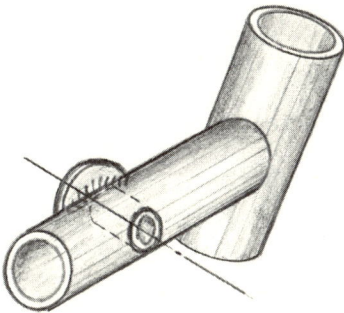

Washer and Tube

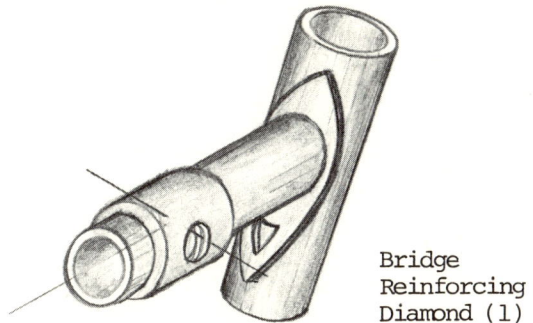

Annulus Type (Tube Within a Tube)

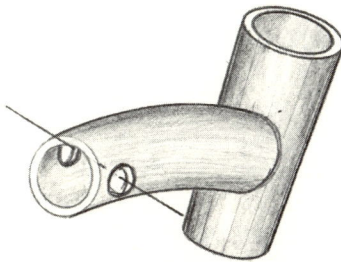

Bridge
Reinforcing
Diamond (1)

Curved Bridge - Also available as
prefabricated braze-on

Notes: (1) Diamonds may be used on
any type bridge.
(2) Also see Figure VI-3.

FIGURE IX-3

PART III
FINISHING TOUCHES

Chapter X

FINISHING THE FRAMESET
OPERATIONS REQUIRING SPECIAL TOOLING

If you have followed the outline of this book — cleaning up and filing most of the joints as they were brazed — there should not be much finishing work left. Some typical tasks at this time are cleaning up those braze-ons you may have added, final shaping of the seat attachment, and touching up the lugs and tubes. If an Allen Key Fastback seat attachment has been used, start filing there. Remove the last traces of any excess brazing material from around the seat stay connections and smoothly flare the joint back into the stays, bolt tube and lug. The attachment is particularly difficult to finish around the undersides of the bolt tube and stays. Rifflers and diemaker's files come in handy here as does a hand-held grinder equipped with small diameter cutters. When the attachment is contoured to your satisfaction, finish smoothing the joint using very thin strips of production cloth.

Next, slit the seat tube. This is done by first drilling a ⅛ inch diameter hole through the back of the tube 1¾ inches below the top of the seat lug. Mount two blades in a hacksaw, and with the main triangle firmly clamped in a vise, saw through the back of the seat stay attachment and seat tube to the hole just drilled. (P10.1) Keep the cut straight. With an Allen Key Fastback design you will be cutting completely through the seat bolt tube as well. Smooth the edges of the slit with a warding file, and remove all burrs from inside the seat tube with a machinist's scraper. (P10.2) Fold a length of production cloth over your index

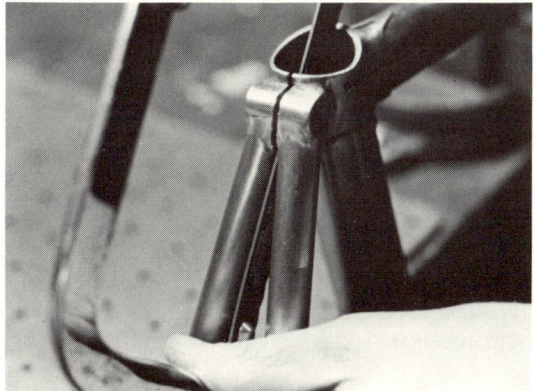

P10.1 Slitting the seat tube. Note double blade arrangement in hacksaw.

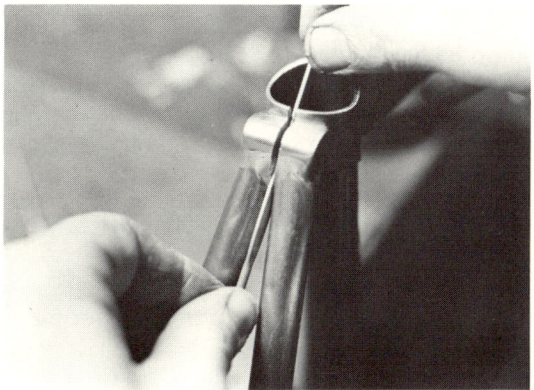

P10.2 Widening the slit with a warding file.

finger and round off the inside edges of the top of the seat tube and the slit. (P10.3) Attention to these details now will prevent seat post scratches later.

P10.3 *Production cloth is used to smooth out the tube ID and top of seat lug.*

Now clean up any braze-on attachments that may have been added. Other areas which may need filing are the top and bottom of the head tube. File away any excess tube that extends beyond the head tube lugs, leaving about $\frac{1}{16}$ inch extra for final facing, which will be done later with a head tube cutter. Also, remove any tube projections or brazing material that may extend inside the bottom bracket shell. Cut away burrs there with a machinist's scraper.

The final lug-edging work may now be done. Rifflers are ideally suited to this purpose. Start with the lug seams. Use a riffler to smooth them out and remove excess brazing alloy. Strive for a smooth, sharp line at the lug edges. Maintain this definition inside the lug cut-outs and windows as well. Sometimes excess filler flows into these areas leaving unsightly blobs. Remove this material completely so the cut-outs and windows stand out as sharply as the outer edges of the lugs. Now dress the edges of the spigots, paying particular attention to joint surfaces normally hidden from view, such as the undersides of the bottom bracket shell. The edges of all lugs and shell spigots should be filed so they are perpendicular to the adjacent tube surfaces, and their corners should be quite sharp. (P10.7)

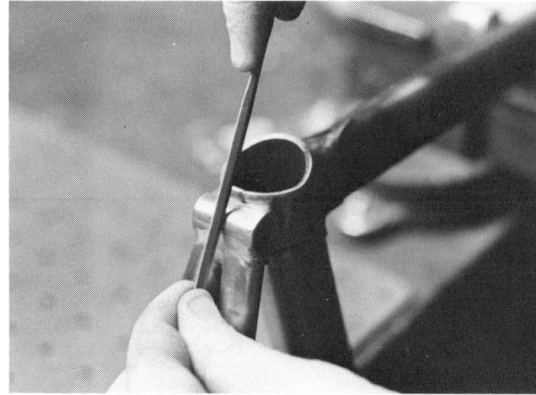

P10.4 *Finish-contouring the seat attachment.*

P10.5 *Special operation for "concealed" brake conduit design. A slot is cut in the seat tube wall to provide passage of the conduit. Seat post must be similarly slotted in this type design.*

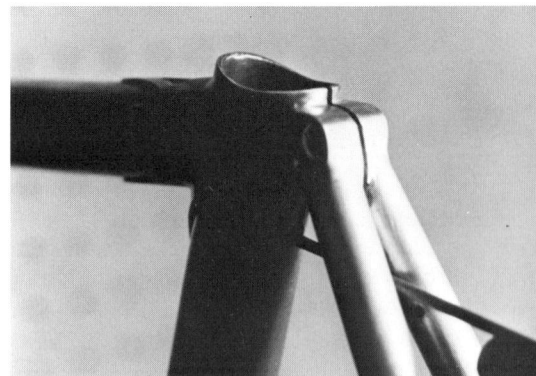

P10.6 *Using a riffler to file the base of the seat tube slit. ("Concealed" brake conduit design.)*

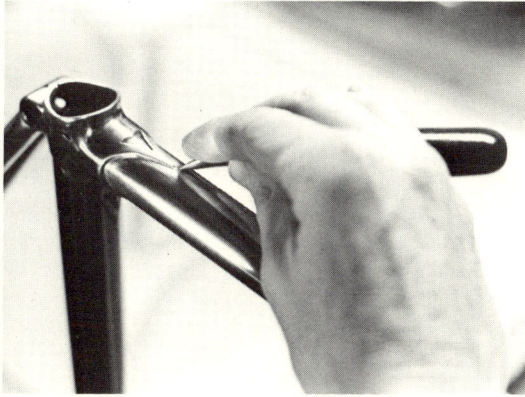

P10.7 Cleaning up lug seams with a curved burnisher.

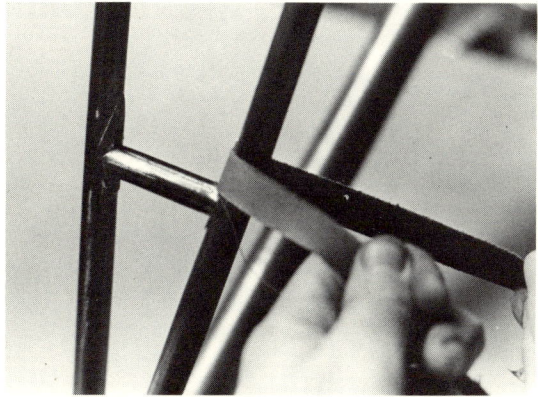

P10.9 Final thinning is done with strips of production cloth.

When the seams are done, finish thinning the lugs and spigots using care so as not to remove too much from their points. These are easily filed away. Thinness with lug definition is the objective. Start the thinning operation with a 10-inch mill bastard file, then switch to production cloth. Use that shoe-shining motion described earlier to maintain a smooth curved surface. (P10.8) Precut several 12-inch

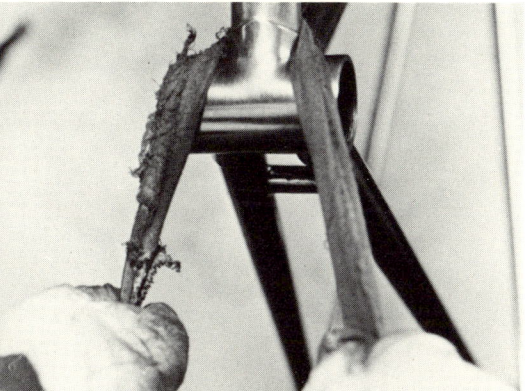

P10.8 Sanding the bottom bracket shell spigots.

long strips of No. 120 grit production cloth into ⅛-, ¼-, and ½-inch widths. Use the narrower strips to round off the smaller lug contours and the wider ones to finish larger surfaces. (P10.9) Lug walls should be relatively thick near the tube joint and then gradually

taper so they are thin near their points. Tapering in this manner permits optimum joint flexibility. Take care not to round off the lug edges.

When the thinning is done, sand all remaining areas of the fork and frame using 1-inch wide strips of No. 120 grit cloth. (P10.10) Keep sanding these assemblies until their surfaces have a bright-metal finish and are free from imperfections. Make a detailed examination of all surfaces under a bright light, looking for any missed spots or lug irregularities, then finish up as required. (P10.11)

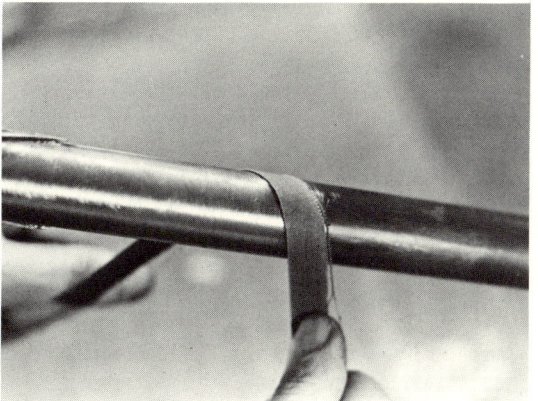

P10.10 Tube sanding with 120 grit production cloth.

105

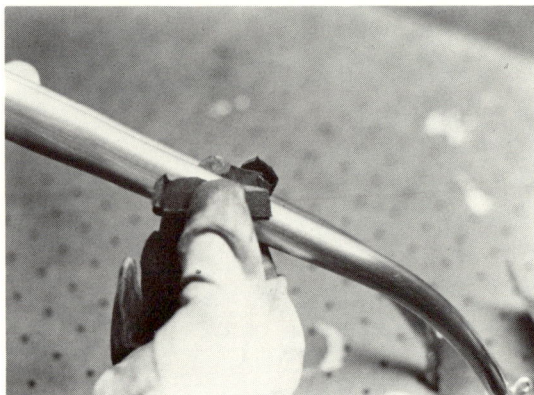
P10.11 Sanding the fork blades.

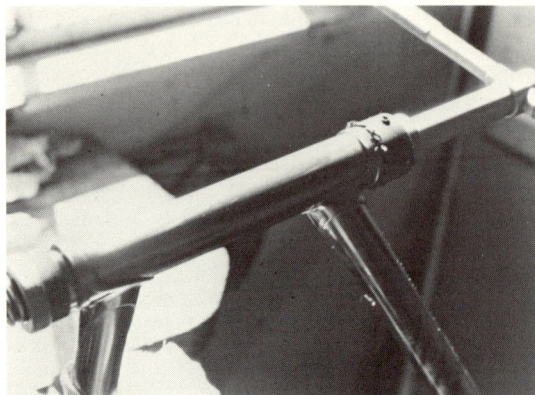
P10.12 Set up for reaming and facing the head tube (Campagnolo No. 733 Milling Tool).

Operations Requiring Special Tooling

Now find a local bike shop that is equipped with a set of bottom bracket taps, a bottom bracket facing tool, a combination head tube reaming and facing cutter, and a crown race cutter. You will have to take the frame and fork to the shop and pay to have the following operations done or pay for the use of the tools while you do the work on their premises. If a shop is not available in your area then ship the frameset to a custom builder to have the work done. Most of those listed in Appendix Table VIII will perform the operations for a nominal fee.

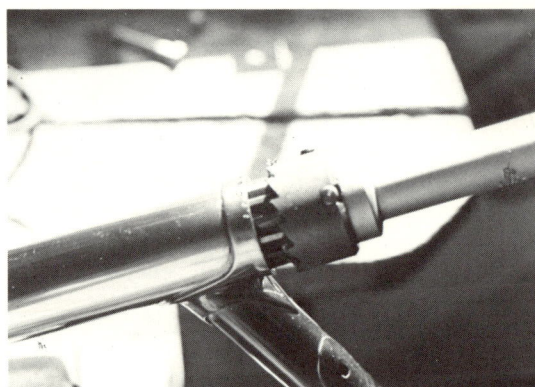
P10.13 Close-up view of reaming and facing cutter. Head tube top lug shown.

Fork Fitting Operations

Assuming you have taken the frameset to a shop, first clamp the frame firmly in a vise.Position it so the down tube is gripped near the head tube lug as illustrated in P10.12. Now, with a head tube reaming and facing tool, ream and face each end of the head tube using an ample application of cutting oil. (P10.13) If a Campagnolo or similar type cutter is used, there is a spring-loaded mandrel that passes through the head tube to keep tension on the cutters as you turn them. If in doubt about how to manipulate the cutter, ask the shop mechanic. It takes considerable hand pressure to keep the tool cutting. (P10.14) Remove only enough material from each end of the tube to obtain a cleanly faced lug surface.

P10.14 Maintain even pressure to keep the tool cutting.

(P10.15) While at the shop you may want to insert the headset races. There is a special tool made for this purpose, although the job can be done in the home workshop using a wooden block and hammer. (P10.16, P10.17, P10.18, P10.19, P10.20. P10.21)

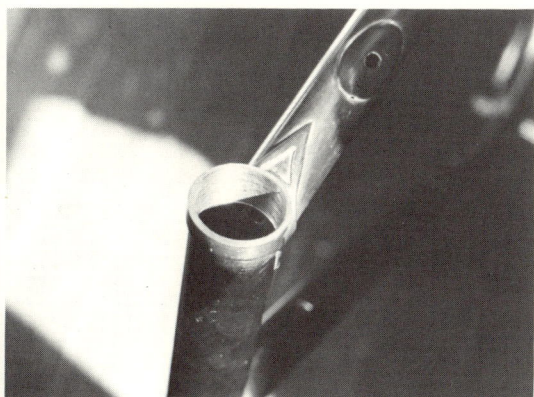

P10.15 Top of head tube. Reamed and faced.

P10.17 Setting the top head race.

P10.16 Set-up for installing the top head race; short aluminum tube is used to prevent damage to race surfaces.

P10.18 The installed race.

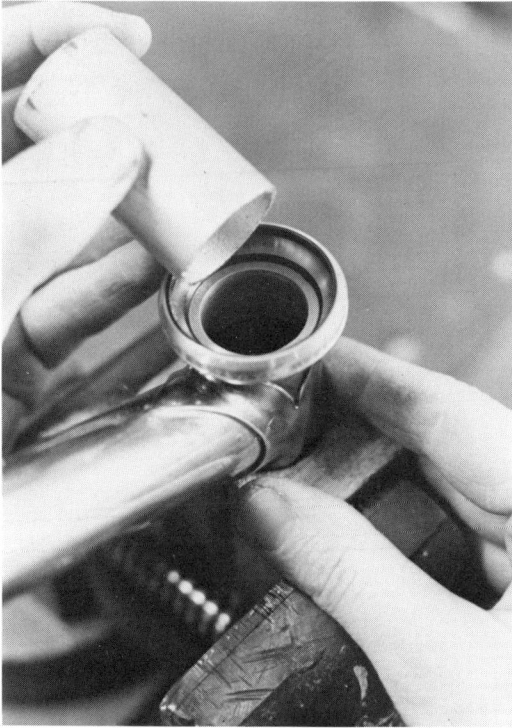
P10.19 Preparing to install the bottom head race.

P10.21 When properly seated, the race should be in firm contact with the faced end of the head tube.

Next, vise the fork, gripping it by the crown as shown in P10.22. Use soft jaw covers to protect the finish. Take a column race cutter and mill the crown's column race boss.

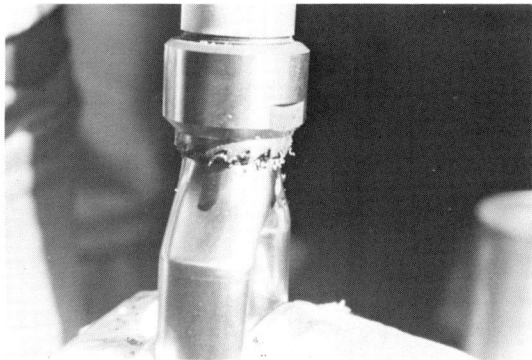
P10.22 Campagnolo No. 718 Crown Race Cutter in operation.

P10.20 Seating the race.

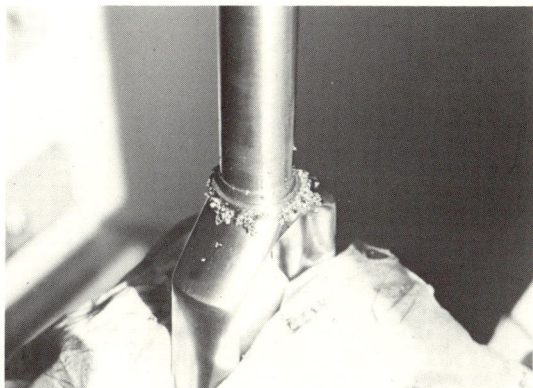

P10.23 Fork crown boss after cutting operation.

(P10.23) Then slip the column race over the steering tube and drive it onto the boss just milled. (P10.24) Use a length of pipe or the special shop tool. If using pipe, place a short piece of aluminum or brass tube against the race to prevent marring its ground surface. The setup is pictured in P10.25. If for some

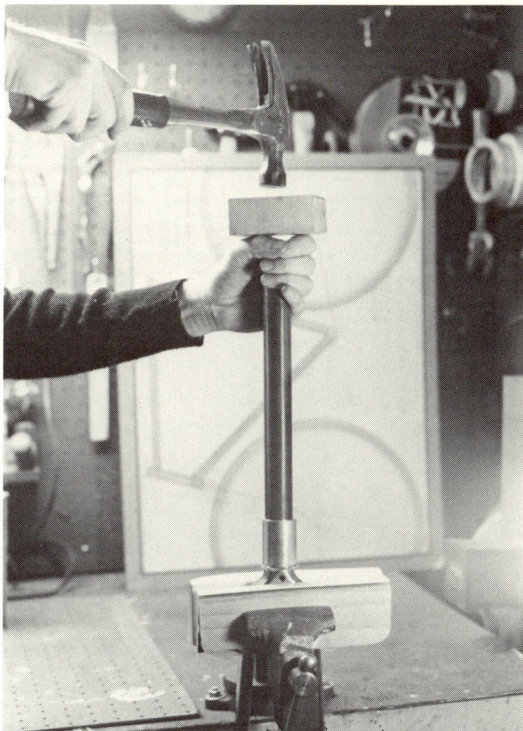

P10.25 Setting the crown race. Lower tube is a short piece of soft aluminum conduit which is used to prevent damage to the race surfaces.

reason the race is not a tight fit on the boss, it may be secured using Locktite No. 2. Another method is to upset the boss surface with a center punch or knurling tool to obtain an interference fit.

Take the remaining headset parts and assemble the fork to the frame. (P10.26) The

P10.24 Set-up for installing the crown race. Note wood clamping blocks to prevent damage to the finished crown.

P10.26 Assembling the fork to the frame.

threaded end of the steering tube should be a bit too long if you have followed the earlier cutting instructions. It will be shortened to exact length later. At this time, just check to see if there are sufficient threads on the steering tube to provide proper seating of the 4 races, bearings, lock washer, and nut. If there are not, use the shop's threading die to cut a longer thread on the tube. If the steering tube is too short you can try shortening the head tube by refacing it on both ends. The amount gained will be very limited — ⅛-inch maximum. If that does not solve the problem, and there are still not enough threads to fully engage the lock nut, you are in the unenviable position of having to replace the steering tube.

P10.27 Starting the bottom bracket tap by hand.

Threading and Facing the Bottom Bracket Shell

Remove the fork and securely clamp the frame either in a vise or in the shop's bike work stand. Grip it at the shell end of the down tube. You can also clamp it to a table with C-clamps. Now select a pair of bottom bracket taps that correspond to the shell's threading — BSA, Italian, or French — and prepare to clean up the threads. A word of caution is in order. If the shell is English-threaded, it will be cut with a right-hand thread on its left side and a left-hand thread on its right side. Italian and French threading is right handed on both sides. Be sure you select the right *nationality* tap and the correct *hand* for the side you will be working on.

It is best to start the tap while holding it in your hand. (P10.27) Shell threads are very fine and it is easy to cross-thread them. You get a better "feel" for the thread engagement and reduce the likelihood of cross-threading by hand-starting the tap. Once the tap is well engaged with the shell's threads, use a tap wrench, or large adjustable wrench, to gain additional leverage. (P10.28) Keep the tap and threads well lubricated with cutting oil. Advance the tap into the hole a quarter turn at a time, reversing its direction at the end of each cutting stroke to break up the chips. Frequently back the tap completely out of the hole and brush accumulated chips from inside the shell and off the tap. Apply fresh cutting oil each time to do this.

Some shells are factory-supplied with

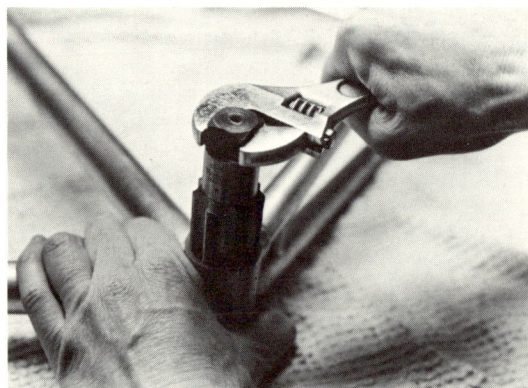

P10.28 Completing the tapping operation. Adjustable wrench is used for increased leverage.

threads only partially cut. These require a fair amount of metal removal during the tapping operation. Sometimes the opposite is true, and the tap may be easily turned into the full depth of the hole. Check tapping depth by intermittently screwing a cup into the shell. When it can be turned most of the way in with the aid of a bottom bracket wrench, you are done. A tight fit is better than one that is too loose. When inserting the cups, the fixed cup (flats milled on its edges) goes on the right side, and the adjustable one (holes on its outer face) goes on the left side of the shell (*right* and *left* are referenced to the cyclist's riding position).

110

As a last step, face each side of the shell using the shop's bottom bracket facing tool. Remove only enough metal to achieve a cleanly faced surface. Test the fit of the cups once more to see if they will still screw into the shell to the proper depth. (P10.29, P10.30) All remaining work may be done in the home workshop.

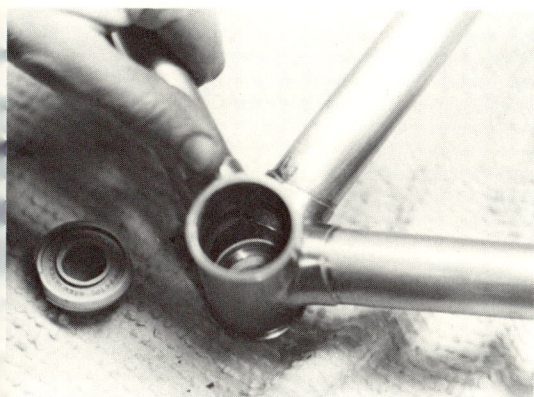

P10.31 The steering tube is marked for cutting. Nut and washer are used to determine proper length.

P10.29 View of tapped shell with adjustable cup in place. Fixed cup on bench.

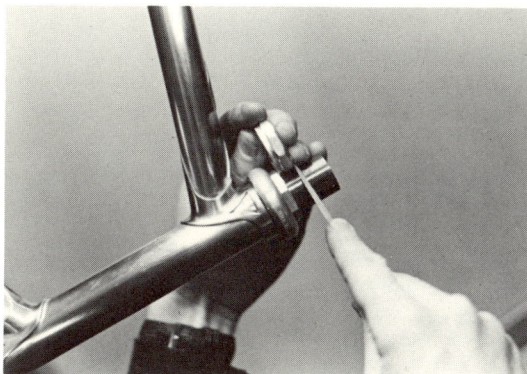

P10.32. The steering tube is cut, leaving a bit extra on the end for filing.

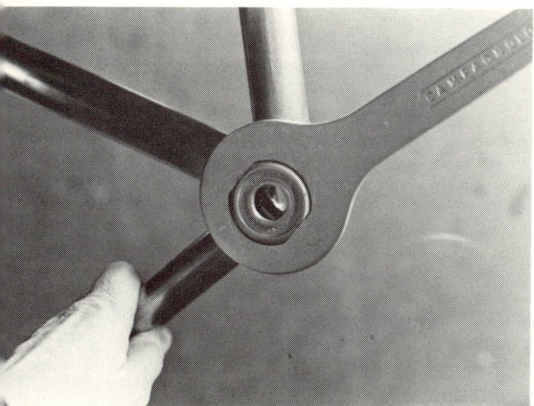

P10.30 Installing the fixed cup. Campagnolo No. 713 fixed cup wrench.

When you are back in your own workshop, reassemble the fork to the frame; then mark and cut the end of the steering tube to final length. (P10.31, P10.32) Also, file a keyway into the threaded end of the tube to accommodate the headset washer tab (or flat, if your particular headset washer requires that type of shape). These operations are best accomplished by removing only a little material at a time, then checking the fit by assembling the fork to the frame using all headset parts. A 10-inch or 12-inch mill bastard file works well for shortening the tube while the keyway may be cut with either an 8 x $\frac{3}{32}$ inch warding file or a riffler. (P10.33, P10.34, P10.35, P10.36, P10.37) Final-check the fit by assembling the headset and mounting the fork, locking it to the frame with the headset nut and washer. A slight clearance gap should exist between the end of the steering tube and the underside of the lock nut, and the fork should smoothly turn through 360 degrees of rotation without binding. (P10.38)

P10.33 A file is used to square off the threaded end of the tube.

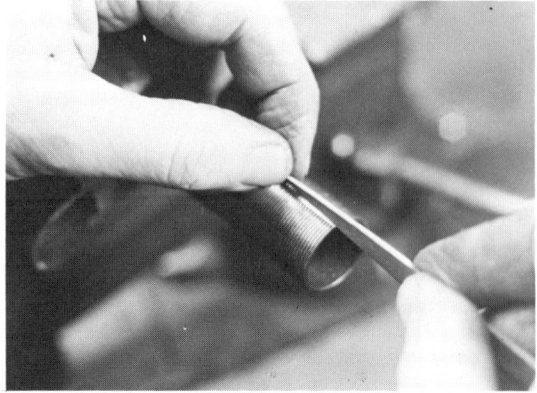

P10.36 Cutting the locking washer tang keyway for a Campagnolo headset. Other headsets may use flat-type washer.

P10.34 Chamfering the end threads.

P10.37 Trial fit-up of the locking washer.

P10.35 Using a machinist's scraper to de-burr the tube ID and clean up the end threads.

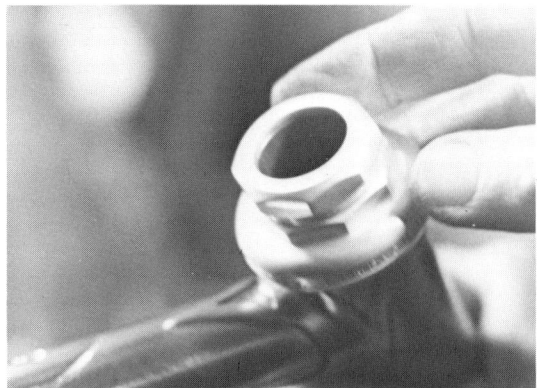

P10.38 The mounted headset assembly. Note slight clearance between end of steering tube and underside of lock nut.

Final Alignment and Tracking

With the fork mounted, make a final alignment check of the entire frameset. Mount the front and rear wheels and the front and rear brakes. First check the frame for alignment using the string test. Next check the fork by measuring the gap between the inside of each blade and the wheel rim. Sight along the front of the frameset and verify that both wheels are perfectly aligned with each other *and* with the seat tube. If the wheels are slightly cocked askew, it is possible to make corrections by selectively filling the drop-out surfaces on which the wheel axles rest.

The "acid" test is to check the tracking. To perform this test, snap a 30 foot long chalk line onto a smooth surface such as a gymnasium floor. Mount a stem and handlebar on the frameset. Center the front and rear wheels on one end of the chalk line and hold the frameset so it is vertical to the floor. (A carpenter's spirit level taped onto the handlebar drops will help here.) Now, slowly push the wheeled frameset along, keeping its front wheel centered on the line while maintaining perpendicularity. After traveling about 15 feet check the position of the rear wheel. It should still be centered on the line. If it is not, the frameset is out of alignment. It could be due to misalignment in the fork, the frame, or a combination of the two. If the rear wheel is still on the line after 30 feet, you can be assured your frameset is aligned. Now, we will proceed to the final phase — surface preparation and painting.

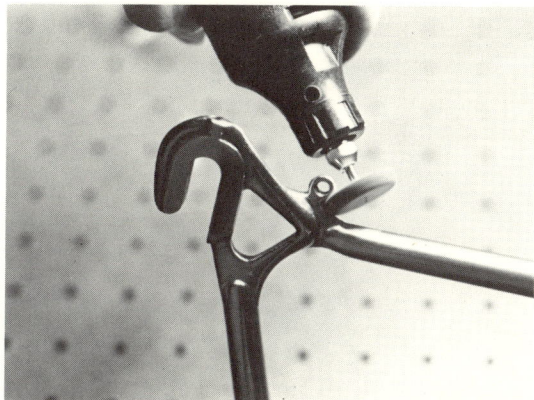

P10.39 Smoothing intricate drop-out contours with a Dremel Moto tool. Here, a small buff is used to round small radii.

CHAPTER XI

SURFACE PREPARATION, PAINTING, AND DETAILING

Before embarking on the task of painting the frameset, give some serious thought to having that job professionally done. Not that doing it yourself is so difficult — if you have come this far, building your frameset from scratch, you have certainly demonstrated the capacity to master the technique of spray painting. The limitation here is more a matter of not having the proper equipment to do the kind of paint job you want.

For example, if a polyurethane two-part finish is desired the popular DuPont "Imron" polyurethane paint may be your choice. Application of this product requires an air compressor, tank, and spray gun. In addition, there is also the expense of purchasing a special primer, thinner, activator, and the "Imron" color enamel itself; these materials are costly and are usually available only in quart quantities. Some alternatives are to shop around to find a local auto body shop that will sell you the small amount needed, or, perhaps, purchase small quantities of "Imron" painting materials from one of the professional frame painters or material suppliers listed in the Appendix.

Another factor you should consider before doing the spray painting yourself is that "Imron" generates fumes that are very toxic and dangerous if inhaled. "Imron" spraying must therefore be done in a properly ventilated spray booth. If you have access to all this equipment, then, by all means, use "Imron" or its epoxy equivalents. They are extremely durable paints and resist chipping and scratches far better than conventional enamels and lacquers. If you lack the equipment but still want an "Imron" job, send the frameset to a

professional bicycle frame painter. Refer to Appendix Table VII for the addresses of these specialists.

If you do not have access to spray painting equipment but still want to do your own paint job, there are two practical alternatives. One is to use pressurized spray cans of lacquer. The other is to use pressurized spray cans of enamel.

Lacquer

Lacquers are fast drying and are quite easy to apply. The lacquer painting process differs from that used with epoxy and regular enamels in that lacquers are applied in multiple coats. Each coat is allowed to dry, and is then rubbed out with a special compound (or sanded with 400 grit paper). In this manner, 20 or more coats may be applied. Each coat bonds to the previous one by partially dissolving the prior coat. Because of the layering and compounding process, lacquer paint jobs exhibit a translucent, mirror-like quality and have a depth, brilliance, and smoothness that is difficult to duplicate using ordinary enamels. Pressurized spray cans of acrylic lacquer are readily available from most automotive supply houses and chain discount stores in hundreds of colors. Schwinn dealers also stock a quality line of proprietary lacquers in spray cans, although color choice is somewhat limited.

All of these factors make lacquer an ideal choice for the amateur builder. However, lacquer does have some negative characteristics. First, because of the layering process, a multi-coat lacquer job takes longer to complete than an enamel application. Depending on the number of coats desired, the procedure could extend from a period of several weeks to a month or more. Secondly, lacquer is brittle and chips rather easily when compared to enamels in general and epoxy enamels in particular.

Enamel

As for enamels, they are available in spray cans in as many colors and at even more outlets than lacquers. Enamels are essentially applied in a single painting session. Usually two, sometimes three, coats are sufficient to give adequate coverage. The last coat is left to dry for a few days to a week before building up the frameset with its components. The chief advantages of enamels are: they are usually less costly than lacquers (although this can vary among sources of supply), and they may be quickly applied in one session with the frameset soon ready for final component fit-up, usually, in a few days' time.

One major drawback of enamels is that because they are applied in fairly thick layers and dry more slowly than lacquers, they are less forgiving of spraying errors. A precise and well-practiced spray technique is necessary. Enamel spray jobs are difficult to do without getting at least a few runs or paint splatters and these blemishes are also more difficult to remedy than those made with lacquer. Also, enamel's longer drying time makes the surfaces more susceptible to dust pickup. Until fully cured, enamel tends to be softer than lacquer and is easily fingernailed and dented. Finally, even a perfectly done enamel job may not match the beauty and brilliance of a hand-rubbed, multicoat lacquer finish. Enamel has a characteristic "orange peel" effect which may be seen even on some professionally done jobs. So there you have it: choose lacquer or enamel. Now I have a few points on surface preparation and priming.

Surface Preparation and Primers

If the frame and fork have been thoroughly sanded in accordance with Chapter X, you have met the first criterion — a smooth, clean surface. Essentially, the metal must be sanded out leaving a perfectly smooth, bright-metal finish. Do not expect primer or paint to cover

up major imperfections. If you want a first-class paint job you must be willing to spend the time required to properly prepare the surfaces.

Primer Functions

Primers serve several important functions, the first of which is to form a protective layer that prevents oxidation of the steel surfaces. A frameset can be primed, then stored until you are ready to spray the color coats, without rusting in the interim. Primers also perform a surfacing function, filling in *minute* surface irregularities in the base metal (not major pits). As successive coats of primer are applied and sanded out these imperfections disappear, leaving a smooth surface. The primer recommended here (for lacquer) is actually a primer/surfacer and does a better surfacing job than common red oxide primers that are frequently used for both enamels and lacquers. Finally, priming provides a bondable surface to which the color coat can adhere.

For optimum results, two additional operations are done as part of the surface preparation and priming tasks.

- Filling in major surface irregularities or joint gaps with automotive body putty or epoxy.
- Applying an aluminum undercoater after the final priming.

While sanding the frameset, you undoubtedly inspected it for any deep nicks, joint gaps, and other surface irregularities that could not be safely removed by sanding alone. These should be filled in with body putty or epoxy, then sanded smooth. Epoxy or body putty may be applied to bare metal directly or over primer or primer/surfacer coats. The only precautions are to apply it in *thin* layers and to allow ample drying time before sanding.

The final surface preparation task is to spray the entire frameset with an aluminum undercoater. This enhances the coverage of all paints, whether enamel or lacquer. If you are going to use one of the new pearlescent or flamboyant colors, an aluminum undercoating is essential. Use the following list to determine your surface preparation and priming supplies.

116

Materials Required for
Surface Preparation and Priming

- Four 9 by 11 inch sheets of 3M "TRI-M-ITE" wet or dry paper — two 360 grit, one 400 grit and one 220 grit. Also, one 3M rubber sanding block. Cut sheets into 3 inch wide strips to fit the block.
- One tube of Underhill or similar automotive body putty, or epoxy.
- Two 16 ounce cans of Sherwin Williams "Zelon" Primer/Surfacer (for lacquer jobs) or two 16 ounce cans of red oxide primer (for enamel jobs). Call your Sherwin Williams regional sales office for a list of "Zelon" distributors.
- One 16 ounce can Schwinn Aluminum Undercoater. If you plan to use enamel, be sure the undercoater is enamel. For lacquer color coats, get lacquer undercoater.
- Lacquer or enamel thinner as required, and acetone.
- Paper towels and plenty of clean rags.
- Masking tape.
- Small can of Acme No. 45 Rubbing and Blending Compound and cotton balls (lacquer jobs only).

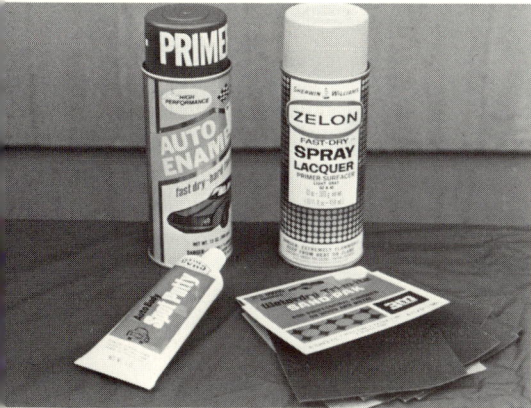

P11.1 Surface preparation and priming supplies. Spray cans of primer (left) and primer/surfacer (right), body putty, and assorted "TRI-M-ITE" papers.

Readying the Frameset for
Priming and Undercoating

If you have not already done so, disassemble the fork from the frame. Remove the headset parts, all fender eyebolts and axle adjuster screws. The fork crown race may be left in place provided it is masked off. Inspect the frame and fork for any irregularities or missed spots, then carefully sand them once more using the 220 grade "TRI-M-ITE." Do all surfaces, applying just enough pressure to remove any oxidation that may have formed since you last sanded them. Wipe the assemblies clean, and blow accumulated grit from holes and the bottom bracket shell.

Next, make four cylinders from light cardboard. Insert one in the bottom bracket shell, slip one into the top and another into the bottom of the head tube. Place one in the seat tube. Trim the cylinder in the bottom bracket shell with a razor blade, cutting it flush with the shell ends. The cylinders in the head and seat tubes should stick out at least 3 inches; these will be used to turn the frame as you paint.

Insert the threaded end of a spoke through one of the rear drop-out axle adjuster screw holes, and thread a nipple fully onto it. Bend the hub-end of the spoke so it forms a closed loop. This will serve as a hanger to support the frame while it is being painted. Take the fork and mask the crown race if you have left it in place; then, take a long piece of brass brazing rod and attach it to the side of the steering tube using masking tape. The masking tape is wound around the tube and serves the dual purpose of holding the rod in place while providing masking for the entire steering tube and its threads. Form a closed loop at the end of the rod, wrapping it around itself several times. This is what you will hang the fork on.

Now, find a good location to paint in. It may even be outdoors, provided temperatures are not much lower than 65 F. A sunny or well lighted location, free of drafts, is ideal. If painting indoors, you may want to screw two hooks into the ceiling, about 6 feet apart, from which the frame and fork may be hung. It is also advisable to use a window fan to maintain adequate ventilation when painting.

Begin by using the body putty to fill in any

imperfections you may have found in the frame or fork and sand them smooth. (P11.2, P11.3) Next, wipe the frame and fork clean using a clean rag saturated with acetone. Do this work in a well ventilated area (preferably outdoors) and avoid breathing in the fumes. All surfaces must be spotless and free from fingerprints before applying the primer.

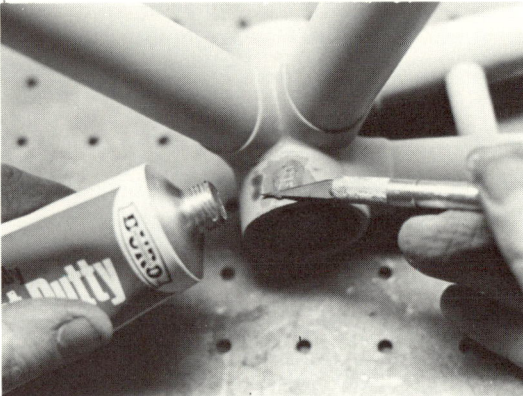

P11.2 Fill in small imperfections with body putty.

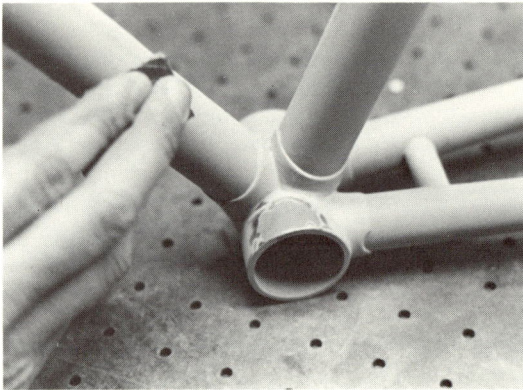

P11.3 Sand out dried putty to a smooth finish.

Applying Primer and Undercoater

Cover yourself with a hat, face mask, goggles, and long-sleeved shirt. Take the spray can of primer/surfacer (lacquer jobs only) or red oxide primer (enamel jobs) and prepare it by shaking as directed on the side of the can. Spray a light coat of primer/surfacer (or oxide primer) over the fork and frame. (P11.4) Your spray technique need not be perfect because primer is quite forgiving. Even if runs form, they may be sanded out using 220 and then 360 grit "TRI-M-ITE" paper.

P11.4 Spraying a primer/surfacer coat.

After the primer has dried, sand all surfaces using No. 360 "TRI-M-ITE" paper. (P11.5) Frequently brush the sanding dust off the paper to prevent loading. Wipe the fork and frame clean, and spray a second coat. The primer/surfacer dries to a dull gray color that highlights any surface imperfections. The dull finish of a red oxide primer will do the same. After each application scrutinize the surfaces,

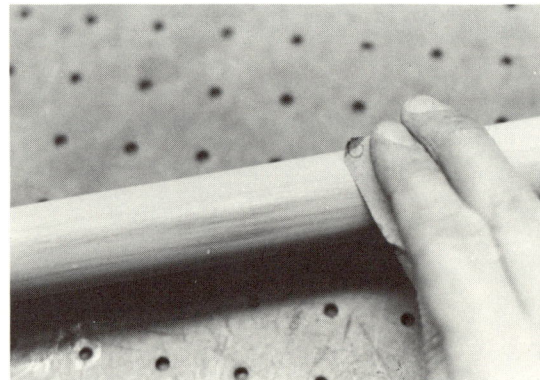

P11.5 Sanding the second coat of primer/surfacer with Grade 360 "TRI-M-ITE" paper.

and if some areas still look rough keep spraying and sanding them until every square inch of the frame and fork are as smooth and pit-free as you can make them. Extra effort spent in achieving a smooth surface now will pay off handsomely later, when the color coats are applied. (P11.6)

P11.6 The primed frameset ready for aluminum undercoating.

When priming and sanding are completed, spray the fork and frame with two thin coats of aluminum undercoater. Be sure the undercoater is compatible with the paint you will be using (either lacquer or enamel) for the color coats. Sand the first coat with No. 360 paper, but do not sand the second coat. If you miss a few spots after the second coat, sand those spots lightly and respray those surfaces only.

Applying the Color Coats

Until now the procedures have been much the same whether using lacquer or enamel. For the purposes of this discussion, the steps for applying lacquer will be covered first because they are somewhat more involved than those used for enamel. Before "color-shooting" the fork and frame, spend some time practicing to develop a spraying technique.

Collect those odd-ball tubes and lugs you brazed together earlier (when you learned to braze) and spray them with primer and a coat of aluminum undercoater. Set aside an extra can of the exact type of color paint you will be using on the frameset, and practice spraying these scrap tubes. Through experimentation, you should soon find the optimum nozzle distance to achieve a smooth even coat without runs. Here are a few tips to help you do a good job:

- Frameset and room temperature should be near 70 F for best results. Heat the spray can in hot water (not over 120 F) for 10 minutes before using, then shake according to instructions on the can.
- Do not spray in a draft or in windy conditions; absolute calm is required.
- Keep an acetone-saturated rag handy and wipe the spray head nozzle frequently. This prevents splatters. Also, shake the can vigorously after every couple of passes.
- Whether using lacquer or enamel, spray in *thin* coats. Start the spray before it hits a tube and leave it on until after it passes the end of the tube.
- If a run forms, it may sometimes be stopped by quickly repositioning the tube.

Applying Lacquer

When you are confident of your proficiency, wipe the fork with a clean lintless rag, hang it on its hook, and apply a full color coat of lacquer. Spray the underside of the crown first, then its top, all around the steering tube. Use short bursts. Next, spray the insides of each blade, then do their outer surfaces. Maintain a controlled steady motion as you sweep the spray along the blades. Avoid interruptions and keep the layers thin. With lacquer it does not matter if the coverage is sparse and a little of the undercoater surface shows through. Subsequent color coats will cover it.

Set the fork aside to dry and hang the frame on its hook. Spray rather heavy bursts into the irregular areas of the frame, such as the seat attachment, the rear drop-outs, bridges, and around the bottom bracket shell. Do these surfaces first, then work along the tubes. Which tube you start with or the sequence used is not as important as controlling the spray and maintaining a constant nozzle distance from the surface. Keep the spray moving along the tubes at a uniform rate. Go back and forth, moving around each tube in sections, finishing one tube completely before going on to another. (P11.7)

Try to work as quickly as you can so that areas being overlapped are still not fully dry. This prevents overspray and promotes a smoother and more uniform coat. Grasp the cardboard tubes inserted in the head tube and seat tube and position the frame to best advantage while you work. Try to keep the spray can vertical at all times and frequently wipe its nozzle with the acetone-saturated rag.

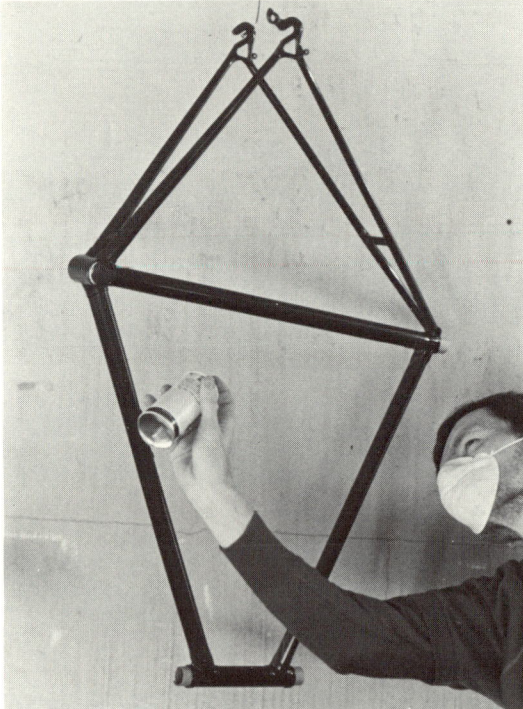

P11.8 Key to a smooth lacquered surface: rubbing compound, cotton balls, and patience (not pictured).

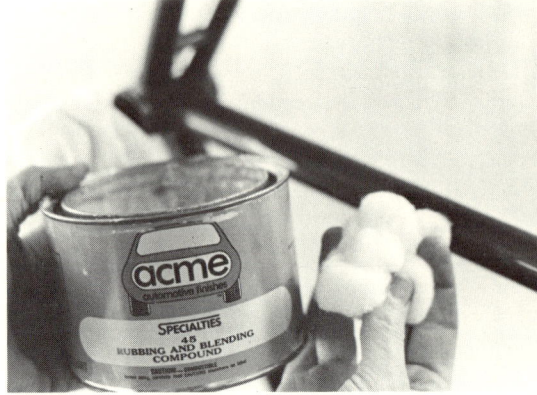

P11.9 Rub with a light back-and-forth motion. Be careful not to cut through the aluminum undercoater.

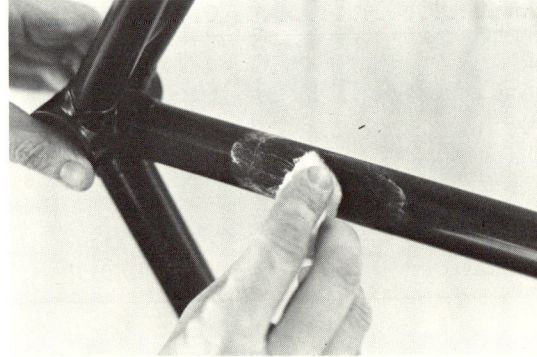

P11.7 "Shooting" a lacquer color coat.

Let the frame and fork dry several hours; then break out some cotton balls and a can of rubbing compound. For lacquer, I recommend ACME No. 45 rubbing and blending compound (P11.8) It may be used straight from the can (need not be mixed with water) and is very fast cutting. Dip a cotton ball into the compound, and, with a light back-and-forth motion, start to "rub-out" a tube. *Use light pressure or you may cut through the aluminum undercoater.* Rub in one direction only, lengthwise, back and forth along the tubes. (P11.9) As one cotton ball becomes saturated with paint, discard it and use a clean one.

Continue working until the frame and fork are fully rubbed out and glass-smooth to the touch. (P11.10) It is no problem if most of the color coat is rubbed away provided the aluminum undercoater is still intact. If you do rub through the undercoater *spray that spot with fresh undercoater.* Because lacquer has a transparent quality it is impossible to completely hide such areas using color coats alone, regardless of how many layers are applied. Do not try it.

Now, wipe the frame and fork with a water-dampened, lint-free rag or chamois to remove all traces of compound. Use a toothbrush and water to get compound out of the tight spots such as the lug seams and around the seat stay attachment. Spray on another coat of lacquer

120

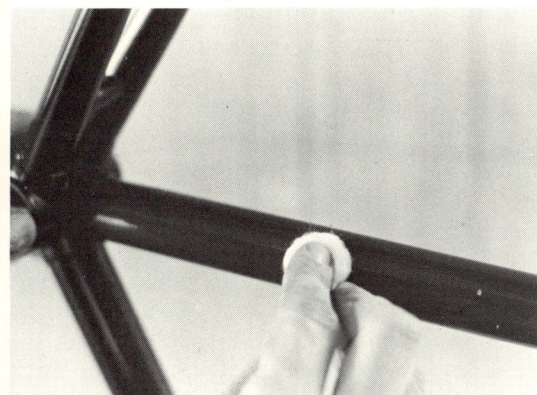

P11.10 Rub until a high luster is obtained.

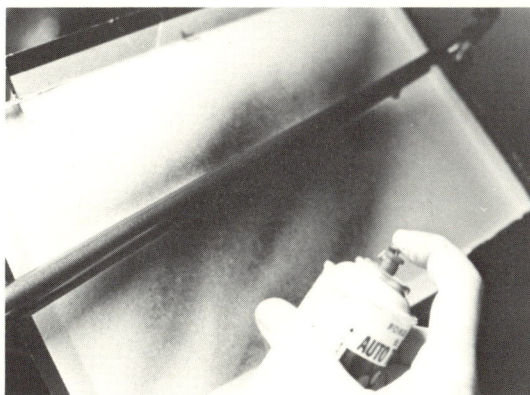

P11.12 Use a cardboard shield to prevent overspraying onto finished sections when touching up.

and rub it out as just described. As the layering process is continued, the lacquer will take on an appearance of depth, like looking into a pool of water. (P11.11) You may continue layering as long as you like, but from a practical standpoint, four to six coats should yield a truly remarkable finish. As an alternate method some painters prefer to sand out all coats using 400 grit "TRI-M-ITE," except for the last one or two which are compounded. Either method will give good results.

P11.11 Six coats of hand-rubbed lacquer.

Applying Enamel

With enamel, the spraying technique is the same except there is no layering. Spray a first coat, keeping it very thin to prevent runs. Let it dry 10 minutes, or until tacky, then shoot a full coverage coat. Wait 15 minutes; check for missed spots, and, if necessary, apply a third coat. That should do it. It is best to let the frame and fork dry out in a warm dust-free room. Check the curing process by occasionally testing the paint's hardness with your fingernail. If you have to apply several thick coats, it may be necessary to wait a week or more before mounting components.

Accenting the Lugs

When the color coats have fully cured, the frameset may be accented by applying gold or some other contrasting paint to the lug outlines and cut-outs. Purchase a small bottle of Pactra or Testors "Pla" in the desired color, some compatible thinner, and a No. 00 red sable pointing brush. A few cotton swabs will also be needed.

Lay the frame or fork on a blanket, sit down, and prop your painting arm and wrist on a steady rest made from some books. Now, carefully apply the accent paint to the lugs and cut-outs using the pointing brush. (P11.13) Keep the accent lines narrow and unwavering, and use some restraint when accenting. It is best to do a modest amount of outlining and

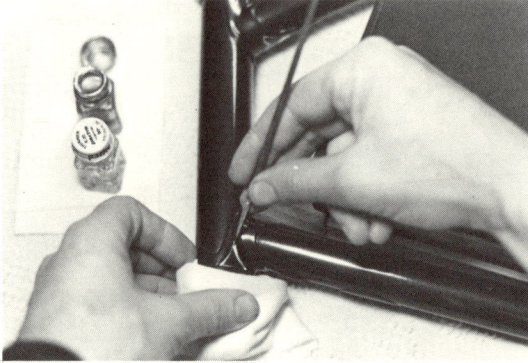

P11.13 "Accenting" lugs with a pointing brush.

let the lugwork rest on its own merits. If you smudge the accent line a sharp edge may be easily restored by sweeping a thinner-soaked cotton swab over the affected area. (P11.14) Also, two thin coats of accent color work better than trying to do the job in a single application.

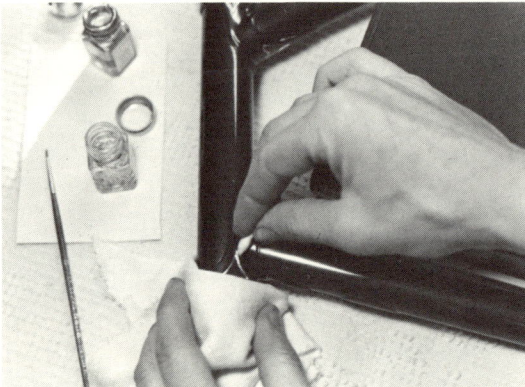

P11.14 Excess accent paint may be removed with a thinner-saturated cotton swab.

Decalcomania

The last bit of customizing you may like to try is to either paint your name on the frame or apply it using decals. Unless you have some experience with hand-lettering it is best to use decals. These are available in sheet form, or as individual letters, from stationers and graphic

arts supply houses. They usually come in at least two styles, Roman and Gothic, and in several sizes. Colors are generally gold gilt with a black outline. The best size letter for a down tube application is 1 inch. If you want to do a really first-class job that will look as though the frame were hand-lettered, try this procedure.

Using a sharp pair of scissors, close-cut the decals so there is no clear decal material extending outside the black letter-outlines. (P11.15) Purchase a small jar of decal setting solution from your local hobby shop. Soak the letters in a shallow bowl of lukewarm water, and liberally brush the setting solution onto the tube where the decals will go.

P11.15 Close-cutting decals.

Carefully slip the decals from their paper backing and onto the tube, locating them by eye as well as you can. (P11.16) The setting solution will prevent the decals from drying in place, permitting ample time to align all the letters so they are spaced just right. If by chance the letters do start to stick, just apply more solution to soften the glue. Once you have the letters where you want them, use a water-dampened sponge and your fingertips to bring them into firm contact with the tube. Stroke out all air bubbles and press the decals' edges down all around. Sponge away excess water and let the decals dry overnight.

When the decals are fully dry, go over them and the entire frameset with a water-moistened sponge to remove all encrusted glue.

P11.16 Applying decals to the down tube. Tube surface is first wetted with decal setting solution.

Now apply the tube manufacturer's transfers. These are usually affixed to the seat tube and upper portion of the fork blades. One or two light spray coats of clear paint, similar in composition to that used for the color coats (lacquer or enamel) may now be applied over the decals and transfers. This will make them more resistant to scratches and abrasion.

Waxing

Before attempting to wax the frameset be sure all paint and decals are thoroughly dry. Use a good quality liquid wax, such as Du-Pont "Rain Dance." Liberally apply a first coat, and buff it dry with a clean rag. After a few hours drying time apply at least one more coat, buff it out, and you are ready to build up your custom bicycle and head for the open road. (P11.17)

P11.17 Persistance and determination rewarded. The finished frameset!

CHAPTER XII

DECISION TIME

As discussed in the Introduction, this book was planned to serve a two-fold purpose: first, to function as a decision making tool for those individuals who are uncertain about undertaking construction of a frameset; and secondly, as a complete manual for readers who do attempt design and construction themselves. If you have just read the previous eleven chapters for the first time, it is decision time.

For those who elect to give the job to a professional builder, a thorough review of Chapters I, II and VI is now in order. The information contained in them will be of assistance in specifying your frameset's geometry and its materials of construction. Reference to Appendix Table VIII should also prove helpful when selecting an appropriate builder to do the job. While not mandatory, it is a good idea to include a half-size drawing of the frameset with your order, keeping a copy for your own records. The drawing will give the builder a clearer picture of your needs and facilitate communications between the two of you regarding any design changes that may be proposed.

If you remain convinced that building your own frameset is the only way to go then get to work laying out a design. Take a course in brazing or make a nominal investment in lugs and tubing, and start some *hands-on* self-instruction using Chapter III as a guide. If you cannot seem to master the skill and decide not to go ahead with the project, do not despair. You have saved yourself some money and the expenditure of a considerable amount of time — both far too valuable to waste on a hopeless cause.

On the other hand, if your brazing does come up to par, then order the frameset materials, and start construction of the jigs in accordance with Chapter V. From that point on it will be a case of putting forth your best effort plus a sizable amount of time, patience, and determination.

Keep the Foreword of this book handy and read it whenever your morale sags. "Silent Cal" probably never envisioned his comments on persistence and determination appearing as prefatory remarks in an amateur framebuilding book. However, I cannot find more appropriate advice to assure success in the venture many of you are now about to undertake.

Good Framebuilding!

APPENDIX TABLES

I. REYNOLDS 531 Butted Tubes — Standard and Heavyweight

II. REYNOLDS 531 SL — (Special Lightweight) Butted Tubes

III. Columbus Chrome-Molybdenum Steel Tube Sets

IV. English Legal Standard Wire Gauges — SWG — Equivalent Thicknesses in Inches and Millimeters

V. Tangents

VI. Retail Suppliers of Bicycle Tubing and Frameset Materials. Domestic Manufacturers of Investment Cast Frameset Parts

VII. Professional Frame Painters

VIII. Professional Custom Framebuilders

IX. Bibliography and Selected Reading List

REYNOLDS 531 BUTTED TUBES
STANDARD AND HEAVYWEIGHT

Tube	Outside Diameter: Figures in Millimeters, Inches in Parentheses — English	Metric	Wall Thickness, SWG — Standard	Heavy	Lengths Available, (mm)	Notes
Steering Tube	25.4 (1)	25	13/16 SB	-	180, 200, 220, 240, 260, 280, 300	Available threaded – 24 TPI x 50 mm long on English and 1 mm pitch x 50 mm long on metric.
Head Tube	31.7 (1 1/4)	32	20 ST.G. English Only	19 ST. G. Metric Only	150, 170, 220, 320, 635	General Note: DB = Double Butted. SB = Single Butted. ST. G. = Straight Gauge. Standard weight tube set for 56 to 60 cm. Frameset weighs approximately 2,445 gms.
Top Tube	25.4 (1)	26	21/24 DB	19/22 DB	600, 635	
Down Tube	28.6 (1 1/8)	28	20/23 DB	19/22 DB	635, 650	
Seat Tube	28.6 (1 1/8)	28	21/24 SB	19/22 SB	635, 650	
Seat Stays	16	13	20	20	550, 600, 625 with 8 mm tip ID	Can be supplied domed and slotted, 5 x 10 mm or 5 x 15 mm.
Chain Stays		22		21	380, 400, 440 with 9 mm tip ID	Can be supplied domed and slotted, 5 x 10 mm or 5 x 15 mm. Can also be furnished fluted, fluted and indented, or round-oval-round. Footnote 1.
Continental Oval Fork Blades	Oval is 28.5 x 16.5.		18/21 taper gauge		350, 370, 400 with tip ID's of 9 or 10 mm	Forks can be supplied bent as follows: Rake 12 x 55 mm offset " 15 x 35 mm " " 15 x 45 mm " " 15 x 50 mm " " 16 x 30 mm " Also can be supplied domed and slotted 5 x 10 mm or 5 x 15 mm. Footnote 2.
"New" Continental Oval Fork Blades	Oval is 27.5 x 20.		19/24 taper gauge		370 mm long, taper to 10 mm bore; 400 mm long, taper to 11.6 mm bore.	Can be supplied bent as follows: Rake 15 x 45 mm Rake 16 x 30 mm Also can be supplied domed and slotted, 5 x 10 mm or 5 x 15 mm.
Track Pattern Fork Blades	22 round		17/20 taper gauge		350, 370, 400 mm x 10 mm tip ID	Can be supplied bent as follows: Rake 13 x 45 mm offset " 14 x 40 mm " " 16 x 30 mm " Also can be supplied domed and slotted 5 x 10 mm or 5 x 15 mm.

Data Courtesy T. I. Reynolds Limited, Birmingham, England.

TABLE I

REYNOLDS 531 SL
(SPECIAL LIGHTWEIGHT) BUTTED TUBES

Tube	Outside Diameter Figures in Millimeters Inches in Parentheses English	Metric	Wall Thickness, English	Wall Thickness, Metric (mm)	Lengths Available, (mm)	Notes
Steering Tube	25.4 (1)	25	13/16 SB	1.6/2.3 SB	220	English is threaded 25.4 mm x 24 TPI for 50 mm. Metric is threaded 25 mm x 1 mm pitch for 50 mm.
Head Tube	31.75 (1 1/4)	32	20 ST.G.	0.9 ST.G.	220	GENERAL NOTES DB = Double Butted SB = Single Butted ST.G. = Straight Gauge T.G. = Taper Gauge
Top Tube	25.4 (1)	26	22/24 DB	0.7/0.5 DB	600	
Down Tube	28.6 (1 1/8)	28	21/24 DB	0.8/0.5 DB	620	
Seat Tube	28.6 (1 1/8)	28	22/24 SB	0.7/0.5 SB	600	
Seat Stays (2)	16	16	24	0.5	600 tapered to 10 mm on English. Tapered to 10 mm diam with domed ends on metric.	
Chain Stays (2)	22.2	22	23	0.6	440 tapered to 11 mm on English. Tapered to 11 mm diam with domed ends on metric.	English and metric both indented for wheel
"New" Continental Oval Fork Blades (2)	Oval is 27.5 x 20 mm cross section by 67 mm long.		Made from 19/24 SB drawn to T.G.	1.0/0.5 SB	397 tapered to 13.5 mm round.	English ends are domed. Blades are made from 24 mm diam x 19/24 SB tube.
Bridge Tube	12.7		20 ST.G.	0.9 ST.G.	100	

Note: Reynolds recommends SL tubing be brazed only by experienced craftsmen familiar with lightweight frameset construction. Silver soldering (sic) is recommended with care being exercised so as not to overheat the tube. Also, one should avoid having to dress the tubes after brazing due to extreme thinness of the tube wall sections. Any finish filing to remove excess brazing material runs the risk of reducing the thickness of the already thin walls, seriously weakening them.

Data Courtesy T. I. Reynolds, Ltd., Birmingham, England.

TABLE II

COLUMBUS CHROME-MOLYBDENUM STEEL TUBE SETS

Tube Set Description	Wall Thickness	
	Milli-meters	Closest SWG Equi-valent
SP - Road Heavy - 2370 grams		
A rigid set used for lap road races over rough ground and touring frame-sets. Suitable for riders weighing more than 155 lbs.		
Main Triangle Tubes- Single and double butted	0.7-1.0	22-19
Head Tubes	1.0	19
Chain and Seat Stays	1.0	19
Steering Tube - Single butted and helically reinforced with 5 ribs	-	-
Fork Blades - Oval	1.05	19
SL - Road Light - 2065 grams		
A medium-light elastic set used for in-line and lap road races over flat and smooth roads. Suitable for riders weighing less than 155 lbs.		
Main Triangle Tubes - Single and double butted	0.6-0.9	23-20
Head Tubes	1.0	19
Chain and Seat Stays	0.7	22
Steering Tube - Single butted and helically reinforced with 5 ribs	-	-
Fork Blades - Oval	0.9	20
KL - 1710 grams		
An extra-light set for in-line races and time trials on flat and smooth surfaced roads		
Main Triangle Tubes - Single and double butted	0.5-0.7	25-22
Head Tubes	0.8	21
Chain and Seat Stays	0.5	25
Steering Tube - Reinforced	-	-
Fork Blades	0.9	20

TABLE III

133

COLUMBUS CHROME-MOLYBDENUM STEEL TUBE SETS

Tube Set Description	Wall Thickness	
	Milli-meters	Closest SWG Equivalent
PS - Track Sprinters 2435 grams		
A light set with stiff chain and seat stays. Used for general track racing: sprint, six-day and pursuit framesets.		
Main Triangle Tubes - Single and double butted	0.7-1.0	22-19
Head Tubes	1.0	19
Chain and Seat Stays	1.0	19
Steering Tube - Single butted and helically reinforced with 5 ribs	-	-
Fork Blades - Round	1.05	19
PL - Track Light - 1845 grams		
A lighter track set.		
Main Triangle Tubes - Plain gauge	0.6	23
Head Tubes	0.8	21
Chain and Seat Stays	0.7	22
Steering Tube - Single butted and helically reinforced with 5 ribs	-	-
Fork Blades - Round	0.9	20
Record - 1650 grams		
An extra light set used only for track record attempts.		
Main Triangle Tubes - Plain gauge	0.5	25
Head Tubes	0.8	21
Chain and Seat Stays	0.5	25
Steering Tube - Reinforced	-	-
Fork Blades	0.9	20

Notes: (1) Quoted tube set weights are approximate.
(2) Amateur builders are cautioned to use only the heavier weight tube sets on their first attempt.
(3) A.L. Colombo recommends brazing temperatures between 600°C. and 700°C. (1202°F. to 1292°F.). Select silver rod with liquidus in the 1150°F. range. DO NOT USE BRASS ROD.

Data courtesy of A.L. Colombo, Milan, Italy.

TABLE III (continued)

ENGLISH LEGAL STANDARD WIRE GAUGES, SWG
EQUIVALENT THICKNESSES IN INCHES AND MILLIMETERS

SWG No.	Inches	MM
9	0.144	3.66
10	0.128	3.25
11	0.116	2.95
12	0.104	2.64
13	0.092	2.34
14	0.080	2.03
15	0.072	1.83
16	0.064	1.63
17	0.056	1.42
18	0.048	1.22
19	0.040	1.02
20	0.036	0.91
21	0.032	0.81
22	0.028	0.71
23	0.024	0.61
24	0.022	0.56
25	0.020	0.51
26	0.018	0.46
27	0.0164	0.42
28	0.0148	0.38
29	0.0136	0.35
30	0.0124	0.32
31	0.0116	0.30
32	0.0108	0.27
33	0.0100	0.25

TABLE IV

137

TANGENTS

$\dfrac{(90\deg - a)}{2}$	tan
6° 0′	.1051
10′	.1080
20′	.1110
30′	.1139
40′	.1169
50′	.1198
7° 0′	.1228
10′	.1257
20′	.1287
30′	.1317
40′	.1346
50′	.1376
8° 0′	.1405
10′	.1435
20′	.1465
30′	.1495
40′	.1524
50′	.1554
9° 0′	.1584
10′	.1614
20′	.1644
30′	.1673
40′	.1703
50′	.1733
10° 0′	.1763
10′	.1793
20′	.1823
30′	.1853
40′	.1883
50′	.1914
11° 0′	.1944

TABLE V

RETAIL SUPPLIERS OF
BICYCLE TUBING AND FRAMESET MATERIALS

Bike Warehouse
21 Main Street
New Middletown, Ohio 44442

Dade Cyclery
3043 Grand Avenue
Coconut Grove
Miami, Florida 33133

Fastab Cycles
Department A
2706 South Glenbrook
Garland, Texas 75041

Proteus Design, Inc.
9225 Baltimore Boulevard
College Park, Maryland 20740

E.U.R. International
P.O. Box 45
Dayton, Ohio 45405

DOMESTIC MANUFACTURERS OF
INVESTMENT CAST FRAMESET PARTS
(All will sell retail to amateur builders)

Henry James Folson
Henry James Bicycles, Inc.
704 Elvira Avenue
Redondo Beach, California 90277

"Cleanline" bottom bracket shells, lugs, drop-outs, and fork crowns.

Proteus Design, Inc.
9225 Baltimore Boulevard
College Park, Maryland 20740

Fork crowns.

Medici Bicycle Company
5937 Sheila Street
Los Angeles, California 90023

Lugs

George P. Wilson
27189 Roger Street
Hemet, California 92343

"Ultra-Light" and "Standard" drop-outs.
"Super Pro" and "Standard" lugs.

NOTES:

1. Tubing and materials may also be special-ordered through bicycle shops and custom framebuilders.

2. When ordering investment cast lugs or bottom bracket shells, be sure to specify exact frame angles. Investment castings are very rigid and more difficult to cold-set than conventional, bulge-formed, or stamped and welded steel parts.

TABLE VI

141

PROFESSIONAL FRAME PAINTERS

*John Anderson
John Anderson Painting
Jail Hill Road
Haddam, Connecticut 06438

Assenmacher Lightweight Cycles
4506 Morrish Road
Swartz Creek, Michigan 48473

Sam Braxton
Braxton Bike Shop
2100 South Avenue, West
Missoula, Montana 59801

The Brielle Cyclery, Inc.
10 Union Avenue
Brielle, New Jersey 08730

Chris Chance
Chris Chance Cycles
11 Windsor Street
Cambridge, Massachusetts 02139

*Jim Cunningham
Cyclart
410 Cribbage Lane
San Marcos, California 92069

Albert Eisentraut
1000 22nd Avenue
Oakland, California 94621

Hugh Enochs
c/o Jevelot Corporation
P.O. Box 349
La Honda, California 94020

E.U.R. International
P.O. Box 45
Dayton, Ohio 45405

Bruce Gordon Cycles
(Painter: Les Lunas)
27729 Clear Lake Road
Eugene, Oregon 97402

Dave Hartranft
11 Windsor Street
Cambridge, Massachusetts 02139

Victor J. Larivee
Custom Frame Painting
Cycle & Sport
400 Broadway
Santa Monica, California 90401

Medici Bicycle Company
5937 Sheila Street
Los Angeles, California 90022
also
1183 West Side Avenue
Jersey City, New Jersey 07306

Osell's Custom Frames
1003 25th Avenue, S.E.
Minneapolis, Minnesota 55414

Paris Sport
136 Main Street
Ridgefield Park, New Jersey 07660

Proteus Design, Inc.
9225 Baltimore Boulevard
College Park, Maryland 20740

Jim Redcay
Jim Redcay Frames
Washington Street
Lambertville, New Jersey 08530

Santana Cycles, Inc.
167 Cascade Court
Brea, California 92621

TABLE VII

143

Ben Serotta
Serotta Cycles
P.O. Box 817
Saratoga Springs, New York 12866

A.D. Stump Cycles
2834 Colorado Avenue, #45
Santa Monica, California 90404

TET Custom Cycles
(Painter: Tom Teesdale)
1121 Brady
Davenport, Iowa 52803

*Ed Weissler
Cyclery North
6322 North Broadway
Chicago, Illinois 60660

NOTES:

1. Most listed painters use DuPont "Imron"; some also offer enamels and lacquers.

2. *Full line paint shops specializing exclusively in bicycle painting, refinishing, and chrome plating.

PROFESSIONAL CUSTOM FRAMEBUILDERS

F.H. Appél Co.
100 West 35th Street, Suite G
National City, California 92050

Assenmacher Lightweight Cycles
4506 Morrish Road
Swartz Creek, Michigan 48473
(T)

Robert Blaedel
Vulcan Velo Works
129 N.W. 2nd Street
Corvallis, Oregon 97330
(T)

Jeffrey Bock
c/o Michael's Cyclery
Kellogg and Main Streets
Ames, Iowa 50010
(Also builds midgets and mixtes.)

Ronald Boi
RRB Cycles
562 Green Bay Road
Kenilworth, Illinois 60043
(T) (Also builds triplets)

William Boston
Bill Boston Cycles
38 Franklin Street
P.O. Box 114
Swedesboro, New Jersey 08085
(T)

Sam Braxton
Braxton Bike Shop
2100 South Avenue, West
Missoula, Montana 59801

Chris Chance
Chris Chance Cycles
11 Windsor Street
Cambridge, Massachusetts 02139

Kurt Cira & Alan Pearce
Rainbow Jersey
2613 E. Hampshire Street
Milwaukee, Wisconsin 53211

John Corbett
Frame Works
521 Fifth Avenue, S.E.
Minneapolis, Minnesota 55414

Bill Davidson
Bill Davidson Cycles
26227 114th Avenue, S.E.
Kent, Washington 98031
(T)

Roland Della Santa
P.O. Box 6771
Reno, Nevada 89513
(T)

Albert Eisentraut
1000 22nd Avenue
Oakland, California 95621
(T)

Hugh Enochs
c/o Jevelot Corporation
P.O. Box 349
La Honda, California 94020

E.U.R. International
P.O. Box 45
Dayton, Ohio 45405
(T)

Fastab Cycles
Dept. B
2706 Glenbrook
Garland, Texas 75041

Doug Fattic
c/o Kettering Bike Shop
3120 Wilmington Pike
Dayton, Ohio 45429

TABLE VIII

Henry James Folson
Henry James Bicycles, Inc.
704 Elvira Avenue
Redondo Beach, California 90277

Frame Works
521 Fifth Avenue, S.E.
Minneapolis, Minnesota 55414

Raymond Gasiorowski
Romic, Inc.
4434 Steffani Lane
Houston, Texas 77041

Bruce Gordon
Bruce Gordon Cycles
27729 Clear Lake Road
Eugene, Oregon 97402
(T) (Also builds mixtes)

Griffon Cycles
(Jim Holly-Builder)
c/o Wilshire West Bicycle Shop
11841 Wilshire Boulevard
Los Angeles, California 90025

Thomas Harper
Thomas Harper Cycles
685 Jason Street
Salem, Oregon 97301

Dave Hartranft
11 Windsor Street
Cambridge, Massachusetts 02139
(T) (Also builds recumbents and
manufactures a 5 speed
"Pocket Bicycle")

T.S. Isaac
1515 East 9th Avenue
Denver, Colorado 80218
(T)

Philip Jache
Jache Cycle Works
2769 North 32nd Street
Milwaukee, Wisconsin 53210

Tom Kellogg Cycles
(Tom Kellogg Builder)
5 Liberty Lane
Wescosville, Pennsylvania 18106

Chris Kvale Cycles
1208 Como Avenue, S.E.
Minneapolis, Minnesota 55414
(T)

Colin Laing
Colin Laing Bicycles
915 East Fort Lowell Road
Tucson, Arizona 85719

Vincent Lanfranca
Brooklyn Bicycle Company
715 Coney Island Avenue
Brooklyn, New York 11218
(T)

Victor J. Larivee
Custom Framebuilding
Cycle & Sport
400 Broadway
Santa Monica, California 90401

Mike Melton
2910 Rosewood Drive
Columbia, South Carolina 29205
(T)(Also builds racing and touring tricycles)

Medici Bicycle Company
5937 Sheila Street
Los Angeles, California 90022
    also
1183 West Side Avenue
Jersey City, New Jersey 07306
(Custom builds touring model only.)

Jim Merz
Merz Manufacturing
2115 N.W. Everett
Portland, Oregon 97210
(Also builds custom unicycles)

Peter Mooney
Mystic Valley Wheel Works
889 Main Street
Winchester, Massachusetts 01890

Marc Muller and Dan Horvath
Phydeaux Cycles
136 West Adams Street
Villa Park, Illinois 60187

Native Frames
(Drew Banton — Builder)
81 Melville Avenue
Dorchester, Massachusetts 02124

Andy Newlands
c/o Toga Frame Company
227 Avenue B
New York, New York 10009

Osell's Custom Frames
1003 25th Avenue, S.E.
Minneapolis, Minnesota 55414

Paris Sport
(Dave Moulton – Builder)
186 Main Street
Ridgefield Park, New Jersey 07660
(Also specializes in midget
and small framesets)

Fred Parr
c/o Bicycleville
306 Pico Boulevard
Santa Monica, California 90405

Stephen K. Perry
Perry Cycleworks
5205 Tally Ho Lane
Alexandria, Virginia 22307
(T) (Also builds midget
singles and tandems)

Platano Cycle Works
Mike Jakiela & Bruce Hecht
14255 Community Road
Poway, California 92129

Proteus Design, Inc.
9225 Baltimore Boulevard
College Park, Maryland 20740

Jim Redcay
Jim Redcay-Frames
Washington Street
Lambertville, New Jersey 08530

Tom Ritchey
1041 Ringwood Avenue
Menlo Park, California 94025
(T)

Richard Sachs
Main Street Box 194
Chester, Connecticut 06412

William Sampson
5052 Corbin Avenue
San Jose, California 95118
(T)

Santana Cycles, Inc.
167 Cascade Court
Brea, California 92621
(Specializes in tandems only)
(T)

Schwinn Bicycle Company
1856 North Kostner
Chicago, Illinois 60639
(T) (Orders may also be
placed through local
Schwinn Dealers)

Ben Serotta
Serotta Cycles
P.O. Box 817
Saratoga Springs, New York 12866
(T)

Paul M. Simison
Simison Cycles
210 Woodrow Street Box 766
Chillicothe, Missouri 64601

A.D. Stump
2834 Colorado Avenue, #45
Santa Monica, California 90404

TET Custom Cycles
(Tom Teesdale—Builder)
1121 Brady
Davenport, Iowa 52803

Bill Vetter
Box 165
Greensboro Bend, Vermont 05842

Vulcan Cycle Works
2388 E. Las Posas Road
Camarilla, California 93010

Peter Weigle
J.P. Weigle Cycles
(At the Goodspeed Airport)
P.O. Box 112
East Haddam, Connecticut 06423

George P. Wilson
Bicycle Frame Builder
27189 Roger Street
Hemet, California 92343
(T)

Clarence W. Witt
Witt's Bicycle Shop
22138 Mission Boulevard
Hayward, California 94541

NOTES:

1. All listed builders construct racing and touring singles unless otherwise noted.

2. (T) indicates builder also makes custom racing and touring tandems.

3. Other specialties in parentheses.

4. Many listed builders also offer custom painting services. See Appendix Table VII for separate list of professional frame painters.

BIBLIOGRAPHY AND SELECTED READING LIST

The following is a partial list of informative books, pamphlets, and magazine articles covering frameset design and construction, and related subjects.

FRAMESET GEOMETRY, DESIGN, AND CONSTRUCTION

Bike Tripping
Tom Cuthbertson
Chapter 14—The Frame, written by Albert Eisentraut, Frame Builder
Ten Speed Press, 1971

Bicycle Frames: A Close-Up Look
Joe Kossak
Bike Book Quarterly No. 4, August 1975
World Publications

Bicycling—March 1978
Vol. XIX No. 3
Page 34
"Road Test: Custom Bicycles for Specific Needs" by Gary Fisher
Photos by Gail Heilman
Published by:
    Bicycling Magazine, Inc.
    33 E. Minor Street
    Emmaus, Pennsylvania 18049

Bike Warehouse Catalog   Parts and Accessories—12, 1979
Frame Specifier F. 7 "Why Should I Build My Own Bike?"
by Peter Morgan
Bike Warehouse, A Division of Nashbar/Associates, Inc.

Bike World—January/February 1978
Volume 7—Number 1
Page 30 "A Framebuilder Talks About Workmanship and Methods"
by David Gioia

Bike World—August, 1973
Volume 2—Number 4
Page 32 "Building Your Own Frame"
by A.D. Stump

Bike World—December/January 1972/73
Volume 1—Number 6
Page 12 "What Makes a Bicycle Good?"
by Kurt Miska
    Published by World Publications
    1400 Stierlin Road
    Mountain View, California 94042

Cycling—1972
C.O.N.1—Central Sports School—F.I.A.C.
Rome, Italy

TABLE IX

DeLong's Guide to Bicycles and Bicycling The Art and Science
Fred DeLong
Chilton Book Company, 1978
Chapter III—Comparison of Bicycle Tubing and Frame Construction
Chapter V—The Custom Frame (Steering Stability and Handling)

The Proteus Framebuilding Handbook
A Guide for the Novice Bicycle Framebuilder
Dr. Paul Proteus
Proteus Press—A division of Proteus Design Inc., 1975, 1976

Top Tubes (Pamphlet)
Published by T.I. Reynolds Ltd. (13 pages)
P.O. Box 232
Hay Hall, Redfern Road
Tyseley
Birmingham, England B11 2BG

BICYCLE MECHANICS AND MECHANICAL ENGINEERING

Bicycles & Tricycles: An Elementary Treatise on Their Design and Construction
Archibald Sharp
Originally published by Longmans, Green & Co., London, New York, and Bombay, 1896
Reprint available from MIT Press, 28 Carleton Street, Cambridge, Massachusetts 02142

Bicycling Science—Ergonomics and Mechanics
Frank Roland Witt and David Gordon Wilson
The MIT Press, 1974

Standard Handbook for Mechanical Engineers
Theodore Baumeister, Editor and Lionel S. Marks
McGraw-Hill Book Company, 1967

FRAMESET COMPONENTS IDENTIFICATION AND DIMENSIONS

Ron Kitching's Handbook—1970
Ron Kitching
Ron Kitching (Wholesalers) Ltd.
Hookstone Park
Harrogate, England

Sutherland's Handbook for Bicycle Mechanics—Second Edition
by Howard Sutherland & John Porter Hart—1977
Sutherland Publications
Berkeley, California

HUMAN GEOMETRY

Gray's Anatomy—1901
Henry Gray, FRS
Running Press, Philadelphia, Pennsylvania, 1974

DRAFTING TECHNIQUE

Fundamentals of Engineering Drawing—2nd Edition
Thomas E. French
Charles J. Vierck
McGraw-Hill Book Company, New York, 1930, 1966

BRAZING TECHNOLOGY

Brazing Manual—1963
American Welding Society, Inc.
United Engineering Center
345 East 47th Street
New York, New York 10017

Low Temperature Brazing—1957 (Pamphlet)
United Wire & Supply Corp.
1497 Elmwood Avenue
Providence, Rhode Island 02910

Low Temperature Brazing Engineering Facts and Data
Bulletin B-80
United Wire & Supply Corp.
Cranston, Rhode Island 02910

Safety in Welding and Cutting—U.S.A. Standard Z49.1
Published by The American Welding Society, Inc.
2501 Northwest 7th Street
Miami, Florida 33125

Welding Handbook—1976, 7th Edition, Volume 1
Fundamentals of Welding
Published by American Welding Society, Inc.
2501 Northwest 7th Street
Miami, Florida 33125

Welding Handbook—7th Edition, Volume 2
Welding Processes—Arc and Gas
Welding and Cutting, Brazing and Soldering
Published by American Welding Society, Inc.
2501 Northwest 7th Street
Miami, Florida 33125

BICYCLE PAINTING

Bicycling—September 1976—Vol. XVIII, No. 9, Page 36
"How to Paint Your Bike and Do It Right" by M.W. Compton

Bicycling—October 1976—Vol. XVIII, No. 10, Page 26
"How to Paint Your Bike, Part 2" by M. W. Compton

INVESTMENT CASTING

How to Design and Buy Investment Castings—1960
Edited by Robert H. Herrmann
Published by:
      Investment Casting Institute
      Chicago, Illinois 60645

Additional informative articles may be found in other back issues of the previously mentioned magazines, **Bicycling** and **Bike World**, and the following periodicals:

Competitive Cycling
      Competitive Cycling, Inc.
      P.O. Box 1069
      Nevada City, California 95959

Velo-news
      Box 1257
      Brattleboro, Vermont 05301

INDEX

Alignment, *also see Tracking*
    final, 113
    fork blades, 68
    set ups for rear triangles, 97-98
    string test, 88
    table-method for main triangle, 79

Alloys
    brazing rod, 24-25
    cadmium-free brazing, 31-32
    in bicycle tubing, 48
    specifications table for silver brazing, 30

Axis of central movement, *see Crank axis*

Axle length
    front, 42
    rear, 87-88

Bibliography and Selected Reading List, 149-152

Bicycle Tubing and Frameset Materials
    retail suppliers of, 141

Bottom bracket shell
    aligning and brazing, 78-79
    height, 5-6, 13, 20
    manufacturers, 53, 58, 141
    shaping spigots, 75
    threading and facing, 110-111

Brake
    bridge designs, 99
    bridge fabrication, 92-94
    front reach, 13, 20
    hole drilling, 69, 92
    rear reach, 13, 92-93

Brass and filler rods, 24-25

Braze-ons, 54, 58
    attaching, 94-96, 99
    cleaning up, 104

Brazing *def,* 24
    color/temperature chart, 29
    five stages in, 26-27
    fluxes, 25-26, 33
    joint clearances, 24-25
    learning, 27-28
    material suppliers, 25, 141
    process, 26
    references on technology, 151
    rods for, *see Alloys*
    rod specifications, *see Alloys*
    safety precautions, 27
    torches and flame temperatures, 23-24

Bridge tube, 13, 22, 56, 58, 92-94
    brake hole reinforcements, 58, 92-93, 99
    locating the, 22
    reinforcing diamonds, 54, 58, 92, 99

Brushes
    paint, 36
    pointing for accenting, 121-122
    wire, 36

Butted tube, 47-49
    configurations, 49
    cross section views, 57
    identification of long-butted ends, 57, 59
    ordering, 50
    properties of, 48-49
    shortening precautions, 50, 59-60
    typical applications in framesets, 56

Cadmium
    hazard, 25

Capillary action *def*
    in brazing, 26

Chain stay, 56, 129-135
    bridge fabrication, 92-94
    chain ring depression, 87
    cutting for stiffness, 86
    end shapes, 70
    length, 7, 13
    mitering, 87-88
    set-up for marking, 97
    slotting and doming, 85-86

Clamping and layout aids, 41, 43

Cold-setting
    fork blades, 68
    limitation with investment cast parts, 52, 141
    main triangle, 79
    rear triangles, 93

C.O.N.1. Method, 4
    adjustments for body anomalies and weight of
      packs, 10, 16
    anatomical dimensions, 9-10
    figure illustrating measurements, 16
    table of tube lengths, 17

"Cooked" tubing, *see Overheating*

Crank axis *def,* 5

Crank length
    and fender interference, 21
    effect on bottom bracket height, 6
    interplay with head tube angle, 7

Cups
    identifying threads, 110

Cyclist's CG and Combined CG *def,* 5

Decals and transfers, 122-123
    close-cutting, 122
    setting solution, 122

153

Dented tubes, 59

Dies
    used in investment casting, 51
    used for steering tube threading, 110

Diffusion *def*
    in brazing, 26

Down tube, 13, 21, 49, 56, 77-78
    gauge selection, 50
    mitering, 72-74
    sizes and weights available, 129-135
    special length problem, 74

Drawings, design
    drafting materials required, 19
    layout guide, 13
    protecting originals, 22
    references on drafting, 151
    scale, 19

Drop-outs, 52, 54, 58
    brazing to blades, 64
    brazing to stays, 86-87, 90-91
    modifying for short chain stays, 85-86
    offset type, 54, 66
    shaping, 64, 70
    thinning, 64-65, 85

Energy-efficiency *def,* 4
    objectives to achieve, 3

English Legal Standard Wire Gauge (SWG)
    table of dimensions, 137

Eutectic *def,* 24

Fender clearance, 13
    front, 7, 20
    head tube adjustments for, 21
    rear, 7, 21

Fork, 13, 20-22, 60-70
    blades, 20, 49, 50, 58, 62-70
    blade vents, 66
    crown, 53-54, 58, 60-61, 66-69
    fitting operations, 106-110
    length, 7-8, 13
    rake, *see Rake*

Frame *def,* 3

Framebuilders
    directory of professional, 145-148

Frame Painters
    directory of professional, 143-144

Frameset *def,* 3

Frameset Geometry, 3
    anatomical fit considerations, *see C.O.N.1*
      Method
    bicycle use considerations, 3-10
    illustration showing principal elements, 13
    references on, 149-150

Head tube, 13, 20-21, 49, 56
    angle, 7
    brazing the, 76-78
    cutting to length, 71
    drilling vent hole, 76
    reaming and facing, 106-107, 110
    sizes and weights available, 129-135

Investment Casting
    bottom bracket shells, 53
    domestic parts manufacturers, 141
    drop-outs and lugs, 52, 54
    fork crowns, 53-54
    precautions in cold-setting parts, 141
    process description, 51
    references on, 152
    "waxes" for, 51

Jigs
    fork, 42, 44
    main triangle, 42, 45
    set-up aids, 41, 43
    use of, 66-68, 77-78

Liquidus *def,* 24
    table for various brazing alloys, 30

Lost wax casting, *see Investment Casting*

Lugs, 50-53, 58
    custom cut-outs, 75
    finishing interiors, 76
    for special seat attachments, 84
    preparation of, 75-76

Melting range *def,* 24
    table for various brazing alloys, 30

Milling the crown race boss, 108-109

Mitering, 71-75, 87-90, 92-93
    files for, 35
    template for, 72

Neutral steering *def,* 6
    cornering effects, 8-9
    graph and formula for, 15

Overheating tubes
    detrimental effect, 25
    heating influence on strength of Reynolds
      "531," 48
    temperature limits for Columbus tubing, 25,
      135
    temperature limits for Reynolds "531," 25

Oversteer *def,* 8 *also see Quick Steering*
    graph and formula for determining, 15
    reasons for, 8-9

Paint
    accent, 121
    brushes for pointing, 121
    enamel, 116,121
    "Imron," 115

lacquer, 115-116, 119-120
oxide primer, 116
primer/surfacer, 116
rubbing compound, 117
undercoater, 116-117

Painting
accenting lugs, 121-122
applying lacquer, 119-120
enameling, 121
rubbing out lacquer, 120-121
sandpapers used in, 115, 117-119
spray technique, 119-121
supplies for surface preparation and priming,
117
surface preparation and priming, 116-119
tips for, 119
undercoating, 116, 118-119

Pinning
of files, 36
parts together, 60-61

Quick steering, 9, *also see Oversteer*
graph and formula for, 15

Rake *def,* 6, 8
as determined by head tube angle, 6-7
graphs and formulas for, 15
influence on fork length, 7-8
laying out blades to fit, 62-63
lines (on graph), 8, 15
selecting blades for proper, 50

Rifflers, 35-36

Sanding
seat attachment, 81-82
supplies, 36-37
technique on lugs, 76
technique on tubes, 60-61, 63-64, 67, 69, 79,
105-106
thinning lugs by, 105

Seat attachments
Allen Key Fastback, 80-82, 84, 88-92, 103-104
various designs, 80, 83-84

Seat stay, 13, 56, 129-135
brake bridge fabrication, 92-94, 99
cutting for stiffness, *see Chain stay*
end shapes, *see Chain stay*
joining to chainstays, 90-91
joining to seat attachment, 91-92
mitering for Allen-type attachment, 88-91
set-ups for cutting to length, 88-91, 98
slotting and doming, 86
vent hole drilling, 90

Seat tube, 13, 20, 49
angle, 6, 10, 13
cross section view, 57
gauge selection, 50
mitering, 74

sizes and weights available, 129-135
slitting and finishing, 103-104
table of lengths, 17

Silbrazing *def,* 24
fluxes, 33
joint clearances required, 25
rods for, 30-32

Soldering *def,* 24

Solidus *def,* 24
table for various brazing alloys, 30

Solvent
for tube cleaning, 59

Special designs
concealed brake conduit, 94-96

Stability
and bottom bracket height, 6
and head tube angle, 7
in a sprint, 7

Steering geometry, 6-9, 13, 15
also see Head tube angle and Rake

Steering tube, 20, 48-50
fitting to crown, 60-61
sizes and weights available, 129-135
threading, 110
trimming and keyway-cutting, 111-112

Stiffness as affected by
chain stay length, 7
fork length and rake, 7-9
head tube angle, 6-7
materials of construction, 10
seat tube angle, 6
wheelbase, 5

Supertorch, 23-24

Swiss Pattern files, 35-36

Tangents
table of, 139

Taper gauge, 48-49

Toe clip interference, 21

Tolerances
for brazing, 24-25
of frame angles and tube lengths, 75

Tools
for layout, 36
special bike related, 37
table of files required, 35

Top tube, 13, 20, 49, 56, 78-79
cross section view, 57
gauge selection, 50
mitering, 71-73
sizes and weights available, 129-135
table of lengths, 17

Tracking, 113
   also see Alignment

"TRI-M-ITE" papers, 117-118, 121

Tube blocks, 41, 43

Tube manufacturers, 47

Understeer *def,* 8
   graph and formula for, 15

Vent holes
   need for, 66

Waxes
   for protecting paint, 123
   used in making investment castings, 51

Weight distribution
   anatomical, 10, 16
   referenced to wheel loads, 5, 21

Wetting *def*
   in brazing, 26
   in decal application, 122

Wheel
   axle lengths, 42, 87-88
   diameter used in rake formulas and graphs, 8, 15
   removal problem with short stays, 7, 21-22, 93

Wheelbase, 5, 13
   reworking in design, 22

Wheel clearance, 13
   front, 7-8, 20
   rear, 7

Whip, *see Stability*

157

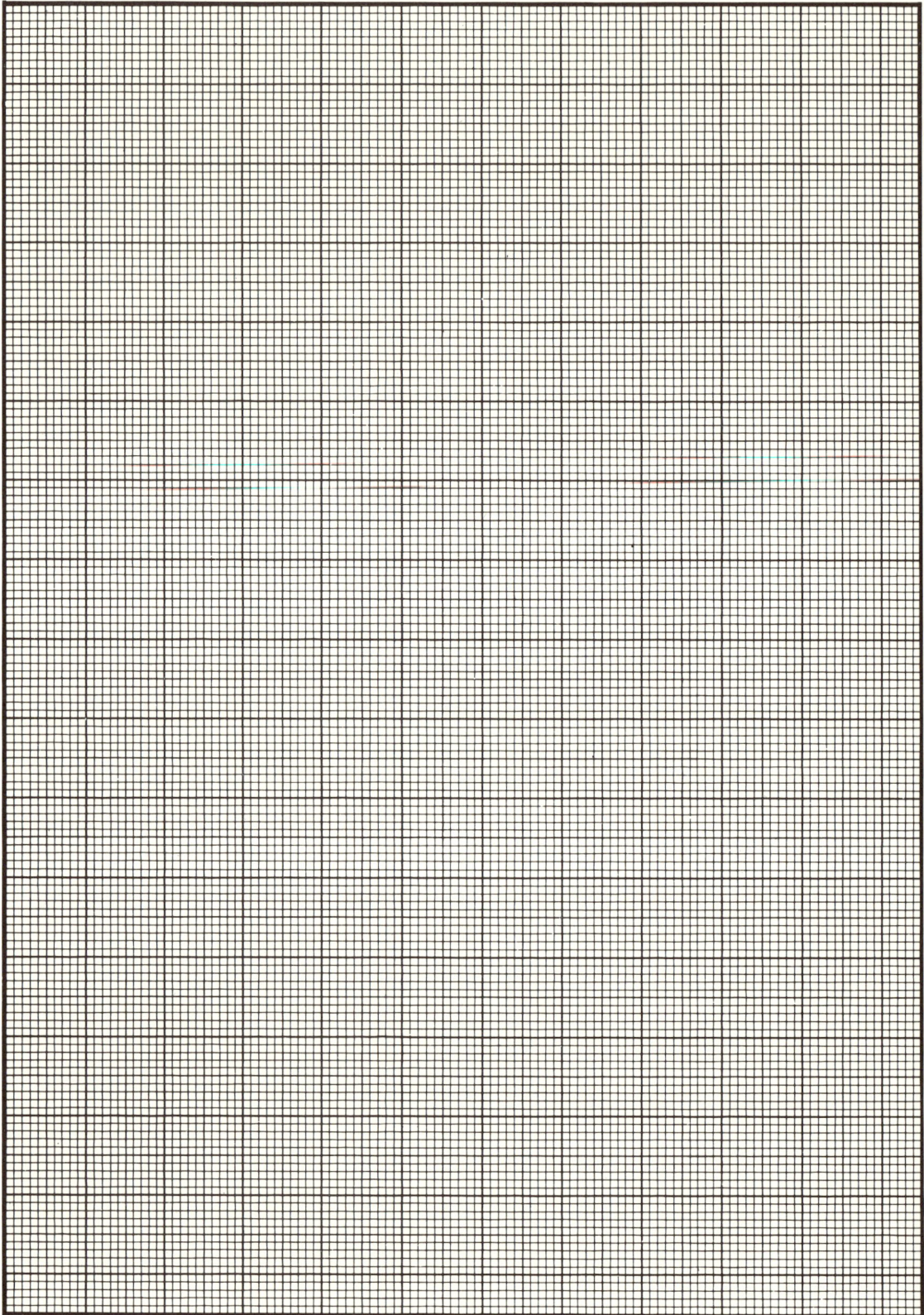

159

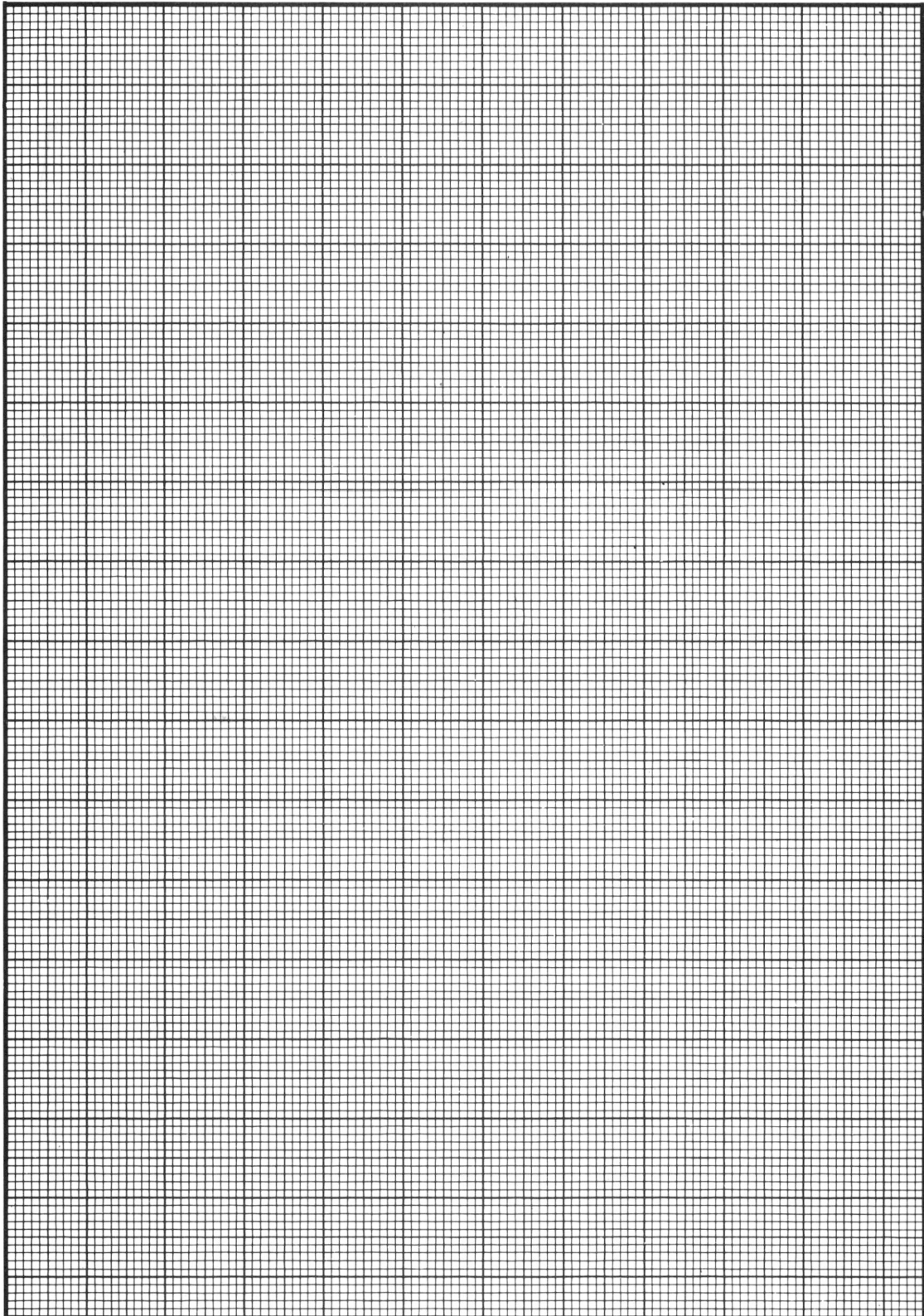

Designing and Building Your Own Frameset has been typeset and printed by Mercantile Printing Co., Inc., Worcester, Massachusetts. The typeface is English Times. The book has been printed by offset lithography on Mohawk Superfine Softwhite Text and has been bound by New Hampshire Bindery.